A YEAR
IN THE
WOODS

A YEAR IN THE WOODS

ASHLYN McKAYLA OHM

Words From The
WILDERNESS

Words from the Wilderness
© 2021 by Ashlyn McKayla Ohm

A YEAR IN THE WOODS
52 Weeks of Growth, Grace, and the Glory of God

For information, contact
www.wordsfromthewilderness.com

Cover design by Hannah Linder Designs

ISBN (paperback): 979-8-9853344-0-1

First Edition: September 2021

21 22 23 24 25 26 27   10 9 8 7 6 5 4 3 2 1

ACKNOWLEDGEMENTS AND DEDICATION

As I consider this dedication, I'm reminded that towering trees raise hands to Heaven only because someone, somewhere, had the faith to press a seed of belief into a soil that held only possibilities. It's with immense gratitude that I testify that the same has been true in my life, and I wish in some way, however feeble, to convey my appreciation for those who have sown the seeds of this book, and of its author.

For Lain Rodgers—the champion of silent, selfless service. Thank you for living surrendered to the Spirit.

For the kind friends who have always encouraged me—the ones who read my first blog posts, who didn't laugh when I declared I wanted to be a writer, who prayed for me and cried with me and repeatedly assured me that God's anointing was on me—thank you. If I began to list names, I could fill this entire book, but know that you are all so dear to me.

For my too-good-to-be-true mother, Derri Ohm. I'm supposed to be able to craft sentences for every situation, but words are weak compared to the beauty of all that you are. I can only say thank you—for soaking me in grace and lavishing me in love, for showing me how to think wisely and dream extravagantly. Thank you for those endless hours spent teaching me—first holding my hand as I traced wobbly letters, then patiently showing me the nuts and bolts of a good research paper, drafts of my infamous report on Dolley Madison spread on the floor all around us. But you've been so much more than my trusted teacher. You're my constant encourager, faithfully urging me upward. You're my guide to godliness, unfailingly pouring the truth and love of Jesus into my soul. And you're my very best friend—the one who has always, always, given me wings. If you could count the summer stars, then you would know just how much I love you and always will.

For my fantastic dad, Ralph Ohm. Again, any words I could write barely even make ripples in the ocean of my love for you. Thank you for countless rereads of *Goodnight Moon* and *Runaway Bunny* (complete with sound effects that, according to you, were responsible for catapulting me from newborn nonentity into sentience; this is debatable). Thank you for always urging me on to adventures—even the ones that did not proceed quite as envisioned. Thank you for having a self-described "midlife crisis" and buying an RV in which we traveled to dozens of wilderness areas throughout the country. And thank you most of all for being the one I could count on—the running buddy no matter the weather, the face in the audience at every recital, the enthusiastic fan of each blog post. Standing on your shoulders, I can see very far indeed.

For my Lord and Savior, Jesus Christ. May my every breath be expended in the praise of Your glory! Please accept this humble offering—please find joy in my celebration of Your world and Your Word. You have done it all! You have brought me into being and have sung my spirit to serenity. You have linked my hand in Yours and led me over every mountain range—not only the ones in my woodland wanderings but also those along the journey of my soul. May I radiate Your majesty a thousand upon a thousand times! I offer You this book with this prayer always upon my lips: "Let the heavens be glad, and let the earth rejoice; let the sea roar, and all that fills it; let the field exult, and everything in it! Then shall all the trees of the forest sing for joy before the LORD, for he comes, for he comes to judge the earth" (Psalm 96:11-13a ESV)!

I close with a quotation from Gene Stratton-Porter's classic *A Girl of the Limberlost*, words that have defined my life: "If I am a woman at all worthwhile, it will be because I have had such wonderful opportunities. Not every girl is driven to the forest to learn what God has to say there."[1] Few in this day have the joy, indeed, and I am forever blessed that I am one of them—that I have breathed the air of the High Places and found joy hiding between the trees and witnessed the clouds tumbling overhead and realized that yes, I will live forever. Thank you, Mama and Dad, for unfailingly replying to my boredom with a suggestion to play outside. And thank You, Maker of Mountains, Weaver of Wilderness, for the beauty and the burning of Your glory in this world. May I sing Your praises well.

– Ashlyn McKayla Ohm
January 2021

Table of Contents

WILD GOOSE CHASE 1

FORGED IN FIRE 6

WINTER WOODS 12

FROZEN FILIGREE 18

TRUE NORTH 23

SLEEPING UNDER SNOW 28

THE PINECONE PARABLE 33

WARMER WINTER 39

GROWING WITH GAILEY 45

THE DAFFODIL DARE 51

GROWING GREEN 57

OF FLOWERS AND FAITHFULNESS 62

BUTTERFLY BLESSING 67

APRIL SHOWERS 72

UNDER HIS WINGS 78

MINI MIRACLES 85

THE TRAIL TO NOWHERE 91

HOPE FROM A HUMMINGBIRD 96

THIN PLACES 102

12,000 FEET 108

HOMESICK 113

SLOW STROLL 119

LOST AND FOUND 125

WHEN THE TREES FALL 130

MIDSUMMER MIRACLE 135

LIGHTS IN THE NIGHT 140

TOADS ON THE ROADS 145

FLOWERS IN THE DITCH 151

SONG OF SUMMERTIME 156

WHEN THE CREEK DRIES UP 162

LESSON FROM A LIZARD 167

ITCHY ISSUES 173

THE MIRACLE OF THE MOTH 178

THE BEAUTY OF BATS 184

TRAPPED IN A PUDDLE 189

DARK SKY 195

THE MISSING MARTINS 201

IN LOVE WITH LECONTE 205

WELCOMING THE ELK 212

FAITH AND THE FOOTHOLD 218

WHERE THE WIND BLOWS 224

DARING TO DREAM 229

WATCHING IN THE WOODS 235

LESSON FROM LEAVES 241

PERSIMMON PROPHECY 247

TRUTH FROM THE TRAIL CAMERA 253

TREASURES IN THE TREETOPS 259

OF CORN AND COURAGE 264

SOARING IN SILENCE 270

ADVENT AND ANIMALS 277

MIDWINTER MIRACLE 282

GOD'S CHRISTMAS TREE 288

ABOUT THE AUTHOR 294

REFERENCES 295

WILD GOOSE CHASE

I t was that dim, uncertain time of day—the time when the sun is just settling behind the trees for the night, but its light still lingers faintly. I was using the last drops of day to keep working on a big task: the eternal chore, familiar to all who live in the country, of collecting and burning fallen tree branches. I'd been working diligently all afternoon, submerging many loads of brush in a roaring fire. Now, with evening creeping over the hills, I was solely focused on retrieving the dead sticks under the last few trees in a certain area before I returned to the fire to watch the sparks collide with the stars.

Storms were predicted for later, and their first messengers were already boiling over the sky in the form of rolling purple clouds. The winds, however, were still gentle and held the avant-garde scent of an approaching thunderhead along with the elusive sweetness of spring. As the day faded, the spring peepers—the tiny frogs that live in the marshes—began raising their chorus.

Then I heard something else. Something different than the frogs, the breeze, the few sleepy birds giving subdued chirps. Something that made my heart beat a little quicker and brought me out from under the trees to examine the sky. As the sound grew louder, I scanned the clouds, searching for the source—a source I recognized.

1

Just as I'd hoped, here they came, a triangle of migrating geese slicing across the sky. Their unmistakable calls echoing from the clouds, they flew so low above my head that for a moment I could hear the rhythmic pulsing of their wings, like the heartbeat of the wilderness. I watched, hardly breathing, until they had vanished over the horizon and the song of the peepers was once more undisturbed by their trumpet calls.

It's migration—a predictable journey, one I've watched on an annual basis. Every fall, I've witnessed geese hastening southward, racing the Arctic air, and I've heard the first frost in their cries. In the spring, I greet them once again as they arrive from the south; without the looming threat of winter, they can afford to linger in Arkansas for a little while, enjoying the lake near my house and basking in the newness of spring. Yet the familiarity of the sight has never made it stale, and each time I see geese overhead, the deep parts of my spirit stir in a way that is half exhilarating and half unnerving. Some part of my soul that will never be fully tamed quivers to life and peers, with restless eyes, beyond the confines of my daily life—into the unknown North where the geese are flying, drawn by a lodestone so strong that even a wingless human can feel its tidal pull as they sweep across the sky.

As I watched these geese soar over my head, I was reminded that we serve a God Who understands these longings, Who knows how desperately we crave—and need—adventure. This desire is natural, and I believe it was programmed into our spirits by God Himself to call us into destinies greater than ourselves. In fact, I believe that when those deep wells of our being are stirred, it's because the Holy Spirit Himself is breathing on our hearts. And no one understands these migratory yearnings better than He.

In fact, although Christians today tend to minimize the importance of the Holy Spirit, this wasn't the case for the Celtic Christians of the medieval period. Profoundly aware of the Spirit's work in the world, these Irish believers gave Him a very special title—*An-Geadh-Glas*. Subtly poetic for its sound alone, this phrase literally translates as "The Wild Goose."[1]

God as a goose? What were these believers thinking? Although at first glance the comparison may seem shocking, even degrading, it is actually one of the most beautiful analogies in all of theology for the work and ministry of the Holy Spirit. Like a wild goose, the Celts explained, the Holy Spirit operates in a realm outside of everyday life.

He is mysterious—His course is inexplicable. He is unpredictable—a God of dazzling adventure. And most importantly, He is uncontrollable—an entity that cannot be manipulated, captured, or tamed—only pursued.

To put this into perspective, imagine for just a moment that you decided to follow a real-life wild goose. Picture yourself taking a car, or bus, or even traveling on foot northward, forsaking your convenience and desires to doggedly pursue this single bird. Following the goose—staying on its course, watching it fly, finding the ponds where it slept each night, contemplating its next move—would become your single goal. Everything else would dwindle in comparison to this one pursuit.

Isn't this how the Christian life was always meant to be?

Not an insane obsession over a bird, but a radical reordering of our priorities and an enormous appetite for adventure. A journey into the depths of the greatest unknown, on an epic voyage, following the only One Who can lead our spirits on the life-giving paths He designed for us.

What an invitation! But how many times do we refuse? It's ironic: our society loves the thrill of a hunt, but we don't seek after God. We *pursue* romantic partners, *chase* dreams, *follow* our heart—but we expect God to come on our terms and eat from our hand. Instead of a Wild Goose, we'd prefer the Spirit to resemble the tame dove pictured in so many church murals—a soft white bird, small enough to be carried in one hand, cooing comfortably on a shoulder. We're uneasy with the thought of the Wild Goose—unwieldy, unpredictable, uncontrollable, demanding our utter concentration, tearing the sleepiness of our souls with strident cries.

And so, as He flies over our heads, we let Him go. As I did, we may pause in our daily activities when we hear His call, glancing up to admire His flight. We might listen to His cries for a moment and hear the beating of His wings. But then we shrug and sigh and grab another armload of dead wood, or fear, or resentment, or whatever keeps us solidly anchored to the ground. We laugh a little at that longing in our souls and remind ourselves to be grown-up and "practical" (a deadly word). And ultimately, our souls become so dry and cracked that we no longer hear the exultant call of the Wild Goose, and the quickening of our spirits His flight evokes dies into a leaden dependence on church attendance and routine prayers and, possibly, a cross decal on our back bumper.

What if there were more?

What if the restlessness in our souls—the small, secret emptiness—was never meant to be ignored? What if the something in our spirit that trembles at the honk of migrating geese was the realest, truest part of who we are? What if God expected not conformity or prosperity but desperation—the desperation of a search for Him?

My friends, *An-Geadh-Glas* will fly over your heads again. He'll give His call, and you'll hear His wingbeats. It could be small journeys He asks at first—perhaps performing an act of kindness for a cantankerous neighbor. Or finding the strength to forgive someone who will never know of your sacrifice. Or choosing to pause and breathe a silent prayer before snapping that sharp answer at your annoying coworker. But whatever the moment looks like for you, it is always the Y-shaped fork of a choice.

The first option is the safest: you can ignore the cry of the Wild Goose and return to gathering dead wood. Choose this route, and you'll never be forced outside your comfort zone. You'll never cross difficult trails in pursuit of something that others ridicule. You can settle snugly into your safe, empty corner of the world, and you can cling to control—or at least the illusion thereof.

But you'll also be dead.

The other choice is more dangerous. Reckless, the world might say. The other choice is to lose your life. To give in and give up and accept that the Wild Goose is higher than you. To die—but to die so that you may live, live fully alive in a throbbing joy that most people never imagine exists.

If you choose this option, then welcome—you are now following the Wild Goose. But let me warn you—the path won't be easy. Following the Wild Goose takes focus, the ability to corral an ever-wandering mind bouncing around a world of distractions and remind it to gaze with pure devotion on one Person only. Toss regrets, ignore fears, and forget failures—there's no time for burdens like these anymore, because the Wild Goose travels fast, and your eyes must not stray from Him.

Hand-in-hand with that focus is trust. In the core of your being must be an unshakable conviction that the Lord Who created you loves you enough to give you a life of adventure, not safety. There will be times when that trust cracks like an empty shell. There will be moments when you cry, moments when you droop on the lonely edge of a wilderness pond, wounded and exhausted, and believe that *An-Geadh-Glas* is punishing you, that He is dragging you through the roughest terrain He can find in a brutal act of sadism. You'll look at that tombstone, or bank account, or lost opportunity, or angry friend, and you'll scream and rage and pound your fist at the heavens and beg to return to earth, to fall from the skies and crawl back to an earthbound existence, which, although bland and unsatisfying, at least doesn't hurt like this.

But then you'll hear the call again—the irresistible lure of the Wild Goose. And He will whisper to your soul, "Peace, My child. This is our journey through the wilderness. Your scars are your strengths. Your hurts are your healing. And your pain is My purpose. Keep following me. Keep chasing me. I see you, and I am pleased, and I will never leave you behind."

I've followed the Wild Goose through some dark places, some paths fringed with thorns and steep with rocks. But I can assure you that for every lonely night and every weary day, there have been miracles of healing, of fiercely-pounding joy, of love and laughter and life and always, always, the beating of wings. The words I write in this book are truths I've learned from Him, either in actual wilderness settings or just in the wild and barren places of the soul. I wish I could say I follow Him perfectly, but I don't. I listen to fears far too often. I chase distractions, I cling to burdens, and I frequently veer from His course. But despite my shortcomings, I can say with absolute certainty that following Him is my best and highest calling. And it is my fervent and heartfelt prayer that you will decide to listen to that migratory stirring in your own soul and join me on this "Wild-Goose Chase."

FORGED IN FIRE

My family and I are blessed to live in a very rural area on a beautiful tract of land. However, we're not alone on the property. This is especially true in the back acreage, which is on the other side of our creek from our house and borders a largely undisturbed tract of wilderness. This section of our property offers refuge to birds, small animals, deer, and the occasional bear. Sometimes, at night, we've even heard the scream of a hunting mountain lion, prowling along the ridgeline, or the hair-raising cries of a wolf pack on the run.

To clear this land—smoothing hills, chopping trees, "landscaping" it into an artificial façade—would be to destroy its benefit as a refuge for the wildlife we love. However, although we aren't seeking a "golf course" look, there is still a daunting amount of maintenance to be done, including bush hogging to keep the meadow areas open and removing invasive species such as the ever-persistent mock orange trees. And there is one chore that never seems to end. That is the building—and burning—of brush piles.

On a property covered in trees, it seems that a single gust of wind can send a shower of dead branches to the ground. If we allowed these to remain where they fall, the land would not only look unkempt; it would eventually be unable to be maintained. Thus, it's necessary to collect all of these fallen limbs in a central location and then dispose of them.

I'm not sure if it's the sense of accomplishment, the opportunity to be alone in the woods, or simply the hypnotizing catharsis of watching a fire burn. Whatever the reason, though, I dearly enjoy this chore and volunteer for it as often as I can.

On a cold winter afternoon, there's no better activity from my point of view than pulling on my coat and boots and driving our RTV—its roomy bed can accommodate ample brush—across the creek, my beloved dog Mercy hitching a ride. Once I arrive in the area to be cleared, I attack it with gusto, dragging brush back and forth and filling the bed many times over. As dusk begins to fall, it's time for the best part yet.

In the midst of the trees, nestled at the foot of the mountain with the old railroad bed not far away, there is an open clearing. The ground is a thick layer of ash, several inches deep—a testament to the fires that have lived and died here. My fingers trembling in the cold, I carefully strike a match, a tiny glow of infant fire, and hold it to a small piece of fuel...perhaps a twig, or a sliver of bark, or even a dry leaf. Then, with the utmost care, I begin tending this tiny flame, carefully balancing more and more bits of fuel on it, bigger and bigger pieces, until the spark that was birthed at the end of the matchstick is now a healthy blaze licking eagerly at the entire brush pile.

Up to this point, I've done the work, but now the fire takes over and amply repays me for my efforts. As the sky turns purple and cobwebs of dusk wrap around the trees, I perch on the tailgate of the RTV and watch the fire. Glistening sparks soar upward, chasing the stars themselves. The hearty odor of pure wood smoke fills the evening air. The warmth of the blaze radiates like a warm hug, protecting me from the chill of winter. And once darkness completely settles, pouring itself out in the little valley where I wait, the fire is truly its most glorious.

I love to watch all the colors of the flames...dull orange melting the logs into chunks of smoky embers...brassy yellow leaping skyward...and more rarely, a shiver of golden-blue, as the very hottest flames dance in the heart of the fire and entwine themselves around each other.

There's something about a fire that we humans can't resist. It is at the same time familiar and fascinating, domestic and dangerous, a workhorse and a wild mustang. To ancient peoples, it was not only the entity that cooked food and warmed dwellings; it was also an animate quality deserving of worship and adoration. Even today, as we supposedly advanced people brag about our taming of fire, pointing to its numerous uses in industry and innovation, an open flame still evokes strong emotional responses—and reminds us that fire will never be under our control.

When I watch those brush piles melting in the flames, I think about these disparities—about the apparent paradox that is this force of nature. And my mind begins to wander to a different fire—the one that came to earth two thousand years ago.

I gaze at the flickering shadows and pretend I'm watching the scene—twelve uncertain men praying hesitantly in an upstairs room. Their leader had left, their numbers had shrunk, and their government was displeased. Surely they tasted the sickening scent of fear. Surely they huddled in the dark corners of Jerusalem. Yet it was at this moment of vulnerability and terror that the flames of the Holy Spirit flooded the room with the roar of an irresistible wind. In an instant, these people who had once seen God now housed God. He was within them—and they could be silent no longer.

And suddenly, these twelve timid men, cowering in a secret room, became twelve courageous men, spilling out of their hiding place, tumbling into the crowds, shouting the praises of the God Who had come to dwell in them. Lives changed…glory revealed…the church born. And all from a holy fire that has never gone out (Acts 2).

It doesn't come as a surprise to me that the Holy Spirit chose to reveal Himself in the form of fire, because fire is one of the closest earthly symbols for the spiritual reality of the Holy Spirit. Indeed, their roles mimic each other in so many ways.

First of all, fire guides. These days, we're surrounded with artificial light—flashlights, phone apps, night watchers and streetlights and headlamps. However, not so long ago, it was flaming torches and fire-bearing lanterns that guided people home. Even now, when I sit beside the fire, I admire the way the surrounding landscape seems to glow, allowing me to see into even the darkest crannies. It was this illuminating effect that Jesus had in mind when He promised His disciples that the Holy Spirit would "guide [them] into all truth" (John 16:13 KJV). Certainly it is the role of the Spirit to help believers recognize false doctrine and discern truth from error. However, it is also His role to guide us literally along the path of our lives. In a labyrinth of many choices, with innumerable futures spread before us, it is the Holy Spirit Who "directs [our] steps" (Proverbs 16:9 NASB).

In addition to guiding, fire protects. There's a reason I make sure that the fire is robust before darkness falls completely. In a forest where wolves and bears and panthers prowl, there's safety in sitting near a fire. Wild animals are innately uneasy around flames and smoke and will usually avoid an area where a fire is burning. Likewise, the Spirit within us is our strongest defense against Satan's attacks. Consider Ephesians 6, in which Paul discusses the armor of God. While many virtues serve protective roles—the shield of faith, the breastplate of righteousness, the belt of truth—the Spirit as revealed in the Word is named as the believer's sword, the only component of the armor that goes beyond providing defense to actually allowing us to go on the offensive against the enemy.[1]

Guidance and protection—valuable blessings, to be sure. However, the Holy Spirit has yet another role. And this is where our human strength ends, because to go deeper with the Spirit, we need a much higher level of involvement—one that not everyone is willing to contribute. Are you ready?

To access the full blessings of the Spirit, we're required to stand within the fire.

You see, when I dump a load of wood on a fire and watch it burn, I am merely a disinterested observer. Certainly, I enjoy the benefits that we've already discussed—guidance from its light, protection from its proximity. These are offered to me free and do not require that I approach any nearer to the center of the blaze. However, if I wanted to go beyond observing to actually participating, I would not be able to keep my distance. I would have to stand within the flames.

Now obviously, I don't recommend trying this with a physical fire. But in a spiritual sense, it is this complete surrender—this throwing ourselves into the flames of the Spirit—that God requests from us. At first, this may sound extreme, ridiculous, even downright terrifying. Perhaps that's why many Christians are satisfied with standing outside the fire and watching it burn—enjoying its light and protection, receiving its blessings with gratitude, but not allowing themselves to be united with the blaze itself. Indeed, inviting the Holy Spirit to pour holy fire into our very selves can sound even more disturbing than stepping into a glowing inferno.

Does this sound terrifying? Uncomfortable? Radical? If your answer is yes, you're not alone. We humans fear complete surrender as much as we fear an out-of-control wildfire—or maybe more. But don't miss this point—God's fire is not for destruction but for purification. The Holy Spirit doesn't want to burn you—He wants to build you.

Indeed, one of the most popular Biblical metaphors for the work of God in the lives of His children presents God as a refiner—a skilled craftsman who exposes contaminated metal ore to flame in order to render it free of pollution. Consider Malachi 3:3, which pictures God as "a refiner and purifier of silver" (ESV). Proverbs 17:3 takes this analogy a step further, likening God's work in our lives to the smelting of precious metals: "The crucible is for silver, and the furnace is for gold, and the Lord tests hearts" (ESV). It was this purification to which Job referred; lost and alone in the midst of his trials, he nonetheless cried out, "When He has tried me, I shall come out as gold" (Job 23:10 ESV).

But just because God is a refiner doesn't mean His purifying influence in our lives is a guarantee. Like all other aspects of our sanctification—our growth into His likeness—the final choice is ours. If we wish, we can stand and watch the flames, enjoying such blessings as we can receive from a distance. Or we can throw ourselves into them—with all our pain, shame, heartache, and fear—and emerge transformed. One choice is safe and sane, easy and convenient. The other is difficult, dangerous, embarrassing, messy—but transformative.

So how do we do it? How do we tap into the purifying power of the Spirit? There is no magic trick, no one epiphany to catapult us into a new level of growth. Instead, there is only the quiet day-to-day humility of consistently, decision by decision, word by word, action by action, choosing His will over ours.

This is what Paul had in mind when he urged his readers to "be filled with the Spirit" (Ephesians 5:18 ESV). The Greek word used here, *plerousthe*, denotes a continual filling, one that must be constantly renewed and replenished as we strive toward His purity—just as a fire needs to be constantly refueled in order to burn brightly.[2] In addition, we must "abstain from every form of evil" (1 Thessalonians 5:22 ESV) in order to not "quench," or extinguish, His movement in our lives, in the same way that we would be careful to not smother a fire with dirt or drench it with water (1 Thessalonians 5:19 ESV). Lastly, a fire cannot be controlled or commanded—so we give Him free rein to be continually "course-correcting" us, gently aligning our actions, desires, and motives with His. And then, in the midst of surrender, we find ourselves dancing in the flames!

My friends, this is a sacred time of year. We've just concluded our celebration of the Savior's birth and thanked God for His gift of love. And now we are taking our first tentative steps in a new year. These midwinter days are days of renewal, of growth, of commitment to transformation. They're also the soil in which our priorities for the upcoming seasons take root. It's my prayer that as we begin this year, we stop hovering on the edges of the embers and instead fling ourselves into the flames. Let's commit to ruthlessly exposing ourselves to the Spirit, allowing Him to burn away our dross and shape our character into His image. And then let's rejoice together— for we have chosen the path of purity, and the light and the love and the letting go that have always, since that famous upper room, amazed the watching world!

WINTER WOODS

W hen was the last time you took a walk through winter woods?

There's a quiet ache in the January forest. All year, the woods have been vibrantly alive—a rich symphony of sound and color and movement. In spring, they don the filmy chartreuse of new leaves and welcome migratory birds back from tropical regions. As the days stretch into summer, they provide a shady shelter where hundreds of insects click in the lazy afternoons and newborn fawns romp, flashing their dazzling white spots. Even in autumn, the season of descent, the woods are still alive—lavish displays of color, arching antlers of nimble bucks, pale grace of birches and the last faded leaves floating gently downstream as the wild geese cry overhead.

But in winter, all the life seems to have leaked away. The chorus of frogs and insects and birds has fallen silent; the only sound is the roaming wind in the barren treetops, with perhaps an occasional peep from the hardy birds of winter—such as the chirps of the little juncos, "snow birds" we call them, or the mournful moan of an owl. And as sound is muted, color is too. The world is washed in neutral hues…beige of withered grass, stark silver of leafless trunks, rusty brown of fallen leaves. Even the sunlight seems weakened and watery, as if the year of life and birth and beauty has left all creation too tired to do anything but sleep and dream of what once was.

I feel it, this sacred silence, when I walk through the winter woods. My fondest memories from hikes taken during this season involve moments of transcendent stillness. Watching the golden perfection of the full moon rise above tangled birch branches. Enjoying a "conversation" with a talkative Barred Owl during velvet dusk. (Over the years, I've learned the calls of several owl species in my region; not infrequently, I can persuade them to answer me.) Running homeward through the fallen leaves, with a slow-burning sunset simmering on the horizon and the first shy stars peeking above me and my breath swirling wild in the ice-born air. These are all moments of indefinable stillness, moments when the heartbeat of the world thrummed slow and all that had rejoiced and danced and laughed and labored under the summer skies drowsed in the piles of dead leaves.

Yes, the winter woods sing a slower cadence, and because of this, there's a sadness in the air—a faint taste of melancholy, elusive and uncertain. After all, it's hard to see the crispy leaves, the bereaved trees, and the barren hillsides without feeling a twinge of regret for summer's lost vibrancy. Yet I love the winter woods, even when they seem most inhospitable. When I shuffle through last autumn's leaves, when I glimpse the deer in their muted winter coats, when I marvel at ice-encrusted streams and twittering chickadees, I am enjoying a commodity that is both rare and mundane, prized and abhorred—quiet.

Our society has a bizarrely paradoxical relationship with quiet. Oh, we pretend to value it highly. When we're overwhelmed, we couple its name with "peace," bemoaning our need for that life-giving combination. We're always speaking of its merits, always remembering its benefits for our health, our concentration, our sanity. Some of us even go so far as to attend seminars or whole conferences on how to apply its principles to our spiritual walk. Quiet is important. We know it is.

Yet on the other hand, despite our professions, we don't actually want quiet. It might be respected, but it is not loved. If you don't believe me, just look at how little space we leave it in our daily lives. We are constantly surrounding ourselves with more stimuli—television shows, radios, Bluetooth devices, even "white noise" machines whose sole purpose is to shatter the stillness. Perhaps this is because, under all our professions of regard, quiet is frankly one of the most frightening states for a human being. Devotional writer Amber C. Haines addresses this concern: "I've been dabbling with the quiet because I need to hear from God, but the truth about the quiet is that it has opened me up wide, turned on my dulled senses, and faced me toward my rawest, loneliest places....[T]he quieter it gets, the lonelier I feel and the more I am left to deal with my own thoughts and what I really believe about God."[1]

Most of us can relate to this confession. Quiet has a strange way of dismantling our defenses and denuding our hidden hearts. We may preach its advantages, but we would prefer to theorize, not experience. However, I believe it is time for us, as the people of God, to make peace with the presence of silence. For it is often in the holiness of hush that the voice of God is most audible.

Consider the episode recorded in 1 Kings 19—a glimpse into the life of God's servant Elijah. When we see the mighty prophet in this passage, a tremendous bout of spiritual warfare has left him victorious but also exhausted—in body, mind, and spirit. He has retreated to the wilderness (a move with which I can't help but sympathize!) and fallen into a despair so dark that he has begged God to take his life! In this time of trouble, God visits this broken man—but not in the way we might expect.

As Elijah huddles in a small cave on a mountainside, a pageant of dramatic phenomena passes before him—a violent wind strong enough to tear chunks of rock off the mountain, an earthquake that shakes the foundations of the land, and even a raging wildfire with flames whipping past that cave of refuge. At the end of these events, though, Elijah hears "a still small voice" (1 Kings 19:12b KJV). Recognizing the One Who speaks to him, he reverently wraps his face in his cloak and goes forth to commune with the Lord.

I read this passage, and I can't help but shake my head. A still small voice? This method of communication seems odd to me, so imagine how much stranger it must have been for Elijah! It's interesting to note that the wind, the fire, and the earthquake were all ways in which God had manifested Himself previously in Scripture.

Indeed, He had a history of appearing to Israel in dramatic ways—the parting of the Red Sea and the subsequent destruction of the world's largest army, the pillar of blazing fire that led the Hebrews through the desert, even the merciless plagues that consumed the doubters and naysayers.[2] Elijah himself had just come from Mount Carmel, where his prayers were answered with the jaw-dropping response of fire shooting from the sky to validate his ministry and his faith.[3] Surely, then, as he waited in that cave, he watched each new display, familiar from history, with expectation. *This is it! Here He comes!* Yet the God of the whole universe, the One Whose breath parts the oceans and Whose word cracks the sky with thunder, chose to speak in a still small voice. Ordinary. Boring. Even anticlimactic.

Yet unmistakably divine.

And if you think that this was a special exception, that God no longer speaks in the quiet, then think again. It's a truth I'm reminded of each time I stand in the winter forest and hear nothing louder than the scuffing of birds in the fallen leaves or the gentle wind sighing through the treetops—quiet is one of God's favorite ways of communicating with His people.

Why? Why would He choose this humble way of speaking to us?

For starters, quiet is often not as drab as it appears. In fact, it's sometimes the only way God can get our attention. Just consider how many noises vie for our scattered focus—humming ceiling fans, barking dogs, creaking doors, yelling people, honking horns, roaring jets, bleeping alarms. My cell phone alone, so my analytics reveal, assaults me with a ridiculous average of sixty-one notifications every day—and that's after I systematically disabled this function for most apps and programs. Moreover, in the spiritual realm, we face another layer of "noise pollution" as we are constantly assailed with Satan's bombardment of fear and doubt, worry and regret, guilt and uncertainty and ever-fluctuating emotional states. Just as a teacher might stop talking in order to get the attention of an unruly class— just as a silent pause in a darkened theater cues the focus of the crowd for what is to come—God sometimes uses quiet as a means of redirecting our focus to Him and making us hungry for His Presence. Indeed, this seemingly mundane medium is often the most dramatic tool God can use!

Once God has our attention, quiet can also become His avenue of compassion. When we are hurting, when our world has been clawed to shreds and it seems no power on earth or heaven can put it together again, the last thing we need is for God to show off. We only need Him to show up—to sit with us in our pain, to hold us with gentle hands, to carefully pull together our sharp and shattered pieces, our raw and bleeding edges, and hug us close to His heart. Think about Elijah's situation again. Confused, alone, dejected, and burned out, he had no use for a raging wildfire or an uncontrollable windstorm. He only needed the still small voice—the invitation to intimacy. And often, that's what we also desire—the beckoning welcome that urges us to crawl out of whatever cave we've hidden in.

And when we come forth from that cave in answer to that still small voice, then the true beauty of quiet begins to blossom. You see, it's an undervalued principle that *quiet equals growth*. In our culture, quiet is viewed passively—as merely a gap to be filled. Indeed, we perceive quiet as an indicator that nothing is happening. However, this is far from the truth. The great periods of growth in our lives happen not during the bright and sunshiny times, but during the long agonizing stretches of silence.

This is nowhere more true than in the winter forest. The trees look dead, the colors have leaked from the landscape, the air is bitter, the birds have flown, and the grass is merely crumbling stalks. To our eyes, the quiet of this season symbolizes death and decay, not vigor and vitality.

But right now, in that "dead" winter forest, blanketed by all that silence, growth is happening. It's creeping up on the world in ways we don't even notice. The sap is circulating in the trees; many of them have already set leaf buds, the embryos of the spring foliage that perch on the deadened branches like patient reminders that spring is on the way. The birds that disappeared in the fall are preparing for their northward journey; in fact, some may have already begun their flight as we speak. Those fawns whose antics I enjoy each spring are, like most of the season's offspring, still developing inside their pregnant mothers through these winter days. And all this growth—the child of the silence—is what makes the miracle of spring possible at all.

Maybe this is what we're supposed to remember when we see the winter woods. Too often, we view silence as a frightening void or even a disgrace—a sign of being abandoned or defeated. Silence means that we are not doing enough, or that our lives are dwindling to stagnation, or even that God is ignoring us and has turned His attention to more deserving children. Yet in the Creator's world, quiet is the opposite of the negative meanings we ascribe to it. Quiet is the lullaby sung lovingly to the growing earth, the blessing poured out on its efforts, the wellspring from which the succession of other seasons flows.

Yes, the winter woods look barren. And at times, so do our lives. We've all crouched in a cave and wept with Elijah. But today, if you find yourself in silence, please know this above all—you are not forsaken. The eye of the Lord does not leave you for one moment. In this season of quiet, embrace His nearness, and enjoy His gentleness, and expect His growth. Great things are coming, slowly building, taking root in ways too small to notice. The quiet is not deadening—it is quickening. So smile in the silence—and when you hear that still small voice, be ready to respond, "Speak, for Your servant is listening" (1 Samuel 3:10 NASB).

FROZEN FILIGREE

I f you want to feel small, stand outside on a winter
night.

Admittedly, I'm not usually out of doors after dark during the
winter. I happily roam the leafless woods all during the abbreviated
afternoons of this season, but when the last drops of sunlight trickle
from the landscape, I view the embers of sunset kindling on the
western horizon as my cue to head for shelter. I'd rather watch the
dusk deepen by looking out a window—protected from its chill by
the cocoon of warmth and light that is my home.

But occasionally, for one reason or another, I find myself
outdoors on a winter night. And when I do, it's an experience unlike
any other.

The darkness is abysmal—a deep, velvety black that seems to
absorb all color. Yet the stars are at their most brilliant, glittering like
a handful of jewels tossed across the canopy of the heavens. The
night is silent, devoid of sound except for the occasional rasp of a
fox's bark or mournful query of an owl. It's so quiet I can hear my
own breath, the swirling clouds floating toward the stars. And on the
bitterly cold nights, the nights when the chill tingles inside my nose, I

sometimes bend down and run my fingers lightly over the dry and wilted grass, feeling the icy resistance of the winter night's most signature feature—frost.

In a strictly scientific sense, frost is nothing more than hardened water. When cooled below a certain temperature, called the dew point, the water vapor in the air condenses into liquid. If surrounding surfaces are colder than the water, it will crystallize into frost—a delicate arrangement of ice crystals that crawl along every outdoor surface.[1] Yet this bare-bones explanation doesn't convey its destructive power. It's cursed by agriculturists from commercial farmers to home gardeners—just one touch from its frigid fingers turns the inherent water content in crops and outdoor plants to ice, rendering even the most vibrant plants a droopy, wilted mess when the sun rises the next day.[2] In addition, frost can create hazardous driving conditions; most of us have known the frustration of a frost-crusted windshield or the anxiety of maneuvering roadways slickened by the ice. And let's not forget the psychological factor: just the sight of the iced-over trees or the crunch of the crispy grass under our feet makes us feel ten times colder!

In many ways, frost is the very embodiment of the bleakness of winter—the congealed breath of the north wind, the tangible crust of cold on every living thing. But in a paradoxical twist, frost is not only deadly and destructive. It is also surprisingly, astonishingly, beautiful.

If you've ever taken a close look at a frosted leaf or grass blade, you've doubtless noticed that far from being a single sheath of ice, frost is actually composed of trillions of individual crystals. And the variety of patterns in which these crystals are arranged seems infinite. Some designs are geometric—cubic crystals jumbled side by side. Others are more abstract—feathery sweeps tracing lacy scallops on folded leaves. Some are like miniature snowflakes—as if each stem of grass has been flocked in velour.

When I see the frost, it's a strange dichotomy. I feel the bracing gloom of winter, the chill and the destruction and the bitterness. Yet I can't help but be captivated by the artistry of the ice—as if angels had stenciled the outlines of their wings on all creation. On one hand frost is grim; on the other, it's glorious. And what a marvel—God takes something that is brutal and harsh, something that is responsible for leaking the life from the landscape, and transforms it into incredible beauty.

Could the same principle be true in our lives?

Perhaps you've never watched your breath on frigid January nights, but I'm sure you've known winter in the way we all do—the winter of the soul. One moment, we can be enjoying a summery life, full of joy and brightness and peace. But in the next breath, the frost arrives—perhaps in the form of a disturbing diagnosis, a shocking phone call, an unexpected confession. Whatever the specific situation, the effects of spiritual frost are the same—shrouding our souls in despair, freezing the life from our spirits, transforming our hitherto sunshiny lives into a bitter winter.

"The most difficult season of the soul for most is winter," notes pastor and writer Miriam Dixon. "The winter of the soul is bleak, cold, dark, and fruitless."[3] Anyone who's ever watched their life take on arctic qualities would agree with these words. Like the frost outside my window this time of year, these frigid days of the spirit cause destruction and loss of epic proportions. Yet they also hold the potential, in the midst of great pain, for great beauty as well.

This idea doesn't settle smoothly into the framework of our thinking. Beauty? In this? We feel that our circumstances are scarcely bearable—let alone beautiful. Moreover, when we stand on the freezing turf of what used to be our life, when hoarfrost has crept into every corner of our souls, the pain is too intense to even imagine trying to find beauty. In fact, the mere suggestion can feel flippant, insulting, and downright disrespectful. When the clouds have blocked all trace of the sunlight, it's too dark to hunt for a silver lining.

If that's you today, then please hear me—in no way am I suggesting that the winters of our souls are not painful. Far from it! In and of themselves, the frosty events that destroy our dreams are far from beautiful. But what I am saying is that our circumstances, no matter how brutal, are being woven into a beautiful story—the intricate pattern that God is creating in our lives.

Over and over again, this idea of beauty nested inside heartache is found in Scripture. Jonah reacted in disobedience, fled from God, and was swallowed by a whale—yet his unlovely actions became part of the redemption of the wicked city of Nineveh.[4] Job lost his fortune, his family, his home, and his friends in one day—yet these tragic events set the stage for one of the greatest dramas of faith.[5] Joseph was kidnapped, abused, enslaved, accused, imprisoned, forgotten—yet with unfailing accuracy, each horrific event became a rung on the ladder to his destiny, and at the end of his story, he was able to gratefully proclaim that "God meant [all the trials] for good" (Genesis 50:20 ESV).

20

"He has made everything beautiful in its time" (Ecclesiastes 3:11a ESV). We read this verse and picture lovely things—butterflies and sunsets and first loves and happy endings. When gazing on these joys, it's easy to agree that yes, God makes things beautiful. But what does the verse say? "He has made *everything* beautiful." Not "some things." Not "happy things." Not "things we like." *Everything*. Even the things that have sharp edges that slice our soul. Even the things we want to scrub from our stories and never remember again. Even the things that wake us up in the middle of the night and leer like phantoms in our most terrifying nightmares. Beauty in *everything*. In fact, God's beautifying touch is most evident not in the things that are already charming but in those things that seem the ugliest—just as it is far more miraculous for His loveliness to be apparent in the cruel frost than in the springtime blossoms.

But even when we acknowledge that God does this, we still don't understand *how*. How can God take the rawest, ugliest pieces of our life and infuse them with beauty? The answer lies in one miraculous fact. You see, God doesn't just inject beauty into our lives. God *is* the beauty—and He steps into our circumstances Himself.

Think about the frost again. If you've ever observed it, then you know that it is most spectacular not at night, but in the early morning—because that's when the sun shines on it. When the first beams of winter sunshine kiss the frost, it is transformed into a fairy palace of wonder—a shimmering exhibition that looks otherworldly. All the colors of the rainbow sparkle above the crispy grass, and diamonds are tangled in the tree limbs. The frost that is so destructive by night is positively breathtaking by day. What makes the difference? The presence of the sunlight—and the way the frost reflects its presence.

My friends, without God, beauty does not exist—and certainly not in the hard and the hurtful. There is no human way that the "frost" in our lives can ever be anything but soul-numbing ice. The frostbitten corners of our hearts hold no attractiveness in and of themselves. But when the Son rises on the landscape of your soul, when the glory of the Lord spills light on your circumstances, then His grace irradiates everything, and the shrapnel in our spirits becomes a dazzling example of His goodness. What once was broken is beautified—all because of the Light.

And just as the frost sparkles in the sunlight, when God pours His love across our winter souls, we respond by reflecting His light. In the joyous paradox of the Kingdom, Jesus transforms the very ice that froze our souls into a priceless jewel that dazzles onlookers. This is why the greatest stories are born in the holy intersection of God's light with your frosty life, for an awe-inspiring purpose: "[God] comforts us in all our affliction, so that we may be able to comfort those who are in any affliction, with the comfort with which we ourselves are comforted by God" (2 Corinthians 1:4 ESV). When God brings beauty from our pain, we then receive the wonderful responsibility of breathing hope into someone else's permafrost soul. And when we look at our life through this lens, the events that brought so much hurt no longer seem like a string of senseless pain. Instead, they become carefully orchestrated opportunities to share the workings of God with those around you.

In the hands of God, the "frost" in our lives is the beauty in our story, the blessing to others—and the beacon to the Lord. You see, when we allow God to work in our bleakest times, He receives all the honor. He's showcased in His splendid glory as the God Who brings beauty even in the dead winters of our lives, the God Who derives growth and life and wonder out of something that seemed to hold only death and disaster.

We've never needed this hope more than now. My friends, in the tumult of our world, we seem to be having many more "frosty nights" than normal. Winter tends to cling to our spirits. The ice on our souls can make it hard to breathe, and at times, all the beauty God promised seems to have fled. Perhaps it's not surprising, then, if the usual tingling eagerness for a new year is muffled this time, replaced by tenuous anxiety and lingering insecurity. We may find ourselves looking at this year with trepidation—the shrinking uncertainty of people who can't bear to be hurt anymore.

And so I want to encourage you today with these words: in the most broken moments, there is beauty. How can I be so sure? Because in those painful times, there is also God. He has always been here—working and waiting and wooing us back to Himself. And as we face this new season, He will still be here. If He can redeem even the most destructive winter force, the grim symbol of bleakness and desolation, then He can transform any painful circumstance we face. Because when the frost in your spirit meets the healing light of the Son, nothing is ever the same.

TRUE NORTH

I received my first compass when I was very young—maybe seven or eight years old. It was a pretty flimsy specimen, more a toy than a tool. It was tiny, about the size of a nickel and attached to a shiny blue carabiner. Oddly enough, I acquired that compass not from an outdoors store or a hiking company but from my local library, where the implements were being used as prizes for children who read a certain number of books during the library's wilderness-themed summer reading program. A voracious reader who needed no encouragement to become lost in a book, I easily met the goal and received the compass as my reward.

That little compass was my friend for several years, my partner in backyard excursions, my companion on family hikes. Thanks to its influence, I fell in love with compasses. They captivated me both with their enigmatic accuracy and their ability to provide a security I found reassuring.

I still have that little nickel-sized compass, and although its dial is a bit wobbly now, I would never part with it. Over the years, however, it's been joined by a collection of other compasses,

23

gathered from here and there. There's the flat black compass with a clear face and guide lines, enabling it to be placed over a map for ease of charting a course. There's also my red wooden compass on its multicolored string—the size of a medallion, it swung from my neck during many an exploratory venture. In my hiking belt at this moment is a sophisticated lenticular compass with brass rods to indicate precise directional variations next to a flat orange compass that cost $1.99. Last but not least is my whimsical compass—a carved wooden ladybug, complete with feet and a painted smile, with a directional dial embedded in her back. This one, a gift from my grandmother, rode in the pocket of my hiking pants for years until I retired her from active service for the protection of her chipping paint.

This list doesn't even begin the enormity of my collection. I've named only a few of my favorites, and that's not counting my other devices, like binoculars and survival tool, that contain built-in compasses. Frankly, I have more versions of this tool than I'll ever need. Compasses are most valuable for topographic hiking, and although I've tried my hand at the sport in the past, I can't help but feel a bit leery of an activity whose main premise is simply to select a landmark on the distant horizon and beat your own route to it. I generally hike on established trails, and while I may need a map to help me decipher the trail intersections, I'm not likely to become directionally confused. Even on the occasions when I do need a compass—rare, in this modern world of safety and sedation—a few quick swipes would open a compass app native to my iPhone.

Yet I won't be scrapping my compass collection any time soon—or ever. You see, a compass is like a memorized emergency number; you may never need to use it, but if you do, it could save your life. Beyond their functionality, though, my compasses mean something deeper to me. They indicate security, stability, certainty. When I stand on a ridge, sweeping the horizon with my eyes, there's a sense of power that comes from being able to consult a compass. I balance the flat disc on my palm, watching the red-tipped needle tilt around the circle, 360 faultless degrees of eternity. And then, if I am patient, if I am very still, if I do not make assumptions or judgment calls or rash choices, the needle will, in its own deliberate way, settle on the almighty N.

And I will plunge into the underbrush with a fearless heart, for now I know my way.

When I first received that tiny compass, I wasn't in great need of directional advice. Life was predictable, simple, and I made my choices with the ease of routine and the reassurance of familiarity. But each passing year seems to bring additional complications, and despite my geeky compass collection, there have been plenty of times when I've lost my way or questioned my direction.

I'm not talking about the white-knuckle war of spirit and flesh, although I've certainly experienced that as well. I'm referring to the times when I've arrived at an intersection where all choices seemed equally viable. I have a passion to follow God's leading, but doing so becomes difficult when His leading is nebulous. In fact, as a teenager harassed by fears about college, I was so afraid of making a misstep that I scrawled an audacious request in my journal: for God to send me a Manila envelope, straight from His throne room, containing the details of His will for the next four years of my life.

Maybe you can relate. Maybe you've been offended by someone's behavior, and you wonder whether to lovingly confront them or simply ignore the pain. Maybe you're unsure about the job offer as you balance comfortable wages and room for advancement against the pressure of competition and the time away from family. Perhaps you've met someone who seeks to unlock your heart, but you hesitate before handing over the key. We've all been in those situations—times when we want to do God's will, but we can't hear His voice. Times when we wish God would send an angel as a divine skywriter and scribble His answer on the rolling white clouds.

Those are the times when we need a compass. We stand on a ridge and look over a dense forest, filled with trees as identical as clones and not a signal fire in sight. The trail forks into a Y, and both angles look much the same. We've talked to other hikers, studied the maps, and examined the options, but we still feel disoriented. The sun seems in the wrong position in the sky, and we can't find our way.

To make things even worse, when we search the Scriptures, we find directions that seem maddeningly vague, even generic. *God, which decision should I make?* "Trust in the Lord with all your heart, and do not lean on your own understanding."[1] *Lord, should I date this person?* "Above all else, guard your heart."[2] *God, what do you want me to do?* "He has told you, O man, what is good; and what does the LORD require of you but to do justice, and to love kindness, and to walk humbly with your God?"[3]

We read those verses, and we sigh in exasperation. *Of course*, we think. Yes, we know to trust God. Yes, we understand to be humble and cling to mercy. But we need specifics for our situation! Why are God's commands so generalized?

I think the clue comes from examining a traditional compass. People unfamiliar with the use of this implement generally envision the compass needle swiveling to face the particular direction they desire to travel—adjusting itself to fit their needs. Yet in actuality, that's not how a compass performs. The job of a compass is not to provide us with tailor-made directions or explicit instructions.

The job of a compass is simply to point us North.

North—because North is the master direction, and if you know where North is, its smaller cousins—east and south and west—fit into their proper positions. North is the greatest direction, 0 degrees on a compass, the place where the horizon's never-ending circle begins. So important is North, in fact, that even maps without room for a full directional panel will always include at least a tiny triangle and an N to orient users. And with stubborn faithfulness, the compass needle will always point to the N marked on its face.

You have to know where North is before you can head in any other direction.

My friends, we are all traveling in a dense wilderness. We could easily become lost—distracted—unfocused—bewildered. But in the moments when confusion holds our peace hostage, all we have to do is fix our eyes on North, and the other questions subside.

Because our True North is God—the Master of the compass, the Maker of the universe, the One Who has hand-drawn each path for our lives and Who guides us as we walk it. He is the fixed point who does not change, never wavers, and never moves. Indeed, God's throne is described in Isaiah 14:13 as being "in the sides of the north" (KJV). God is the Master Director of the master direction. And as our True North, He has provided us with a compass to point us to Him—the Holy Spirit.

Within your heart, you hold the compass to point you North. You've experienced this. Think about a time when you chose to help someone, regardless of the inconvenience to you. A time when you gave a little more money, or time, or love than you thought you could spare. A time when you tentatively embraced a dream you'd cherished and used one of your gifts for God's glory. In those moments, my friends, your compass was pointing you to True North—just as Jesus promised.

It has been said that "God is the answer no matter the question." The phrase sounds cliché, but beneath the façade of banality is a rock-hard base of truth. And maybe that's why God doesn't scrawl words on the sky or whisper the answer in our ear or mail us Manila envelopes full of plans. Maybe life isn't about always making the right turning on the trail—after all, God promises He'll use all our decisions for His glory and our good,[4] so perhaps there's more room than we realize for flexibility in the specifics. Maybe life is more about simply getting our directions straight—about choosing to look North, over and over and over, as many times as it takes to find our bearings and force our questions to shrink into their secondary roles. Perhaps that's why the Bible holds truths to enjoy, not lectures to memorize.

So, if you're at a fork in the trail, pause for an instant. Breathe deeply and don't allow yourself to panic. Listen to the voice of the Holy Spirit within your heart, and keep your eyes on the horizon, 360 faultless degrees of eternity. And then, if you are patient, if you are very still, if you do not make assumptions or judgment calls or rash choices, the Great Compass will, in His own deliberate way, settle on the N.

And then you will plunge into the underbrush with a fearless heart, for now you know His way.

Sleeping under Snow

All around me, the world is asleep.

The trees that rustle and whisper during most of the year are now silent, stripped of their leaves. Most of the birds have migrated, taking with them the melodic soundtrack of summer days. Even the deer are subdued, ensconced in the protective arms of forest thickets.

The depths of winter are a holy hush. After the riotous color and action and life of all other seasons, winter is soaked in a silence so pervasive that when I roam the silvery hillsides or watch the sluggish trickle of the ice-encrusted streams, I imagine that I can almost, *almost*, hear the gentle breathing of the dreaming earth.

But for many animals, this sleeping isn't merely figurative; it's literal. Right now, in holes and dens and burrows, many animals are slumbering in a very important yet enigmatic form of sleep—hibernation.

You see, winter is a perilous time for wildlife. The cold temperatures are dangerous for small animals, and snow and ice render their usual patterns of travel more difficult. Perhaps most seriously, winter brings a reduced supply of food. The nuts, seeds, and berries that were so plentiful in the growing season are now depleted.

28

Thus, hibernation serves as an escape for many species of animals, from woodchucks and chipmunks to hedgehogs and mice. Beginning in early fall, they frantically gorge themselves on all the food they can find in order to build up a thick layer of subcutaneous fat. When winter begins to nip the earth, hormonal changes signal the animals to retreat to their burrows and sleep the winter away. While they may wake fitfully from time to time, this sleep is mostly undisturbed for the duration of the winter, and the fat layer provides energy for their survival as well as insulation from the cold. By spring, the fat store is depleted, and the animals rise with the awakening world—hungry, emaciated, but no doubt relieved to have survived another long winter.

The concept of hibernation is referenced in stories, artwork, and the collective mythology we weave about the natural world. The cultural interpretation of hibernation evokes images of gophers and ground squirrels spiraled in nests of grass, reliving dreams of summer—warm, safe, and blissful. (A hibernation-themed article by the website Environmental Education for Kids reflects this myth with its title: "Snug in the Snow.")[1]

However, in reality, the picture is a bit bleaker. Hibernation is more than ordinary sleep; it's a state of dormancy accompanied by a dramatically lowered metabolism. In other words, the animal's body shuts down to the point that they are, for all practical purposes, lifeless. In fact, if you stumbled across a hibernating animal in the middle of winter, you wouldn't be able to find any sign of life. The animal would be cold to the touch, perhaps even ice-covered. It would be stiff, its muscles rigid, its limbs locked into position. Its breathing and heart rate would be so slow as to be nearly undetectable. For an example of how dramatic these changes are, just consider the woodchuck. Its body temperature while hibernating is a frosty 38 degrees, and its heart rate, normally a rapid 80 beats a minute, slows to an incredible 4 or 5 beats a minute![2] Yes, if you found a hibernating animal, you'd feel a pang of pity and sadly label it another casualty of winter.

But despite all appearances, despite the frost on their fur and the rigidity in their limbs and the almost-nonexistent heart rate, these animals are very much alive. They're not even injured or ill. When spring smiles on the earth, they'll defy all logic—opening their tight-shut eyes and shaking the ice from their coats and scurrying up from their underground dens. The animals that frolic in springtime meadows are ones that could have easily been mistaken for dead only a few weeks earlier.

When I consider this, I wonder how many times in our lives we make the same mistake. Okay, so we probably don't have a lot of experience with judging the vitality of hibernating animals. But haven't we all looked at people, or places, or situations and only seen death—when in reality, hope was still very much alive?

I'm reminded of the story of Ezekiel 37. This prophecy is perhaps one of the most bizarre in all of Scripture. In this vision, the prophet Ezekiel was taken by God to a valley filled with a macabre scene: a tangled mass of scattered human bones. Ezekiel recounts the exchange that followed: "He [God] led me back and forth among them, and I saw a great many bones on the floor of the valley, bones that were very dry. He asked me, 'Son of man, can these bones live?' I said, 'Sovereign Lord, you alone know'" (v. 2-3 ESV).

Ezekiel's reply resonates with me. He doesn't make an extravagant profession of faith, but neither does he negate the chance of a miracle. Instead, he places the possibilities right where they belong—in the hands of a God he rightfully calls "sovereign." With his simple statement, he acknowledges that to his eyes, resuscitation is far out of reach—but he also affirms his trust in the power of God. And how does God respond? By doing the impossible: taking the lifeless jumble of bones and resurrecting them into a mighty army.

My friends, we've all stood in a valley of dry bones and gazed at situations that seemed to be totally, completely, unquestioningly, dead. Perhaps it's a wayward child that won't return, a family member that can't be pleased, a health condition that can't be managed, a marriage that's been shattered, or a career that can't be salvaged. These circumstances can seem just as helpless as the dry bones—as hopeless as the hibernating animals. Regardless of the specifics, when we gaze at dreams that seem so totally dead, our natural human instinct is to give up—to fling our last shreds of hope to the whipping wind. Our souls are fragile, shockingly so, and somehow, this tendency can masquerade as protection—choosing to surrender our hope rather than have it yanked mercilessly from our hands. But whether we're motivated by fear, or grief, or frustration, the danger of this human weakness is great: we often declare the situation dead long before God is finished working.

Renowned author Andy Andrews once wrote, "There are no hopeless situations…only people who have grown hopeless about them. You still have choices you can make."[3] My friends, nothing is ever too far gone for God! He brought a nation out of a 400-year bondage;[4] restored life to a man who'd been lying in a tomb for three days;[5] and (best of all) put His Spirit in our sinful hearts.[6] If there is just one thing I can say with certainty about God, it's this: He is in the business of resurrection. He has always delighted in bringing new life out of seeming death and breathing hope into the bleakest circumstances. When the situation looks frozen in death, His power is revealed in its most dazzling glory.

And in the kind of paradox only God could invent, sometimes, apparent death is the exact opposite: the path to life.

Just think about the hibernating animals again. In the midst of hibernation, they're hovering in the twilight areas on the fringes of life, camping on the very doorstep of death. And yet, in the beautiful irony of God's creation, it is this journey through the valley of death that is responsible for their life.

You see, it would be impossible for these creatures to survive the winter if their metabolism were operating at the normal rate. There simply wouldn't be enough food available to sustain them. They would suffer an agonizing death through starvation, and they would never see the spring. But in His mercy and wisdom, the Creator endowed them with the ability to conserve precious resources by entering this dormant state. By "dying," they're actually living.

It sounds outlandish, and it defies our logic, but it is the way of the Kingdom that quite often, apparent "death" is a necessary ingredient to an outpouring of blessing and life greater than what we can imagine. Just think of these examples. As Christians, we must first die to ourselves to receive new life in Christ;[7] we "die" in baptism to symbolically take part in Christ's atonement;[8] and we die to our sinful desires daily to appropriate the life Jesus won for us.[9] Of course, the most dramatic example in all of history is the death and resurrection of Jesus Christ—by His death, He opened a path to eternal life for all who would believe on Him.[10]

This is a repeating pattern, my friends. Oftentimes, what we classify as dead is not only very much alive, but preparing for a rebirth we would never expect or imagine.

However, I know that if you're staring at the frozen figures of your dreams—if you can no longer distinguish between dormancy and death—if the white silence of winter seems to have shrouded your soul—then no words I could say would salve your heart. You may be thinking that I don't know how bad things are, or how long you've waited, or how unanswered your prayers have been, or how utterly bleak your situation is. And you're right…I don't have a window to your particular pain. But I've carried my own. I've stood in the valley of dry bones. I've searched in vain for any trace of life in circumstances that seemed graveyard-ready.

And I know this: even when it looks as if things are dead, even when there's no symptom of life, even when we have every reason to turn and walk away with granite grief in our hearts—there is still abundant hope to be found. God can reverse any situation. And sometimes, surprisingly often, what mimics death from our point of view is actually the launchpad for new life.

THE PINECONE PARABLE

Y ears ago, my mother, an accomplished artist, was enrolled in a litany of classes at a local college. These art-focused classes taught techniques of design composition, the use of various artistic media, and special drawing styles, to name a few. For one class, she received a standard assignment: create a large drawing of a "still-life" subject (basically, an interesting object or grouping of objects). Looking for a truly unique item to draw, my mother chose something that was doubtless inspired by her love of the woods—a pinecone. The drawing she produced is beautiful, and my grandmother was so entranced by it that it hung on the wall of her house for years. That simple assignment is now part of our family lore.

My family members aren't the only folks for whom pinecones hold a special meaning. Indeed, these humble objects make a plethora of appearances throughout our culture. As a result, most of us are quite familiar with pinecones. Even if we haven't seen a real one, we've at least noticed replicas—embossed on greeting cards, embroidered on pillows, or dangling from a Christmas wreath. And living in the woods, I'm certainly no stranger to pinecones. I've kicked them on forest trails, I've passed them swinging on evergreen branches, and I've even admired cheeky squirrels nibbling away at their seeds. They're so common that, if I'm not careful, I can tend to take them for granted. However, every now and then, one will catch my attention, and I'll notice it in a deeper way.

I've found that there's something satisfying, somehow, about finding a pinecone that hasn't been gnawed by squirrels or worn by the elements or crunched under someone's foot. The scales are perfectly patterned, spiraling around and around in a way that reminds me somehow of feathers on birds or scales on fish or even rungs on Jacob's ladder. The aesthetics, the symmetry, make it easy to see why the exterior of the pinecone receives all the attention. But what most people don't realize is that the most valuable part of a pinecone is found deep inside—the seeds of future pine trees. I hold that pinecone in my palm, and it's only papery bark, and it's only dull-dirt brown, but it's precious and it's beautiful and it's meaningful. And there in the winter woods, fingers wrapped around the sharp-pronged scales, I wonder how it can weigh so little but hold so much.

You see, the scales of a pine cone aren't simply for decoration. They actually cover and protect the seeds, nestled underneath them. In fact, it's not uncommon for a pine cone to remain on its parent tree for an entire decade in order for the seeds to develop fully.[1] Even after the pinecone falls, its primary purpose—protecting those seeds—remains its top priority. And to accomplish this goal, it can do something amazing—open and close itself.

It sounds unbelievable, but if you want to see for yourself, you can try this experiment sometime. Visit the winter woods and look for a pinecone that's recently fallen and still intact. Bring it inside and expose it to a heat source. You could hold it near a radiator, gently warm it with a hairdryer, or even place it in an oven. (Keep in mind that pinecones can burn if the heat is too intense; be sure to perform this experiment safely.) As the pinecone becomes warmer and drier, you'll notice something surprising. The scales will actually unfold, and the pinecone will open completely.[2]

Now, let's say that you removed the fully open pinecone from the oven and submerged it in a bucket of icy water. After only a short time, the expanded pinecone would be almost unrecognizable as the scales tightened and pinched themselves over the seeds.

Why does this happen? The pinecone is specially designed to respond to changing conditions in its environment. Seeds have the best chances of survival if they're released in warm, dry conditions. Thus, warmth and dryness trigger the pinecone to open wide, allowing the seeds to escape. However, cold, wet conditions are not only unsuitable for future trees to take root; they're also potentially damaging to the seeds themselves. Thus, in this kind of environment, the pinecone seals itself up tightly, preventing harm to its precious cargo.[3]

As I watch this odd behavior of the pinecone, I realize that it seems a bit familiar. Perhaps that's because my heart can perform much the same defense mechanisms—opening wide when I feel safe, yet closing off at the first sign of danger. We humans aren't carrying valuable seeds, but we often feel the need to conceal far more precious items—like our emotions, ideas, affections, and even our deep pain.

"Put [my] heart in a shell; put the shell in a box;/Don't let anyone see/That the small quaking shriveled-up thing in the box/Is the heart inside of me." I scribbled these lines down several years ago to help me cope with a difficult time, and as I read them now, I can't help but realize that I've taken this "advice" many times during my life. And I suspect I'm not alone in this. During times of prosperity, people tend to be expansive, friendly, and welcoming. We laugh with friends, confide in our family, smile at strangers on the street. But when we're hurt, we retreat. Suddenly the people around us seem not like potential allies but possible threats waiting to inflict even deeper wounds on our fragile psyche. And like the pinecone, we respond by sealing the deepest parts of ourselves out of sight.

Why do we do this? Sometimes this is a natural response when our openness has been rewarded with hate. When we've been wronged by a close friend, a spouse, or a family member, when someone we love has betrayed our trust, then it's easy to withdraw. If we hadn't been so open and trusting, we reason, we would have never been hurt. And if being open caused the problem, then surely locking our heart away will fix it. So we huddle over our pain and block out those around us.

Or perhaps we've experienced a traumatic situation that has shredded the fabric of our world. Abuse, neglect, accidents, crimes, intense loss and incredible grief—these are some of the darkest lows of the human experience. To survive the holes they rip in our lives, sometimes closing ourselves off feels like the only option. One of the most simply impactive quotations I've ever read on this topic came from an anonymous woman whose story was detailed by Max Lucado in his book *Cast of Characters*. As a child, she endured horrific abuse at the hands of her Satanist parents, who used her as an implement in their heinous rituals. In Lucado's book, she described her survival strategy as "crawling down deep inside herself."[4] Those of us who have experienced an agonizingly painful situation find her words to be terribly true.

And sometimes, we're not facing trauma or rejection but simply encountering a rough season, and we feel no one understands—or even cares to. Our culture is largely to blame for this—the insistence on keeping up appearances, the urge to be constantly rendering our messy lives Instagram-worthy. In a world where we mandate picture-perfection, all we achieve is chronic loneliness. We don't have a culture of authenticity; we have a culture where the mother whose child is battling chronic illness, the man whose faith is wavering, and the teenager seized with doubts about the future all shake hands in the church foyer and politely assure the others that they're doing wonderful, thank you for asking. In reality, everyone is dying inside—and no one wants to be the first to pull off the mask. And in all that loneliness, that inner conviction that judgment accompanies disclosure, we conceal our pain with our Sunday smiles.

I'm sure that like all of us, you've felt that urge to hide. Retreat from a sharp and painful world and seal off your heart. Build a wall that no one can penetrate. There's a problem, though. For the pinecone, closing itself off in less-than-ideal conditions is a God-given design that allows it to protect its purpose. However, what is a marvelous defense mechanism for a pinecone doesn't work so well for humans.

You see, when we close the door to others, we actually open the door to Satan's attacks. The devil loves it when we withdraw from each other—because we have just made his job easier. Perhaps this is what Peter had in mind when he warned his readers that "your adversary the devil prowls around like a roaring lion, seeking someone to devour" (1 Peter 5:8 ESV).

Weakened. Alone. And the lion attacks. Haven't you heard his snarls while you were hiding inside yourself?

Imagine if everyone knew about this. They'd hate you.
No one else has this problem.
You're such a fake.
There's no way to fix this.
If only your kids could behave like hers. Look how perfect that family is.
And you call yourself a Christian!
Don't tell anyone. Do you want the whole church to know about this?
Shame. Guilt. Silence.

And then, Satan's real work begins. Because in isolation, there is only emptiness in which his lies can echo. When we are alone, with no one to give us another perspective, we believe his words much more readily. Slowly, he can destroy us—just like the roaring lion stalking his prey.

"Not neglecting to meet together, as is the habit of some, but encouraging one another, and all the more as you see the Day drawing near" (Hebrews 10:25 ESV). We hear this verse applied to corporate worship, and certainly it is very applicable for that situation. However, it's important to note that there's no number specified in this verse. The "meeting" could have been a hundred people. Or it could have been three—just a handful committed to encouraging each other and speaking truth into each other's situations. "As is the habit of some." Persecution was beginning to rumble underneath at this time. Perhaps the believers were beginning to become discouraged—and withdrawing. At any rate, the author of Hebrews knew that in their pain, as conditions worsened, they needed others more, not less. The very thing they feared—vulnerability—was actually the wellspring of one of their greatest strengths.

So yes, like the pinecone, we're often tempted to close up tightly and hold that pain inside. Yet when we do so, we're only making matters worse. We may be wounded. We may be fragile. We may be terrified—and the thought of revealing our secret pain might feel impossible. But when we open ourselves—even to just one compassionate person—and share our scars, we may be surprised at what happens. The world might not be as threatening as we thought. There's nothing that erases the power of the devil's words as much as these gentle words: *I understand. I'm here. You are not alone.* And even greater than the benefits of opening up to other people is the healing power of sharing our pain with the Lord. No matter what's hurting you today, remember the words of the psalmist: "You keep track of all my sorrows. You have collected all my tears in your bottle. You have recorded each one in your book" (Psalm 56:8 NLT). Your pain is His priority.

In these bleak winter days, most pinecones I locate in the woods are closed up, scales locked over seeds, sharp edges pointing outwards. When I pick one up, I nod my head, because I understand the need to feel protected. Perhaps that's why I enjoy bringing them inside—watching the light and the warmth and the gentle care unfurl the scales and release the jealously guarded seeds. The scales relax, and the bands around my soul loosen—and I smile, because I have learned the pinecone's lesson. In the midst of a frightening world, I am only truly safe when I am living with an open heart.

WARMER WINTER

I n winter, I see angels…in sky and snow.

There's a lacy loveliness about the making of snow angels, a sparkle that has always captivated me. After the earth has been kissed by snowfall, I rush out the door into the winter world and flop backwards onto the fluff of pristine snow. The sky is rapturously blue, the soaring hue of holiness. I gaze at its vaulted dome while sweeping my arms and legs in the signature pattern. Then I peel myself carefully from the impression I've made, trace a halo with a small stick, and admire the angel smiling from the snow.

It's a favorite activity for me, one that embodies the sugar-spun wonder of winter. Yet I don't often enjoy this simple pleasure. Why? For one disappointing reason: I don't have enough snow.

Here in Arkansas, our average winter snowfall is—wait for it!—*four inches*.[1] Four inches??? For a whole winter? To an inveterate snow lover like myself, that statistic is maddening. And many seasons, even that four inches is optimistic.

It's not the temperatures that prevent us from receiving more snow. We have times when frost crackles on every branch and cold seems to creep from the earth itself and the clouds frown on a shivering world. We have nights when the stars themselves quiver in the frosty darkness, and days when the watery sunshine is too weak

39

to thaw the ground. But instead of coming during these subfreezing periods, the precipitation waits until days with slightly higher temperatures—perhaps in the upper 40s or even 50s—and arrives not as snow, but rain.

This pattern generally repeats for the duration of the winter: a long stretch of bitterly cold but dry days will be broken by three or four days of precipitation, with the temperature just high enough to guarantee nothing more glamorous than a cold, churlish rain. The temperature drops following the rain, and the cycle begins all over again.

I find this maddening, because I love snow with a passion. Granted, I'm aware that this form of winter weather is somewhat of a polarizing topic, with its fair share of detractors. I also admit that on the rare occasions when snow has downed power lines or impeded travel, I've been less than thrilled. And yes, part of my attraction to snow may stem from its novelty; perhaps if it were common in an Arkansas winter, it would cease to be magical. But even with these practical considerations, I can think of few natural phenomena more delicately beautiful than a snowfall. The handful of serious snowstorms I've experienced have transformed our property into a fairyland, and their snapshots still fill my memory: a pristine blanket of whiteness over the nakedness of the winter landscape…slanting sunbeams sparkling on the drifts…forests flocked like Christmas trees…the hushed holiness, filled with miraculously perfect snowflakes whirling from the heavens…animal tracks stamped into the snow, perhaps the zigzagging trail of a fox's dainty pawprints or the tiny triangles of bird feet. Peace and beauty and the solitude of winter secrets…all these settle to earth with the swirling snow.

In fact, one of my favorite aspects of Estes Park, Colorado (my "heaven on earth" and favorite destination to visit), is the amount of snow that falls there each winter. In the Rockies, the snow begins flying in October, snowflakes and golden aspen leaves swirling together in the misty air. And the snowstorms can continue well into May. Altogether, the town receives over eighty inches per year![2] As a result, the inhabitants of Estes Park are able to enjoy incredible outdoor sports I'll never see in Arkansas—skiing, snowshoeing, tobogganing. And at Christmas, all the snow makes for an epically perfect holiday landscape.

As I watch weather forecasts with useless hope and scowl at a drab landscape being pummeled by icy rain, it's no wonder that I pine for the snow that blankets Estes Park every winter. To my mind, it's the perfect winter weather. Imagine my surprise, therefore, when I met a woman in Colorado who held a completely opposite viewpoint.

During a visit to Estes Park a couple of years ago, I was browsing a small store and simultaneously chatting with the cashier. In the course of our conversation, I mentioned my dissatisfaction with Arkansas winters and how much I wished we experienced the snow that Colorado did. I was shocked when the woman immediately and grimly informed me that I should be grateful for Arkansas's climate; she loathed Colorado winters. She insisted that they were harsh, bleak, and unforgiving. The snow was excessive. Driving was hazardous. Outdoor recreation was limited. And, she emphasized, even her childhood in gale-swept Kansas had not prepared her for the fury of the winds that roared down the mountainsides all winter long.

And in this conversation, as I observed the look of dread that crossed this woman's face at the very mention of winter, the irony struck me. I found Arkansas winters uninspiring; she envisioned them as a welcome reprieve. I longed for the snow and ice of Colorado; she hated such weather. Each of us was dissatisfied with our own winter, certain that the other one was enjoying the best option.

Isn't that just like us humans? We always want exactly what we don't have. I dream of her snowdrifts and squalls; she thinks snow-free days in Arkansas sound like paradise. The old proverb "The grass is always greener on the other side of the fence" may be hackneyed, but it's undeniably true. Our society has a hard time with a simple virtue—contentment.

"Contentment is natural wealth," sagely observed Socrates.[3] Thousands of years later, Benjamin Franklin echoed this truth: "Content makes poor men rich; discontent makes rich men poor."[4] We read these quotations, and we nod in unfeigned agreement. After all, we know the value of contentment. We praise it in our pulpits and urge it to our children and add it to wall décor.

Yet despite our lip service, we're incredibly skilled at disregarding this simple concept. We dwell in a culture that grasps with greedy fists. "Mine" is usually among our very first words, and we never outgrow its shadow. We turn all of life into a frantic race to have and do and be more than the runners we seek to outstrip. We're willing to dash ourselves to death in pursuit of elusive happiness, and we're sure our efforts can guarantee it for us.

Yet look at us. Competitive? Yes. Confused? Certainly. Combative? Undoubtedly. But content? That's a different story. Somehow, the glittering light of what we don't yet have is always enough to distract our gaze from the gentle glow of the candle of happiness right in front of our eyes.

Contentment is a hard trick to learn. King Solomon, the wisest man who ever lived, is an example of that. He was used by God to pen many proverbs, among them these: "A tranquil heart gives life to the flesh, but envy makes the bones rot" (Proverbs 14:30 ESV) and "The fear of the Lord leads to life, that one may rest content, without visitation from harm" (Proverbs 19:23 BSB).

Yet in his private life, even this most renowned philosopher couldn't implement the advice of his own prudent words. The king who wrote such glowing tributes to contentment never used the word in his daily life. His reign was one of decadence—he lived in extravagant luxury, collected a massive harem (700 wives and 300 concubines), hosted lavish parties, and levied enormous taxes on his subjects to support his hedonistic lifestyle.[5]

But before we judge Solomon too harshly, let's examine our own lives. How often do we want what we don't have? Just as I fantasize about living in another climate, we constantly daydream about different circumstances, mentally superimposing ourselves on new jobs, new relationships, new vacations, new homes, new hobbies. In a process that's been greatly assisted by social media, we hold our lives side-by-side with those of others, and we always seem to come up lacking. And if we're not careful, dissatisfaction with our current state can burgeon into an unending urge that sends us roving restlessly, fruitlessly attempting to transform novelty into peace, looking for an elusive feeling of "enough" that never comes. "Just as Death and Destruction are never satisfied, so human desire is never satisfied" (Proverbs 27:20 NLT).

Discontent may be human, but it isn't healthy. So detrimental is it, in fact, that God included a warning against covetousness in the Ten Commandments![6] At first glance, this might seem a bit excessive to us. After all, does pining after someone's else's belongings or status truly deserve to rank with murder, idolatry, and adultery? This question, however, reveals a lack of understanding about how serious discontent is. In its most elemental form, it's a permanent suspicion of God's good plan—a constant question if He will truly provide us with all we need. And although it may seem subtle, left unchecked, it lies at the root of every other sin listed in the commandments—the seed that sprouts a black and bitter fruit.

The opposite of this, the oxygen to our soul, is contentment. There's a common misunderstanding that contentment is a state of mind, but in actuality, it is a skill. It's not a destination at which we arrive when all our circumstances are perfectly aligned. Instead, it's the pathway that leads our humble footsteps through the meadows of peace. But in this sin-cursed world, when everything in us is always screaming for more, how do we learn to practice this skill?

The first step is to express gratitude for what we have right now. Grace is born in a grateful heart. Although I admit it rather grudgingly, there are reasons to be thankful Arkansas doesn't receive Colorado weather—milder winters allow for a longer growing season, less time spent indoors, and less hazardous conditions. And when I begin to be thankful for these things, I set the wheels of gratefulness in motion. You see, we humans have a strange tendency to hold our gratitude hostage, as it were (*I'll be grateful when You perform my miracle, God!*). But as with most virtues, when we pour out our thankfulness—however small it may be—to God, we find that instead of lessening, it has only increased. "Give thanks in all circumstances," Paul instructed the Thessalonian believers, "for this is the will of God in Christ Jesus for you" (1 Thessalonians 5:18 ESV). We are not told that we must thank God *for* everything, but *in* everything—finding a reason to rejoice in the midst of undesirable circumstances. You see, God doesn't urge us to practice gratitude for His sake, but for ours. It's not a homage He demands to inflate His ego; it's an exercise of trust without which we could not survive.

In addition to practicing gratitude, we acknowledge that God's plan for us is continually unfolding. We trust the wisdom of His designs over ours, and we accept His sovereignty over our lives. From my perspective, constant snow would be a wonderful idea—but that doesn't fit into Arkansas's climate. If that were to occur, the balance of our ecosystem would be upset, and native plants and wildlife would suffer. Transplanting Colorado's weather to Arkansas would destroy our ecology. Could it be that sometimes, God bars events, people, and circumstances from our lives because they don't fit—because they would create waves of destruction to the pattern of our lives that we could never imagine? When discontent whispers to us the need to reach for more, we must commit ourselves to embracing God's plan and walking within the parameters that He has placed around us. Instead of rushing ahead, we pace ourselves to await the unfolding of His designs, certain that He knows best.

Lastly, we balance future ambition with present joy. It's good and healthy to have goals for the future, but we can't allow those goals to detract from today. Perhaps one day, I'll live in a mountainous area that each winter receives all the snow I could desire; but for right now, I dwell in Arkansas, and I can't sacrifice the present beauty around me for future phantoms of bliss. However, this doesn't mean I can't daydream about the future at all. You see, contrary to popular belief, contentment does not equal stagnation; we don't plop down on the trail of our lives and decide we've come far enough. Nor is it equivalent to resignation, to shrugging our shoulders and deciding that since we can't get what we like, we'll just try to like what we were able to get. Instead, contentment is like climbing a mountain. When we pause along the journey, we look forward with eagerness to the peak we are climbing, but we also take a moment to look back at how far we've come and revel in the joy of the journey.

My friends, I've wished for snow more instances than I can count. Our weather patterns in Arkansas have been a constant source of discontent for me. But I've also felt the burn of dissatisfaction on a much larger scale, admiring someone else's lifestyle or longing to exchange my circumstances for some that seem less painful. But each time I feel that aching pull, I have a choice. I can wallow in what I think God should give me—or I can open my eyes to the blessings that surround me. Because you see, as believers, we truly have no reason for discontent; we already have all we need in the Presence of Jesus Christ. Or as C. S. Lewis so aptly stated, "Look for Christ and you will find Him, and with Him everything else."[7]

GROWING WITH GAILEY

It was December of 2018, in the burnt-out end of what had been one of the most agonizing and painful years of my life, that I was finishing a run one night on the road near my house. In the dark of the bitter winter evening, my heart nearly stopped beating when what I believed to be a white phantom-like creature appeared suddenly on the road in front of me. By the glow of my flashlight, I quickly discerned that the "ghost" was actually a pitiful puppy—a whimpering little guy who was skin and bones, with a wound on his front leg. What I wouldn't find out until we later visited the vet together was that he had been shot with a BB gun, was severely neglected, and had apparently been the victim of abuse.

At any rate, I couldn't bring myself to leave a vulnerable dog on the road on such a cold, dark night; when he chose to follow me home, I made no objections. And so Gailey became a permanent part of my life.

Named for his happy disposition, Gailey approaches each day with a *joie de vivre* that is both heartwarming and hilarious—and occasionally disastrous. He adores my black Labrador Retriever, Mercy, and somehow believes himself to be a superior being despite her much larger size. He also possesses a catlike agility and enjoys leaping onto and exploring surfaces far above his head. He's a wonderful dog who brings me so much joy in many ways. However, when he first joined our home, I realized he had one serious problem.

My observational research has confirmed that when bored, Jack Russell terriers daily consume five times their body weight in irreplaceable, invaluable possessions. Ok, the figure may be exaggerated, but the general truth remains. Gailey has so much energy that our veterinarian once remarked that we must have to "peel him off the ceiling" at times. And all too often, especially at first, that energy combined with his intelligence to spark some very, very creative methods for entertaining himself. I was at a loss; I knew that "a tired dog is a good dog," but frankly, tiring Gailey seemed impossible.

On a whim one day, as I was about to depart for a hike in the woods, I grabbed Gailey's leash. I wasn't planning to go far, and I couldn't stand the thought of leaving him behind to devour his bed, shred his toys, spar with Mercy, splash his water all over the floor, or dig in the potted plants (these are not hypothetical scenarios).

When we headed out the door that day, I wasn't hoping that he'd fall in love with hiking or become an avid fan of the outdoors. I was only trying to burn at least a fraction of his extra energy. However, Gailey was delighted with his outing. Today, I need only open the cabinet where I keep my hiking belt for Gailey's excitement quotient to instantly double. He will leap around, making a difficult-to-describe noise that sounds like a mashup of guinea pig squeals, seal barks, and whale calls. He lives for our excursions into the woods.

And while one might think that a dog barely weighing fifteen pounds would not be a great asset in a wilderness area, he's a surprisingly valuable companion. His greatest gift is something unexpected—a new perspective.

Too often, I apply mathematics to the trail. The relaxation of hiking becomes quantified, the trail chopped into minutes, miles, steps. And even if I manage to refrain from approaching the hike with the robotic determination of a gym session, I'm still woefully pathetic at allowing my soul to settle into the present moment. Everything else—from long-ago regrets to a hypothetical future catastrophe to my options for dinner tonight—tends to intrude.

Yet Gailey combats this entire tendency. You see, Gailey has his own pace and his own rhythm. He stops many times—sometimes to roll in dry leaves, sometimes to painstakingly examine a fallen log, and sometimes to perform the sacred art of, ahem, territory marking. In his own delightfully and maddeningly unhurried way, he weaves back and forth across the trail—or leaves it altogether for a momentary investigation. He slows me down and holds me back and trips me up. But at the same time, he sets me free.

You see, what started as an exercise for him became an exercise for me—a workout for my sense of gratitude, an object lesson in noticing blessings. If I am patient—if I allow myself to release the distractions and watch the world through Gailey's eyes—I see wonders. My soul expands and my worries shrink. I slow down and look up and breathe in and reach out. And at my fingertips is a world I sometimes forget—a world of beauty and wonder and too much excitement to ever experience in one hike or even one lifetime. And at the end of the day, I thank Gailey for a great trip—a hike in which he was my protector, companion, fitness buddy, but most importantly, my tour guide in the blissfully simple yet delightful world in which he lives.

We all have places in our lives like this—places where the gentle sweep of joy has been crushed by the tyranny of urgency. In days of old, life had fewer sharp edges. Today, bleeping alarm clocks have replaced the simplicity of sunrise. We rush about with our heads down, earbuds in place, eyes glued to screens, and minds doggedly chasing the next item on our to-do list. In the process, we're missing the miracles—the wonder of the beauty of our lives.

And we're aware of it. We know we're missing out. But we don't know how to make it any different. For the single mom, the college freshman, the busy executive, or simply the stressed-out American, life is too frenetic. If there are miracles along our path, we're too tired to notice them and too harried to seek after them.

Like my former hikes, our life is quantified—tasks completed, bills paid, money earned, promotions received, days survived.

How do we find another path? I'm convinced the secret isn't necessarily to *do less*. The secret is to *do different*.

I'm reminded again of my hikes with Gailey. When I hike with him, he doesn't demand that I shorten my course; he's well able to hike for five or six miles, even on his stubby legs. He also doesn't require me to choose easier terrain; he can scramble over rocks, plow through underbrush, and is famous for his deerlike leaps over fallen logs. The complexity and difficulty of my hike doesn't change. What does change is the way I approach it. My plans aren't compromised—they're reimagined. The hike becomes not a race or a test of skill, but a journey of discovery.

What if the way I hiked with Gailey was the way we lived our lives?

Not catering to the whims of a small dog, but submitting to the requests of the Holy Spirit. Not marveling with our pet at a funny toadstool or herd of deer, but opening ourselves to receiving the blessings that God has tucked into our lives for us to find.

Certainly, sometimes adjustments are necessary. We may have taken on too much at work, made too many commitments, or have time-wasting habits we need to kick. However, I'm convinced that most of the time, our chronic dissatisfaction with our lives doesn't stem from a lengthy to-do list; it comes from a beauty-starved heart. If we shifted our attitudes, we might find ourselves living a completely different life—without making any external changes.

If you're still unsure, just consider the example of Jesus. What we tend to overlook when we read the Gospels is that Jesus was an incredibly busy Man. We're told that the people who wanted to be healed clamored so loudly for His touch that He interacted with them from morning till night with no time to eat.[1] He preached to crowds so massive that once the only way to keep from being thronged was to deliver His message from Peter's fishing boat.[2] He traveled from town to town on foot, was constantly accosted by His enemies, and spent painstaking hours training His disciples. Yet in the midst of His insanely hectic life, He didn't streamline His schedule; He made His every deed and word a prayer. He lived His earthly life from a place of compassion, dedication, and constant communion with the Father.

If, then, we are going to live this way—if we are going to walk in the saturation of the Holy, as Jesus did—then a major adjustment is required. We have to learn to move in the rhythm of the Spirit, traveling at His pace.

I don't set many records when I hike with Gailey. Fastest mile, fastest hike, fastest trip up a mountain and back down—those have been in other times, other places, when I wasn't accompanied by a dog. And since I have such a strong competitive streak, I have to admit that irritated me at first. When he would wander off the trail or scamper onto a rock or stop to play in crunchy autumn leaves, I would tug on his leash and urge him to keep up. My (already limited) patience would drain. My temperament would sour. My frustration would begin to simmer. But that was before I learned to move at his rhythm. If I slow my pace slightly, we're both happy—and I'm aware of the beauty I'm otherwise passing by. Even when he stops altogether to investigate a most interesting smell or close his eyes and enjoy the wind blowing his ears, I only smile. What at first seemed like needless distractions are now the moments of connection and enjoyment I cherish.

And so it is for us as we learn to move in step with the Spirit. You see, the Spirit is not in a hurry. He doesn't work on our timetable or deliver on demand. And at first, learning to move in His rhythm is frustrating and feels counterproductive. We're not getting there fast enough! We're not doing enough, saying enough, being enough!

But then we begin to realize something. As we move with the Spirit, we notice blessings along our trail that we might otherwise have blown right by. They are sometimes small gifts of grace—a smile from a friend, a lovely sunset as we drive home, a bird that landed right outside our office window. Frequently, they come in the form of opportunities to be nearer to Him. Perhaps we begin to pause before we make an important decision. Perhaps we backtrack to hold a door for someone carrying a heavy load. Perhaps we even begin to breathe brief prayers throughout the day as we go about our duties—a prayer for safety while driving, for discernment when offering advice to a friend, for diligence in our workplace and healing for a sick coworker and patience with our difficult spouse.

And when He brings us to a halt, we notice that there's always a reason. Sometimes He might stop us for our good. Maybe He forces us to pause and consider our route—to recognize when we're rushing ahead of Him. Maybe He gently requests that we rest for a moment when we're soul-sick from the world. Other times, He's interrupting our plans to inject moments of meaning into our days. The chance to talk to a friend who's hurting. The conversation we had with a stranger. The homeless man we were able to bless. Distractions? Interruptions? Far from it. These are planned encounters—for His glory.

Miracles. They are everywhere. Gailey will tell you that. From his point of view, each time he discovers a path of a soft moss or a tree with scaly bark, each time he splashes in a shallow stream or roots in a hole in the bank, he has found another one. And if I stay in step with him, then I smile the whole time I hike—because through his eyes, I'm finding them too.

Sometimes we get to see miracles—sometimes we get to be miracles. But either way, we will only find them when we are watching—when our eyes are open, our ears are tuned, our hearts are waiting. Perhaps that's why it's so important to move at the pace of the Holy Spirit—not rushing ahead, not staring at the ground as we check off another mile and another and another. His cadence is slower, His rhythm sustained, His timetable radically rearranged. But it is His schedule—orchestrated in the light of eternity—that we must keep if we are to glory in the gifts He has laid in our path.

THE DAFFODIL DARE

G ood news: it's finally spring!

Now, I have to admit that at this point, the signs of spring are still somewhat sparse. The nights are still chilly; after all, in Arkansas, we're told to expect nighttime temperatures well below freezing all the way until mid-April. Also, although the buds of future leaves are beginning to swell on tree limbs, there isn't much green yet. Even the birds on my feeder are still those of winter—the colorful springtime songbirds haven't yet begun their migration. And of course, as any meteorologist will tell me, I still have to wait another three weeks before the "official" vernal equinox.

But even before I can expect to see spring in full bloom— before the calendar believes it possible, before the weather is amenable, before any other springtime harbinger graces the world outside my window—there is one sign that arrives early, a promise of what's to follow. Today, I couldn't prove that spring is coming by the weather, or the birds, or the barren trees. But the daffodils are blooming.

Daffodils have always been part of our family's story. Entwined around my earliest associations with spring is the memory of seeing the ravine in the eastern section of our property become glorified seemingly overnight by creamy-colored daffodil blooms, as lovely as woodland angels. Smaller but no less stunning than these are the jonquils; these delicate plants still bless me each spring with their star-like flowers at the base of a rock or foot of a tree. My mother planted all of these in their current locations over fifteen years ago, and to this day, they continue to reward her, and us, with lavish blooms.

My favorite daffodils are the ones in the woods behind our house. A gift from a dear friend many years ago, the first few bulbs we planted have since spread across the entire ridge. Each spring, they add a tidal wave of color and beauty to the surroundings. Every variety—from the large King Alfreds of silky petals to the ruffled intensely-yellow ones to the spectacular double-layered ones in dozens of golden hues—is its own special surprise.

It's not only our property that boasts daffodils in the spring. These flowers have even taken to the woods and wilderness. I've been surprised by them quite frequently during my excursions into the forests and hills near my home. Sometimes I can understand the reason—two particularly prolific patches, both a little over a mile from my house, mark the now-empty spaces where grand homes once stood. More often, though, their presence in the forests is a mystery—the last vestige of a story I'll never know.

Yes, I love daffodils. Their petals are beautiful. Their scent is sweet. Their promise of spring is inspiring. But the best thing I love about daffodils? They remind me to be brave.

You see, daffodils' glorious position as the first flowers of spring comes with some adverse conditions to surmount. By blooming now, the daffodils miss out on the benefits the other, later-blooming flowers enjoy—warmer temperatures, more abundant sunshine, gentle spring rains.

And so the daffodils face a struggle. For one thing, there isn't as much sunlight right now. The days are shorter, and our hemisphere of the earth isn't tilted toward the sun yet, so what light does arrive is weakened. Also, animals are hungry during this time, scouring for every last vestige of food, and daffodils are an easy target. And don't forget that the air can still be bitter; those nighttime freezes and chilling winds are a challenge for young foliage.

And sometimes conditions are even worse than normal. A few years ago, I remember seeing the daffodils swaying in the early morning breeze—right after a bitterly hard frost. Another time, they were a bit droopy—though not crushed—from an unexpected round of sleet. A friend of mine once reminisced about an early-spring snowfall in her hometown. As untimely as the event was, the image she remembers most is that of the daffodils, nothing daunted, peering elegantly from the snowdrifts. In fact, she even used two of their flowers for the eyes of the snowman she built that day!

It's not easy being a daffodil. Yet when I look at them, I have a feeling that if they could choose, they'd still want to flower now instead of later. Because you see, the daffodil—rising through snow, ducking under sleet, bracing against whipping wind—is doing something far more glorious than just surviving. It's reminding us of a powerful truth—ideal timing does not require ideal conditions.

I've struggled with this, and I suspect many of you have as well. It's so easy to succumb to the lure of coming perfection—that someday we'll be braver, stronger, better, and *then* we'll undertake the calling God has sown into our hearts. Reared on catchphrases like "perfect timing" and buzzwords like *trained*, *qualified*, and *prepared*, it's a short step to begin to see perfection as a qualification for servanthood.

We have the dream; we've received the word from the Lord. And make no mistake—we'll do it someday. Most assuredly. But right now—well, right now is not a good time. The kids are having problems. Our marriage is struggling. Our health is precarious. There's so much on our plate already. One day—when things are better—then—

But instead of gently settling us in the midst of perfect conditions, life simply keeps throwing more curveballs. Before we know it, the opportunity has slipped beyond our grasp. Conditions are no longer imperfect—they're now impossible. And the dream has died.

Don't get me wrong—preparation is vital. It's rarely a good idea to throw ourselves into a half-baked idea or rashly commit to a project that we haven't considered closely enough. It's been my experience, though, that most of us have more than enough preparation, information, and understanding. We're just waiting for that "magic moment." The problem is this: that moment may never come. And elevating our calling to a mystic rite, only available under perfect conditions, robs us of obedience in the nitty-gritty of everyday life.

You see, when we allow this thinking to cloud our minds, we give in to the pressure of fear. Fear reminds us that we're not enough. It shouts that we're not ready and it suggests the possibility of failure and it wonders why God would choose us anyway. Aren't there people who are much better suited for this—people with picture-perfect lives and impressive spiritual resumes? Who are we to think God chose us? Can we truly bring this calling to life?

With no answers for the questions fear asks, we shuffle the responsibility onto our circumstances. "When I get a job..." "When I retire..." "Once I get this situation under control..." We set a hypothetical marker of our own maturity, and we determine that then—and only then—will we step out in faith—ironically, at a time when that very faith won't be stretched so much.

But the secret to stifling fear's words is to remember a startling truth, one we often overlook. Victory isn't found in stepping into our calling with no mistakes and no regrets. Victory is found at the moment we launch ourselves—just the way we are, at just the time we are positioned, with just the fears we carry—into the wide-open doorway God has prepared for us. Victory comes when we, in the words of Suzanne Eller, "do it afraid."

"Do it afraid." Eller explains this impactful slogan in the following way: "Years ago when I was a young mom, I was afraid...I'd never get it right....One day these words whispered somewhere deep in response: *Do it afraid, Suzie.* Looking back, I believe that God wasn't asking me to embrace my fears, but to trust that He could somehow use this ill-equipped, work-in-progress woman[.]"[1]

Work-in-progress. Ill-equipped. Doesn't that describe all of us at times? Haven't we all identified with struggling to scrape up enough courage to survive the day, let alone strike out on a new venture? And when we feel ill-equipped, or weak, or vulnerable, or unworthy, the most frightening thing is assuming a responsibility from God. The good news? Our obedience isn't dependent on our emotions. We can plunge forward in faith—and do it afraid.

For an example of this, just consider Andrew and Peter, receiving a summons from Jesus to become fishers of men. These men were poor—they lived at a subsistence level. They were

54

uneducated—fishing was the extent of their skill set. They were busy—he caught them in the middle of their workday. Can you imagine the uncertainty they must have experienced? Yet it didn't stop them. They tossed down their nets on the spot and followed Jesus into their future.[2]

Or what about Paul? He wrote over 48% of the New Testament, but four of those books were written from prison. Surely he felt unqualified to write about Christian freedom when he was chained to two bodyguards and denied all privileges. Yet he was able to calmly pen these words, "I want you to know, brothers, that what has happened to me has really served to advance the gospel" (Philippians 1:12 ESV). He did it afraid.

Perhaps the most amazing example is Mary. Nothing could have prepared her for Gabriel's arrival in her hometown. The news he brought sent shock waves that destroyed her relationships, her family dynamics, her hopes, her dreams, her reputation, and her conceptions of God. As a young teenage girl, she was unprepared for motherhood at all—let alone motherhood of such an exceptional baby. Yet when Gabriel finished his proclamation, she didn't insist on more details or demand reassurance that all would work out right. Instead, she resiliently replied, "Behold, I am the servant of the Lord; let it be to me according to your word" (Luke 1:38b ESV). She did it afraid.

You see, sometimes we have to be like the daffodils. We have to choose to bloom, even in the midst of conditions that seem to spit in the face of all God has promised us. And if we make that hard choice—if we "do it afraid"—then we might begin to notice something amazing. We might notice that once we step into the unknown, the fear takes a backseat. Slowly, it dwindles. It may never fully disappear, but our hours spent staring in the face of fear are replaced by times of gazing into the eyes of Jesus. As we press through the layers of pain and fear and uncertainty, we find a healing and a hope and a strength that we could never have experienced any other way. Yes, the wind may blow. Yes, the ice is sharp. But look— we are growing.

I was never reminded of this more strongly than when the daffodils bloomed in the spring of 2019. As the daffodils waved outside my window that year, I was dealing with a chronic illness, frightened about my future, overwhelmed with schoolwork, and preparing to graduate college in two months. My highest aspiration was to survive—nothing more. Yet somehow, God had placed this crazy desire in my heart to create a nature blog—a place where His world would be used to spread His glory.

You see, I'd dreamed of doing such a thing—but I'd always pictured myself doing it later, when I was wiser and braver and more ready to take on this work, when school was over and my health was restored and I was writing fulltime. To my human side, embarking on such a big venture in the midst of my circumstances was near lunacy.

But God's calling refused to be put on hold.

And in between reading ancient literature selections for school and handling the endless details of graduation, I worked on that dream. I built a website from scratch without any idea of what I was doing; most of my instruction came from YouTube videos, and the rest was birthed out of agonizing errors. I hesitantly drafted a first blog, "The Wild Goose." I told a few friends (not many!) what I was planning and spent a lot of time asking God to help me not fall flat on my face and scrawled pessimistically in my journal, "Let's hope [this] doesn't sink instantaneously." I was scared, I was small, and I was definitely uncertain.

But as the daffodils pushed through the ice, so did I. As they stood there bravely, I sought for courage as well. And by the time Words from the Wilderness officially launched on April 1, the daffodils were still blooming, but in a world much less hostile. Spring had caught up with them. They'd outlasted the turbulence of winter. And I was smiling. Yes, I still had struggles, and yes, I was still unsure. But in the teeth of every obstacle that shoved me back, I'd set my face on my calling, and I'd moved forward. I hadn't done it perfectly, but I'd done it—done it afraid.

The daffodils bloomed brightly that spring. And it's my prayer that this year, no matter what God has asked you to do and how crazy it seems, they bloom brightly for you as well.

Growing Green

P ause for just a moment—wherever you are—and gaze out the nearest window. (I'll wait here while you do.)

Take some time to ponder the landscape. Notice the swells of the land, the shape of the clouds, and the angle of the sun rays. Most of all, examine the colors. Which slice of the color wheel predominates in your view?

I don't know where you are or what your surroundings may be, but I can hazard a very reliable guess as to what color caught your eye. The color green. This time of year, green is inescapable. It wriggles with the grass and drapes from the trees and swirls in the mist of the morning sun. If you're in the country today, your view will be saturated with the color, fields and trees and mountains blending harmoniously in a thousand different shades. Yet even if your window opens onto a cheerless thoroughfare in the heart of urbanity, the Great Artist will have left a touch of green somewhere—a swipe on a curb, a splatter on an ornamental tree, even a drip in a window box.

The green of spring can be surprising—as though during the winter, we forget how intense the color truly is. It can be soothing—a restful scene that calms our souls. But most of all, it is startling. After

57

all, a few weeks ago, green was scarce. The world was still wrapped in the garments of winter, dove-gray and sand-brown and chalky white. Trees were silver skeletons. The fields were crunchy with the withered stubble of last summer. The miracle of birds and butterflies was yet to come. Indeed, the world seemed entrenched in winter, and a visitor from another planet, unfamiliar with our cyclical earth, might have supposed spring was a myth—a legend invented by a cold-weary people, a phantom of useless hope.

Then suddenly, we look out our windows one ordinary day, and the landscape is green!

Every spring, I determine that I'll note the exact moment when green begins to seep up through the earth. I watch, scrutinizing the world daily, even hourly. But that moment can't be caught. It's as if some crisp, calm night, heavy with the heralding of crickets and spring peepers, a gossamer angel strikes a divine match, and a wild riot begins in the cold soil and naked trees and forsaken birds' nests again. Then when we wake, a laughing sun is rollicking over the horizon, the trees are racing each other to put out leaves, the birds are singing, "Eggs! Eggs! EGGS!"—and the whole world is green. Not the surface green of a painted façade, but a real, deep, living green, a juicy green that soaks into everything until the grass is dripping, saturated with green. It's a renewal from the roots, a total transformation.

How can it be that one day, everything is old and tired and asleep—and the next, it seems, God has poured immortality onto the world, and all is young and bright once more? When is the magic moment?

It's no wonder the question intrigues us, for the lure of "magic moments" captivates us all. We love the split-second victories, the instant solutions, the overnight answers—celebrity diets and express checkout lanes and quick-cooking oatmeal. And many of us, if we're honest, are waiting for a "magic moment" of our own.

What does your moment look like? When you wake up and your world is green, what is the first sight that meets your eyes? Maybe your spouse is watching you with eyes of love instead of apathy. Maybe the disease that's tormented you has folded its wrinkled wings and flown away. Maybe you can finally fit in those jeans, kick that habit, call that friend, make that decision.

The moment is there for all of us, a delicious dream in the back of our minds—the moment that everything changes, the moment our confining circumstances are snipped in two. It's a moment of confetti and balloons and fanfare, a moment of "happily ever after." But if we're not careful, we can spend our entire lives waiting for that moment without realizing the truth.

My friends, I'll keep watching every year for the "magic moment" of spring—but I no longer believe I'll actually catch it. That's because I've started to understand that the moment is a myth. Yes, the transformation may seem sudden; however, the miracle of spring isn't "going green" but "growing green."

What's the difference? "Going green" is a quick fix, a snap of the fingers. "Growing green," on the other hand—that's a process. A process that's usually not glamorous, sometimes invisible, but always creates transformation. It's the athlete's hard-fought game behind the last-minute point that wins the match—the long years of education and practice behind the entrepreneur's success—the quiet moments of devotion behind the pastor's inspiring sermon.

You see, the story of spring doesn't begin when we notice the green. The story begins long before there's any external change at all. While the trees are lifeless sticks and the ground is brown and withered and the air is frosty, the process has already begun. Sap is circulating in the trees to meet the demands of new growth; I once noticed almost imperceptible leaf buds on an expectant tree during a snowstorm. Birds are beginning their migratory paths from southern regions; in fact, research has revealed that the purple martins near my house began their journey to Arkansas as early as late January![1]

All winter, when we see only death and barrenness, the world is in fact readying itself for the coming of spring. That's why, when the moment is right, the landscape is able to be transformed in such a strikingly sudden time period. The moment of green looks effortless from our perspective, but a long journey has led to this point.

Growing green isn't just for plants. It's for all of us. It's the process of healing, of restructuring, of change and acceptance and decisions. It's long and it's tedious and sometimes it's downright painful.

For proof, just open your Bibles and take a quick peek at the story of Joseph. Genesis 41 is the greatest overnight success story ever told. A forgotten prisoner languishing in a dungeon is suddenly lord of the land! In a matter of hours, Joseph leaves his cell, his poverty, his obscurity, and his hopelessness. In exchange, he receives prestige from Pharaoh, authority over Egypt, material prosperity, and opportunities beyond his wildest dreams. If ever there was a moment when the world turned green, this is it. Imagine how many people gawked at Joseph, envying his fairytale story.

But what the rumors didn't mention and the jealous onlookers never knew was the fact that this particular golden boy had been betrayed by his brothers. Sold into slavery. Exiled from his homeland. Bartered like livestock. Falsely accused. Forgotten by those he tried to help.[2]

Overnight sensation? Yes. But overnight success? Hardly. Joseph had spent thirteen years "growing green." He'd been in God's refining fire—and his heart is the proof.

It's hypocritical for us sinners to judge the protagonists of biblical accounts too harshly. But let's be honest—there's nothing in the story of teenage Joseph to indicate that he did anything besides relish his father's favoritism and manipulate his talents to impress (and irritate) his brothers. A man that self-centered could never have been trusted with his own welfare, let alone that of an entire society. But during his period of "growing green," the deadness of Joseph's heart blossomed into soft verdure. When we see him after his trials, he is no longer the impulsive, indulgent adolescent but instead a righteous, discerning man wise enough to shepherd a nation through disaster and magnanimous enough to forgive his greatest enemies. This change happened not overnight, but over years—lonely and painful and scary years. When Joseph's world saw him in his glory, they couldn't begin to estimate how high the cost of his journey had been.

Don't be deceived, my friends. When you suffer through another gym workout, you are getting stronger. When your efforts to love your spouse go unnoticed, you are getting kinder. And in those dreadfully dark times—on the nights when your prayers feel like lead weights that could never rise to Heaven—during the days when another thing can't possibly go wrong—when you wake in the morning and dread the coming hours—you are getting braver. This is not death, but the beginning of life. Your world may look like dead sticks to you, but inside your spirit, greatness is growing. Greenness is coming.

I wish I could tell you that there truly is a magic moment, but there's not. No miracle pill or DIY hack or bypass route exists. God won't flip a switch and erase your pain, but He does promise that He will lovingly, tenderly, guide you through it. And He assures you that in His economy, nothing is wasted. It will take time. It will take trust. But one day, you'll wake up, and your world will be green. The temptation will be weaker. Your marriage will be stronger. Your work will be more meaningful, and your spirit will be lighter. You may even be able to fit in those jeans. You'll look back and wonder when it happened, and then you'll realize: it's been happening all along.

So bask in that truth today. And rejoice in the miracles of nature all around you. It's spring, and the wild, fierce melody of life and birth, joy and pain, running water and upwelling sap, leaf and bud and shoot and root and green, has begun once more—following its ancient course, still obeying a word slung from the lips of God at the beginning of time. Listen closely to the song the green grass sings, for it's in your heart as well. Right now, in this moment, as long as you have made the decision to follow God, then you are already growing green.

OF FLOWERS AND FAITHFULNESS

T he world is being born again.

I've watched the seasons slip from winter to spring every year of my life, yet each time I witness the transformation, it seems more miraculous. For many weary months, the world has slumbered, encrusted in winter's ice. Churlish winds have muttered gloomily in the barren treetops. Animals and humans alike have shrunk from the bone-numbing fingers of frost. The clouds have been low and leaden, the colors have been faded to sepia shades, and even the daylight has been stingy. But now, the unbreakable fist of frost is easing its grip, and the light and life and color are swirling back into the world.

And slowly, gently, like the first hesitant notes of a symphony, the signs of spring are arriving. One day, there's a forked tongue of crocus stretching from the icy earth. And then, there's a surprising patch of blue sky shyly peeking between those surly clouds. Next, there's a robin, prompt and pompous, hopping across my backyard on a studious search for worms. The miracle is unfolding.

And the world is laughing, the flowers bursting into song around every corner. Spring boasts so many showy blooms—a riot of color and beauty. Fire-throated lilies open their mouths in praise. Daffodils lift their golden trumpets to the warm spring wind. Tulips sway in their scarlet skirts and jonquils scatter like stars and the tall purple lanterns of hyacinths glow in the shadows.

This floral pageant takes center stage, dazzling onlookers with vivid hues and fragrant scents and elegant shapes. Yet my favorite spring flower isn't the lovely lily or bold daffodil or swirling tulip, the starry jonquil or the radiant hyacinth. It's one that's much smaller, much shyer, and much easier to overlook entirely.

You see, one day in late February, when the wind is still a bit chilly and the skies are still rather gray, I step outside my door, and I notice a little white flower blooming in my backyard. It's tiny— smaller than my thumbnail, huddled on the frozen ground—yet it's strikingly beautiful, with five snowy petals enfolding a center streaked with the pink-purple hues of a blushing sunrise. And as the flower smiles at me, I smile back—and I know spring is at hand.

That first flower is just the beginning. With every passing day, there are more and more and more of these blooms—all delicate, all beautiful, all gazing with adoration at the spring sunshine. I know that by the first of April, there will be such a great multitude that my yard will appear completely white with the "springtime snow" of this carpet of stars.

It's funny—I adore these flowers, I venerate them as the heralds of spring, I seek for their presence every year—yet I don't even know what they are. I have always referred to them simply as "the little white flowers." I am totally ignorant regarding their germination process or their origins or their scientific name and classification. My only feeble assumption is that they are grass flowers, but even that is uncertain.

The little white flowers aren't conspicuous and eye-catching. They're humble. They're simple. They're easy to unwittingly bypass or accidentally stomp underfoot. Compared to the more eye-catching flowers, they might seem bland or plain. Yet I believe that they are one of the loveliest members of God's garden.

My friends, this is true in the human world as well. Our culture has no shortage of divas and darlings, idols and icons, stars and somebodies. Influential leaders, talented ballplayers, beloved singers, and glamorous actors command our adoration. These names are scattered across silver screens and splashed over tabloid pages. Yet although it's the glittery and glamorous that snags our attention, it's often the unsung, behind-the-scenes people—the "little white flowers" of the world—who are the true stars of the show.

This flies in the face of everything our culture embodies. We're taught that success is found in the spotlight and that popularity equals progress. We're trained to revere the high-profile positions and to sneer with distaste at the ordinary. But while the wealthy and worldly may dazzle the audience, it's often the folks in the shadows who deserve the accolades—because although their actions are unsung, they're incredibly important.

We see this principle frequently in the Bible. Moses challenged Pharaoh and delivered an entire nation from bondage—but Aaron served as his spokesman and helped him lead the people.[1] David was Israel's greatest king, founding an empire and slaying a giant and birthing a legacy—but it was the prophet Nathan who kept him on the right path and restored him when he strayed.[2] Mary was visited by angels and entrusted with the care of God's own Son—but Joseph was at her side to shield her from the rumors and provide for the family and give her the gift of trust.[3] You see, for every Moses, there's an Aaron. For every David, there's a Nathan. For every Mary, there's a Joseph. And for every Jeremiah, there's a Baruch.

That last pairing isn't too familiar to many people. But just because the story is obscure doesn't mean it's not amazing. Jeremiah was the last prophet to Israel before the nation was conquered by Babylon and dragged away into captivity. Living during a time of crisis, both from external political pressure and internal spiritual decay, Jeremiah preached virulent messages of repentance and coming doom. As a result, he was often unpopular with the people and despised by the rulers, and he faced agonizing persecution and rejection. God must have known that the burden on Jeremiah's shoulders was just too much for one man. And in His mercy, He provided Jeremiah with a helper—his faithful scribe, Baruch.

Baruch isn't a well-known figure. He's not frequently mentioned in Bible studies. He doesn't have his own book in Scripture. He's virtually unknown today, and he was no less invisible in his lifetime. So was this man unimportant because he didn't have a flashy role? Far from it! Baruch may have been overlooked by the world, but he was certainly not ignored by God. Indeed, the Lord gave Jeremiah these special words for Baruch: "Thus says the Lord, the God of Israel, to you, O Baruch: You said, 'Woe is me! For the Lord has added sorrow to my pain. I am weary with my groaning, and I find no rest.' Thus shall you say to him, Thus says the Lord....And do you seek great things for yourself? Seek them not" (Jeremiah 45:1-5 ESV).

At first, this message left me scratching my head. Why would God tell Baruch not to seek great things? Then the answer came like a flash of lightning: *because he was already doing them.*

Baruch wasn't famous, but he was faithful. He wasn't conspicuous, but he was conscientious. He didn't command the attention of man, but he enjoyed the gaze of Heaven. How could Baruch have done anything greater than this? There was no finer role he could have filled than faithfully helping to spread God's Word and cheerfully obeying, even in small and seemingly unnoticed ways.

I think again of those little white flowers. They seem so humble—smaller and duller than the brightness of the other blossoms. And we've all felt that way at times—as if we are insignificant, as if our lives pale in comparison to the glittering glory of those around us. We echo the words of Baruch, mourning the weariness of seemingly unnoticed obedience. But my friends, if you have ever felt like those little white flowers, then mark my words: if you are serving faithfully, if you are exalting God, if you are making your life a blessing to the people around you, then you have no need to seek "great things." You're already doing them! Whether you stand on a stage or a factory floor, whether you address large crowds or envelopes for your boss, whether you've written a book or just a loving note to your spouse—you're doing great things. The size of your audience in no way determines the value of your contribution.

And make no mistake: your contribution is valuable. Just think of the little white flowers again. An inexperienced observer might assume they had no role to play. After all, how could blooms so tiny fulfill any important functions? But in actuality, these flowers make incredibly vital contributions to the world around them. For one thing, they prepare the soil for other vegetation. The barren winter ground needs the stirring and enriching of these forerunner flowers before it can support the lush grasses and vibrant blooms of summer. Furthermore, these flowers are a lifeline for one of spring's most quintessential and foundational species—honeybees. As the days grow warmer and sunnier, I sometimes go outside and kneel in the flowers, face against the fragrant earth, and I see the zigzagging dance of the honeybees as they peek into each tiny flower, wings whirring diligently, sprinkled with pollen like fairy dust.

You may feel like those white flowers—small. Unknown. Insignificant. Perhaps no one knows your name or gives you praise or sees your work. But I promise you that you are chosen, beloved, and exquisitely valuable. Your role is bigger than you know, and your obedience means more than you realize.

In a culture that constantly tells us we aren't enough, that we must do and be and perform at a pace no human could maintain, peace comes as we settle into the roles God has given us—no matter how "unimportant" or "insignificant" they seem. How do we do this?

First, we prioritize God and His Word, following Him and His commands to us regardless of the opinions of the world or the dictates of the culture. Secondly, we honor others before ourselves, squashing our self-seeking tendencies and instead focusing on ways to encourage and uplift those around us. Lastly, we remember that we are in the service of God, and as His trusted followers, we work cheerfully and diligently at whatever assignment He has placed before us.

There are hundreds of those little white flowers—tiny stars sprinkling the world with laughter. I still don't know their name. Perhaps I never will. But I know this: they may be small, they may be humble, but their role is far from unimportant. And just as there are hundreds of those flowers, there are hundreds of people throughout the world faithfully serving God in mundane roles. These people may never stand in the spotlight or receive an award or feature in a newspaper headline, but the God of all the earth promises that they are doing great things. In God's world, there are no unimportant roles or bit parts or seconds. If you are a servant behind the scenes today, then rejoice—because you are doing some of the greatest things of all for His Kingdom.

BUTTERFLY BLESSING

Butterflies are the soul of spring.

And now, in these dainty vernal days, I see them everywhere—fluttering on the soft spring breezes; floating above the first trembling sprigs of grass; balancing for a brief rest, their wings opening and closing in the rhythm of a gentle heartbeat, on the swelling buds of flowers to be. And each butterfly is a masterpiece—their wings the canvas on which the Great Artist splashes living color in a thousand designs. There are the elegant black swallowtails, swathed in the shadowy blue of twilight, and their cousins the tiger swallowtails, streaked like their namesake with bold black-and-yellow stripes. There are the painted ladies, their wings a mural of earthy tones with white stipples that glow like stars. There are the sulphurs that seem to waft through the air with gracefully curving, lemony yellow wings. And last, but certainly not least, are the spring azures—they're no bigger than my thumbnail, but the friendly flutter of their tiny purple wings always brings a smile to my face.

No matter what color or size or design, every butterfly is breathtakingly gorgeous—the swirling soul of the laughing, flower-haired Spring. But when we're admiring these gossamer-winged

67

creatures tiptoeing on the sprays of seasonal blossoms, it's easy to forget that they haven't always been this glamorous. In fact, the butterflies that sparkle in springtime skies actually begin their lives as some of the most awkward, homely, and absurd creatures on the planet...caterpillars.

You see, a butterfly's life cycle begins inside a pinprick-sized egg, usually attached to leaves or twigs. When that egg hatches, the creature is introduced to the world as a wormy, wriggly caterpillar with no higher aspirations than scooting along the ground and munching on the tender new leaves. To see this inglorious, even comical, creature, you'd never dream it would become an object of beauty.

But after the caterpillar has lived for two to five weeks, a shift occurs. Dangling itself from a tree branch, the caterpillar spins a silk lifeline from which to hang and encases itself in a hard skin, or chrysalis. And for a time (usually between ten days and two weeks, although some species can take as long as two years), it waits silently in the dark—until the glorious day when the chrysalis cracks and a gorgeous butterfly emerges.

This process is known as *metamorphosis*—a word whose Latin root literally means "change."[1] But *change* seems too mild a word to do justice to such a marvelous happening. You see, this process involves much more than simply attaching wings to a worm. As incredible as that alone would be, the act of metamorphosis is even more dramatic.

Isolated in its chrysalis, a caterpillar is literally remade. In a complex chemical mixture, key enzymes are activated that dissolve its tissues, breaking down its body. Meanwhile, important genetic clusters called imaginal cells begin absorbing the energy and nutrients from the disintegrated tissues. These imaginal cells contain the blueprints for the adult butterfly, and the dissolution of the caterpillar's form gives them just the energy they need to begin dividing rapidly.[2] And thus the miracle unfolds, as the formless tissue of the erstwhile caterpillar is reconstituted into a breathtakingly beautiful butterfly.

So you see, butterflies are not just recycled caterpillars—they're entirely new creatures. They're not transitioned—they're transformed. But the truly striking principle at work is this: the glorious transfiguration is only possible after the creatures have been, for all practical purposes, destroyed. The death of the caterpillar is requisite for the birth of the butterfly.

68

Isn't this so characteristic of the work of God?

Perhaps today, you feel rather like the caterpillar in the chrysalis. Perhaps you're huddled in the dark, completely isolated while everything you thought you knew, everything you believed you were, is dissolving. Perhaps, even now, you're gripped by the torture of a change you didn't request, won't escape, and can't control.

My friend, if that's you today, then take courage. You see, God loves us far too much to watch us stagnate as caterpillars, trapped in a ground-level life. He'll do anything to prevent us from staggering through this world in an image that's not His, following a plan He didn't design for us. He wants us to become butterflies—to soar to new heights, to fly free in worlds we can't even imagine. And to make that possible, He is constantly in the business of transforming us—smoothing out the rough edges of our character, filling the gaps in our souls, polishing the love in our hearts. And sometimes—quite often, in fact—His work cannot be truly perfected until He blasts through the mistaken identities we've built and takes us all the way back to square one.

Just consider the life of Paul. When we hear his name, we envision a venerated saint, a successful evangelist, a fiery preacher and a brilliant intellectual and a prolific writer who authored nearly half of the New Testament. But the man whose name is almost synonymous with Christianity began his religious career not as Paul, but as Saul—a zealot, a Pharisee, a scrupulous Jew who tortured, arrested, imprisoned, and even murdered the early Christians in the name of misguided religious fervor.

And then God stepped in. "As he [Saul] journeyed he came near Damascus, and suddenly a light shone around him from heaven. Then he fell to the ground, and heard a voice saying to him, 'Saul, Saul, why are you persecuting Me?' And he said, 'Who are You, Lord?' Then the Lord said, 'I am Jesus, whom you are persecuting....Arise and go into the city, and you will be told what you must do'" (Acts 9:3-5a, 6b ESV). Blinded by the vision and decimated by its message, Saul spent three days in a friend's house, until God sent a believer to pray for him, restoring both his vision and his soul.

This must have been the lowest point of Saul's life. One moment, he was renowned, successful, and important. Then, in an instant, his vocation, his friends, his purpose, and his eyesight all vanished like an early morning mist. The three days of waiting in the dark chrysalis of the friend's house must have been agonizing. But

God didn't desert this broken man. After his encounter with Jesus, Saul wasn't just changed; he was completely transformed. And don't forget this: *only when Saul was dead could Paul have been born.* And Paul experienced a joy, a wonder, a life of passion and purpose like nothing of which Saul could have ever dreamed.

Is this process lifegiving? Absolutely. But is it pleasant? Far from it! We humans are reluctant to enter our own states of metamorphosis. For starters, we don't understand what God is doing. His methods seem erratic at best and downright cruel at worst. Moreover, it's uncertain—requiring changes we don't welcome, sacrifices we won't yield, and time we feel we can't afford. Being a caterpillar is boring, certainly, but it's also safe and comfortable; we're not sure we want to exchange humdrum security for the unknowns ahead. Furthermore, the process is painful—oftentimes, it requires us to squarely face some of the most jagged and soul-tearing concepts in the human existence, like broken hearts, illness, suffering, loneliness, or the white-hot flames of longing unfulfilled. And when we think of all these things, all these stacked-up terrors, it's easy to conclude that no future joy can repay us for the present despair. *Whatever God is doing,* we think, *it can't possibly be worth all of this!*

Just think again about the caterpillar. Amazingly, in many species, the imaginal cells begin to activate in a rudimentary fashion before a caterpillar ever enters its chrysalis.[3] This means that many of the goofy-looking caterpillars hunching across new leaves are wearing embryonic wings just under their skin! But those wings are not a reality yet; they're only a possibility. The caterpillar is carrying its future on its shoulders—but it can't be activated until the old is destroyed.

My friends, how true this is for us. God has scattered our souls with potentials that would take our breath away if we were only aware of them. Within us, we carry the seeds of divine plans for our lives. But so often, we don't know this. We don't feel the weight of our wings, and we don't grasp the magnitude of our future. In order to open our eyes to our purpose and give us the capability of embracing it, God has to remake us. Thank God that He sees more than we do and that He's willing to make sure we don't short-change ourselves. Thank God that He is willing to temporarily destroy us— to push us beyond where we would ever venture on our own—in order to develop a greater good we could never imagine. Surely Paul was thinking of his own metamorphosis when he penned these encouraging words: "Though our outer self is wasting away, our inner self is being renewed day by day. For this light momentary affliction is preparing for us an eternal weight of glory beyond all comparison" (2 Corinthians 4:16b-17 ESV).

Because, you see, destruction, no matter how utter it seems, is never the end of the story. God is not a God Who bulldozes our lives and melts our aspirations and then abandons us in a pile of rubble. He doesn't tear down without building up. He doesn't *raze* our lives without also *raising* them. The dark chrysalis isn't the end of the caterpillar's story; it's simply part of the journey. And in similar fashion, God will lead us through our seasons of painful change and to the joy of rebirth that waits on the other side.

And if you don't believe me—if you're sure that the destruction is too complete, the situation too hopeless, the time too dark—then remember this: God is the Author of the most amazing act of metamorphosis in the universe…salvation.

When we put our faith in Christ, God isn't concerned with trying to make us look better or talk cleaner or even act nicer. Instead, He makes us into entirely new creatures—transforming sinners into saints. And to do that, He starts over. In a mysterious transfer that we will never fully understand, the act of salvation requires us to die and come back to life. Our old nature—the sinful, the selfish—died with Christ on the cross and was buried in His tomb. And with that old nature destroyed, our new spiritual selves are born. We come alive in ways we could have never imagined. We no longer bear any resemblance to the creeping caterpillars we once were. Instead, we are soaring as beautiful butterflies! The ground-level life of a caterpillar is vanished in exchange for a freedom we could have never imagined in a sphere we never knew existed.

Trials aren't meant to reduce us; they're designed to release us. As you watch the jewel-winged butterflies floating through the spring sunshine, remember they haven't always been this way. To unlock their full potential—to become who they were designed to be—they had to die and come back to life. And in the same manner, God is transforming us. No matter how painful the process may be, have faith in the result. Believe that even now, He is working in mighty ways. The same God Who mysteriously transforms us at salvation is still leading us through metamorphosis today. He's not destroying us; He's unlocking us from caterpillar lives and preparing us to fly freely with Him.

APRIL SHOWERS

Dear God, just wanted to let You know that You had better check on your garden hose. I think someone left it running, and we don't need any more rain in Arkansas. Okay? Okay. Oh, and we wouldn't hate some sunshine either. Thank You!

Obviously this note to Heaven is tongue-in-cheek, but I think the general sentiment holds true—not just for my family and me, but for all of us who inhabit the currently flood-ridden areas. Just look at the date—the first week of April. We're ready for warm sunshine, fleecy clouds, beautiful blooms, and sweet afternoons in the garden. Days of steel-grey clouds and dripping trees seem like the antithesis of all our hopes.

I have to admit that the rain, though unwelcome, is expected. Always, as winter melts into the first green grass and gentle winds, the rains begin. We even refer to them as "equinoctial rains" because of their uncanny timing right around the vernal equinox. And over the past few weeks, there have been far more soggy days than sunny ones.

And frankly, I'm done—*so done* (in what seems to be modern slang's ultimate expression of exasperation). You see, at first, it was actually a bit exciting. The rain annually signals the beginning of spring, so when the frowning clouds first moved in, I saw them as a promise of a season to come. More than that, the rain itself was subtly, sweetly poetic—the silver sheets washing all the frost of winter from the delicately greening hillsides, the rushing sound of the droplets in comforting background noise, the new shoots and swelling buds drinking in the moisture.

But now? Now I can't see that beauty in it. Now it's just a major inconvenience, for several reasons. First of all, it's seriously inhibiting my outdoor activities. Although I know many people who enjoy running or hiking in rainy conditions, I'm not one of them. And even during the rare moments when rain isn't falling, the constant threat of imminent showers remains, so trying to plan outdoor activities for rain-free times is tenuous. Even with my best efforts, I've been caught more times than I'd prefer in a spring shower while running; I've grimly slogged home with shoes squishy and clothes cold and heavy and a general, unmistakable resemblance to a drowned rat.

But the rain isn't just inconvenient; it's also dangerous. The bodies of water in this region are sated with rainwater, spilling over their banks. There's concern about weakened levees and overtaxed dams. Even the humble creek in my backyard looks more like a raging river than a gentle stream right now; its waters are coffee-colored with sediment, and it's at least four times its normal width.

Also, I know it only gets worse from this point. Today marks the official beginning of severe weather season. All too soon, this annoying rain will be accompanied by the rollercoaster of severe weather in Arkansas—powerful thunderstorms, gale-force winds, tornados, and even the occasional hurricane meandering up from the Gulf.

So yes, we are all *so done*, and for those blessed souls who don't live in flooded areas and want to offer "encouragement" to those of us who do, here are some friendly tips. Don't tell us the weather forecast is showing improvement for next week; we are emotionally fragile, and we can't handle false hope at this point. Don't make jokes about Noah's ark; we've heard them all, and they are not funny. And for goodness' sakes, do not, *do not*, tell us that "April showers bring May flowers."

Because I'm tired of this rain. I want it to move on. I'm ready to trade the rainy season for sunny skies. I want my creek to stop being transformed into the muddy Mississippi. I want to walk through the yard without the ground making squishing noises. I want the puddles in my driveway to leave and the low-hanging scowling clouds to lighten. And most of all, I do not want to be running two miles away from my house and hear the dreaded pattering sound of a curtain of rain moving in my direction.

This is how I've felt for a while now. But the other day, something occurred to me that has begun to change my perspective on rain.

I was picking my way across my soaked yard, trying to keep mud off my shoes and muttering to myself about the rotten weather, when this Bible verse popped into my head: "I will send down the showers in their season; they shall be showers of blessing" (Ezekiel 34:26b ESV).

At first I rolled my eyes and dismissed it as an ironic attempt at humor by my subconscious. But then I remembered something important about rain, and about why it was considered a sign of God's favor.

You see, Israel is not a fertile land. More than sixty percent of it is a desert wasteland, and even the portions of the country that are suitable for agriculture have been enhanced by Israeli scientists and farmers; Israel is famous for ingenuity in irrigation techniques.[1] In Biblical times, the Jews, living at a subsistence level, were at the mercy of the rainfall to ensure their defense against starvation. No rain translated to no crops and thus no food.

So important was rain that God included sending seasonal rains as part of His gift to the people in return for their obedience.[2] And so desperate were the people for the rain that they unfortunately seldom waited for God's timing. Instead, they often turned to pagan rituals and superstitions to try to force demons to send the rain that God would have freely provided, if they'd only waited.[3]

This much I already knew from Bible studies and sermons. But the other day, as I grimaced at my saturated yard, I had a sudden realization: rain, in and of itself, was not the blessing. In fact, it was probably downright unpleasant, much as rain is today. Yet it still symbolized God's favor, for this simple reason: although it was not the miracle, it was the preparation for the miracle. The gift of the harvest would have been impossible without the trial of the rain.

We don't have to live in a flood zone to have rainy seasons in our lives. There are days when we run out of patience, weeks when gratitude feels far away, months of waiting for a breakthrough, and sometimes whole years when we don't want to get out of bed. And as we plod through these rainy seasons, it seems only natural to ask for sunshine. *God, why aren't You listening to me? God, I need peace! God, please heal me! God, make this go away.*

But the sun doesn't arrive, and our hearts continue to be pelted by cold, hard rain. Rain that soaks into our souls and crushes the feeble sprigs of hope and forces us to watch all our dreams of how life should be floating away on a swollen river of despair. And in those times, *showers of blessing* seems like a cruel joke. *In everything give thanks* makes us cringe. *All things work together for good* fills us with rage. This, a blessing? This, something to return thanks for? No way!

But what if we could look at things with a different perspective? What if we could remember the reason for the rain?

Think back again to that verse: "[T]hey shall be showers of blessing." It's fascinating to me that God didn't say "harvest of blessing." He didn't say "crops of blessing." He essentially asked for the people's gratitude for the harvest *before* they saw the harvest. When the crop they needed was still out of reach and the sky was dark with rainclouds, they were to praise Him then. And why? Because by doing so, they demonstrated their trust in Him and their belief that what He had sent, although it might seem unpleasant, was exactly what they needed.

I'm not saying it's easy. I'm not saying it doesn't hurt. I'm certainly not saying it always makes sense. But what I am saying is this: sometimes what we think is the darkest, blackest situation is actually the introduction to the miracle.

Just as the harvest would not be possible without the rain, so often great victories in our lives would not be possible without trials and suffering. The "rain" that drowns our joy might not be a setback. It might actually be the foundation for something marvelous.

In the glorious economy of the Creator, nothing in the universe is wasted. Every tear, every moment of pain, is carefully sown back into our lives like seed into fertile ground. When we pass through difficult times, God is preparing us, not punishing us. If only we could see from His perspective, we'd realize that the very things in our lives that make us feel most abandoned are often the very things that should make us feel the most loved, because they are setting the stage for our miracle.

How does this happen? How does the "rain" in our lives create space for the harvest? Sometimes, it's God's tool to mold our characters, whether through washing away sinful tendencies or simply strengthening His work in our lives. After all, it is in difficult times that our faith, our courage, and our dependence on God are deepened. With no opportunities to practice being brave, or patient, or trusting, we would have only a shallow faith. As I look back over the difficult patches of my life, I realize that God has grown me tremendously during those seasons as compared to days when circumstances were more pleasant and growth didn't seem as vital.

Other times, God is enriching our testimony. "Blessed be the God and Father of our Lord Jesus Christ, the Father of mercies and God of all comfort, who comforts us in all our affliction, so that we may be able to comfort those who are in any affliction, with the comfort with which we ourselves are comforted by God" (2 Corinthians 1:3-4). We wallow in misery during our rainy seasons, but when the monsoon is over, we find that we have developed a depth of empathy and understanding for other rain-soaked souls. Sometimes in our rainy seasons, we are living the testimony that one day others will need to hear. Our cross to bear is also our story to share.

And at still other times, it is in the rain that God is realigning our circumstances—cutting some threads of the story while adding others to weave the glorious tapestry He has planned. The painful breakup you're struggling with now might be designed to protect you from a marriage to someone who doesn't share your priorities. The unwanted diagnosis might be a cue to focus on your health before additional years of bad habits could accumulate. The cross-country move for your work might be the way God introduces you to a wonderful new friend. These are the times when we question God's wisdom in the moment, but later we look back and say, "Aha! Now I see…"

Building our character, deepening our story, rewriting our life—there's so much good in the way God uses the rain. No, it may not be a blessing right now—but it's the preamble to one. And when we view the rain in that light, it changes everything. We understand Bible verses like this: "For I consider that the sufferings of this present time are not worth comparing with the glory that is to be revealed to us" (Romans 8:18 ESV). We nod when we read, "Count it all joy, my brothers, when you meet trials of various kinds" (James 1:2 ESV). Not because the rain is pleasant. Not because it's what we prayed for. Not because He doesn't empathize with our pain or enjoys seeing us suffer. But because the rain is a sign. *Look! The miracle! It's on its way! Not now…but soon…* Right now all we see is rain. But we can rejoice, because harvest is coming.

And so, here in Arkansas, the ground is still mushy. The creek is still turgid. The trees are drippy and the sky is frowning. But somehow, I'm not as irritated by the rain. Because you know what? That hackneyed adage is true after all. I see April showers now, but I know those May flowers are on the way.

Under His Wings

Every year around this time, my family and I welcome a special pair of visitors.

As winter slips into spring, I begin awaiting the arrival of these honored guests. I peer out the windows, wondering when I'll catch my first glimpse of them. I feel the anticipation of their coming. And as the trees turn green and the blossoms open, they appear, as though they too are part of the spring symphony. These guests are a pair of Eastern Phoebes.

Those of you who live in the eastern half of the United States are probably already quite familiar with phoebes. They're energetic songbirds from the flycatcher family whose range impressively stretches from Mexico into Canada. As far as their looks are concerned, they're relatively drab—simple grayish-brownish plumage with white stomachs.[1]

However, what they lack in appearance, they make up for in personality. They're bold little birds with boundless energy. Even when they're perched, they can't simply sit still; one of their telltale features is their habit of continually flicking their tails up and down. Of course, it's rather rare to see them perched; they're almost constantly on the move, darting here and there to capture insects

78

(their primary food) mid-air. I've seen them in a myriad of acrobatic stunts—flying through the tiny gaps in fences at full speed, chasing each other among the trees of wooded areas, making grand swooping dives over lakes. This time of year, I hear their signature "fee-BEE!" calls constantly, and I'm always on the alert for the little birds, tails flicking restlessly, hovering on fence posts and telephone wires.

And so it is that March rides in on rough winds and flying clouds and nights that still crackle with cold, but as it yields to April, it leaves in its wake trees white with fluffy flowers, bees muttering in every bloom, winds gentle and fragrant, and a sky scrubbed to the perfection of blue. And in this springtime splendor I hear it—the shrill whistle of the phoebes, proclaiming their name. "Fee-BEE! Fee-BEE!" And for me, this doesn't just mean that a particular songbird species is once more announcing its presence. It means my friends have come home.

Of all the springs I've welcomed on my land, I can't recall a single one when the phoebes have not come. They flit about our shrubbery. They perch on our balcony railing. They especially enjoy lighting on the dwarf Japanese maple outside my bedroom window and loudly serenading me (usually about thirty minutes before my alarm clock would have rung!). Best of all, though, they're not here for a temporary visit—they're here to live.

Many, many years ago, the phoebes apparently decided that the rough-sawn overhang of our front porch was prime real estate. Since our porch is sheltered by the roof and also by walls on three sides, it's a very protected area, safe from rains or strong winds. With no posts or columns, it's impossible for predators like snakes or cats to climb up the walls and reach the overhang. And so the phoebes chose this perfect site to build their nest.

It looks very picturesque, actually. It's cleverly built, a cup-shaped creation of dried grass and moss, anchored securely to the porch with mud. It appears so idyllic, in fact, that I wonder if guests sometimes mistake it for an artificial decoration. Of course, if they do, they realize their error as soon as they step foot onto our porch. The phoebes take great delight in crouching deep within the nest, perfectly motionless and invisible, until an unwary intruder—say, the delivery man or mail lady—steps up to our front door. Then, they swoop down toward the unfortunate individual, deliberately missing them by mere inches while giving loud calls that must be phoebe war-whoops. It's a very startling performance, especially if you're not expecting it, and it has certainly elicited some dramatic reactions from the people we've forgotten to warn!

We don't blame the phoebes for their territorialism, though, because they're simply trying to keep invaders away from the nest. That nest, indeed, becomes the focal point of their lives during the warm seasons. Every April, when the phoebes first arrive, their immediate priority is refurbishing the nest—a few extra strands of moss here, a bit more mud there. Then the female takes up residence. All summer, we enjoy a front-row seat to the rhythm of life in bird families. Every spring, I've seen the mother lay her perfect eggs. I've marveled when those eggs gave place to scrawny chicks with unsightly pin feathers and gaping yellow beaks. I've cheered on those same chicks when they became fledglings and both parents worked tirelessly up and down our front sidewalk to teach them to fly. And in the fall, when the nest is finally empty, I keep an eye on it over the winter months, making sure it remains in place—because I know April is coming again.

What I find most heartwarming about the phoebe nest, however, isn't the nest itself or even the excitement of watching the baby birds. It's the knowledge of what the nest represents—the trust the phoebes place in our family.

You see, the phoebes have learned that we aren't the kind of people who will tear down their nest or demand they move out. We won't terrify them by being noisy, we won't cause them harm by using harsh chemicals on our landscaping, and we won't annoy them with curiosity about their private affairs. In short, the phoebes have determined that we symbolize safety. And as a result, they keep returning to us.

When I look at the nest, I'm reminded that, like the phoebes, we are all searching for safe places. With every passing day, our world seems to grow more dangerous, more uncertain. And sometimes, we simply want a place of peace, a location where the roar of fear is forbidden to enter, where we know that we are protected and valued. That humble little bird nest reminds me of Psalm 91:1-2, 4: "He who dwells in the shelter of the Most High will abide in the shadow of the Almighty. I will say to the Lord, 'My refuge and my fortress, my God, in whom I trust.' He will cover you with his pinions, and under his wings you will find refuge; his faithfulness is a shield and buckler" (ESV).

My refuge and my fortress. Just as the phoebes find shelter under the overhang of the porch, we are told to seek our covering in the shadow of God's protection. The blessing of the Lord sounds strong and sure in these verses: *refuge, fortress, faithfulness, shield, buckler.*

Under his wings you will find refuge. I read these words, and I envision pressing close to the heart of God, the way the young phoebes cuddle under their mother's embrace. There's peace in these words—a peace that fills our restless souls. A peace that holds us close and whispers, *There's no better place to build a nest.*

But there's a problem.

The problem is that for many people, these words, comforting as they are, simply don't ring true. These verses remind them not of a safe place to be sheltered, but of a time they expected God's protection and didn't receive it. Or a time when God's power seemed to only reach so far. Or worst of all, a time when it appeared that God couldn't care less what became of them. *If God is my refuge and fortress,* they reason, *then where was He when my husband cheated on me? What was He doing when my daughter was in that car crash? Didn't He care when I received that diagnosis? Was He paying attention when my father abused me?*

I understand this feeling, because it's one I've had. When a mysterious health condition taunted me for over six years and continued to baffle more than a dozen doctors, I often questioned the wisdom of God's plan. When I wallowed in the torment of deep depression and an anxiety that felt as if it had swallowed everything that had once made me valuable, I felt far beyond the reach of grace. And when I was powerless to protect those I love from disaster and defeat, I was filled with rage at the One Who could have chosen to stand in the gap and didn't.

Some would have us deny these feelings, pretend that we never falter in our faith. Yet to do so makes us less than human. Following Jesus doesn't automatically seal our lives in an insulated bubble and outlaw all pain and suffering. Our spirits are eternally saved, absolutely. But our bodies still live on a sin-cursed earth. And suffering, in mysterious ways that often hover beyond our comprehension, is still part of God's plan to refine and strengthen us.

Suffering asks hard questions, questions with sharp edges that can slice our faith to pieces. I know. I've asked them too. And it's with great humility that I confess I have no answers for our pain, no secret formula for understanding the *why* behind every tear. But what I do believe, a lesson bitterly learned over years of trials, is this: answers are not necessary.

Now, I know that when everything in your world is broken, it seems that an answer is the only remedy that will put it all right again. I know that when white-hot wolves of pain are tearing your soul to shreds, one thought consumes you: *If God won't fix this, He needs to at least tell me what went wrong.*

But in the long run—in the slanted beams of eternity that spill backwards across our dimension of time and space—answers don't salve the wounds. Answers don't salvage our lives. And answers certainly don't save our souls.

I'm reminded again of the phoebes. I've learned much from watching them. But I think one of their most valuable lessons has been how to press forward in trust.

You see, all has not been easy for these brave bird parents. Nearly every year, they lose one of their young; when the nestlings begin scrambling about inside the nest, one usually falls out and onto the concrete floor below. Sometimes, the fledglings don't learn to fly in time to outwit sneaky predators. And one devastating year, the entire nest, eggs and all, suddenly, inexplicably, fell.

From the phoebes' point of view, our house must be linked with loss and uncertainty. Yet that doesn't seem to negate the safety and hope it also holds for them. In the face of all they've undergone here, they keep coming back. They keep trying again. When the nest fell, they calmly went to work on a new one, in the same spot, the very next day. Their bad experiences have never been enough to cancel out their faith.

And this is where I find myself. The nest has fallen for me many times, yet I keep coming back. I'm well aware of the knowledge of God that is "too great for me to understand" (Psalm 139:6 NLT). I won't pretend to comprehend His workings, and I am certainly not going to presumptuously offer you cut-and-dried explanations for your heartache. There are so many wonderful theological arguments and exegetical reasonings and philosophical musings on the purpose of pain and God's role when all goes dark in our lives. But today, I want to set all of that aside and simply offer this: we do not have to understand to believe.

Because in spite of all our questions, all our demands to know why, this is reality: we may never understand. In this lifetime, much of what God does and how He works will remain a mystery. Our minds could never encompass all of His plans.

But we can still believe.

And what do we believe? That He is faithful. That He is love. That He has our best interest at heart. Like the phoebes, we recognize that the cruel and tragic things that plague us are not from the heart of God. Yes, they may be part of His plan for us, and yes, He will use them to refine our character. But although He recycles pain, He does not prescribe it. Never, never, does He delight in our sufferings.

I'm reminded that when Jesus began to preach on His crucifixion and atonement, His only reward was to witness the desertion of the majority of His followers. And He asked His disciples a heartbreaking question, "Do you want to go away as well?" (John 6:67 ESV). It was a logical question. The same message that had been a stumbling block for the intellect of the shallow fans was also mind-boggling for the Twelve. It wasn't unthinkable that they would also shrug their shoulders and drift away and find a faith that made a little more sense. Yet Peter's answer still rings true today: "Lord, to whom shall we go? You have the words of eternal life" (John 6:68 ESV).

This isn't a resigned, "Well, we have nothing better." Nor is it a grudging, "I guess we'll stick around." Instead, it's a faith-filled declaration, born from a heart for Jesus that clings to a confidence in His love. It's a courageous decision to believe the promises of God even when everything around us seems to hiss that He has lied. It's an affirmation that acknowledges that we will wonder, we will question, we will accuse, we will despair, but we will not leave. And in the end, it's a choice to simply say, "Lord, I don't understand, but I know You love me. And I love You. And for now, that is enough. I would rather have Your love than Your logic."

And that's why my hope is not shaken. I'm not talking about blind faith—as if I were required to turn off my intellect to maintain my belief. I maintain that God invites our emotions, our doubts, our questions, even our distrust. No, the faith I hold is a faith that understands that I am small. I know I serve a God Who is infinitely larger than my fears and infinitely greater than my pain. I'm not God's judge; I don't demand that He explain Himself. Yes, I've been hurt. Yes, I've been wounded. But I know there was a reason—I just may not see it for now, or for ever. And while I wait on the plan to be made clear, I rest in this truth: He loves me, and what has hurt me has hurt Him too.

This year, when the sun turned its face toward my corner of the planet once more, when tiny flowers began peeking up from the tender new grass, when the world looked to spring—the phoebes came back. I heard them, heard them singing their name and remodeling their nest. And now I'm avoiding my own front porch, because I know I'm in danger of being dive-bombed by the over-zealous parents. But that's ok. I'm glad they're back. I'm glad they know that although they have been hurt, it was not our doing. I'm glad that although the nest fell, they chose to build again. I'm glad they still see us as their place of refuge. Their perfect home. And watching them under my porch inspires me to press a little closer to Jesus. After all, to what other love would I possibly cling? Only He holds my heart.

MINI MIRACLES

I love the sounds of spring.

They're so beautiful, and there are so many of them. I'm thinking of the gentle swish of breezes through papery new leaves. Or what about the warbling songs of birds just returned from their sojourn in warmer climates? And I can't forget the soothing patter of equinoctial rains or the low growl of distant thunder before a spring storm.

But of all the sounds of spring, the one that truly symbolizes this season more so than any other is the chorus of the spring peepers.

Perhaps you've never heard the peepers, or perhaps you've heard their song but didn't realize from where it originated. They're a tiny member of the tree frog family, barely an inch long. Their coloring is a drab brown—designed for camouflage—and they have excellent climbing abilities, thanks to unique gripping pads on the soles of their feet. However, despite their aerial prowess, they seem most content on the ground and spend much of their time there.

They prefer to be near standing water, and that's why I often hear them most strongly near the fields just down the road from me, where a pond and surrounding ravines boast all the comforts of home from a peeper's point of view—still water, abundant algae, tall water plants, and moist ground. Last fall, these tiny frogs burrowed deep into the slimy mud and hibernated all winter, protected from hypothermia by a natural "antifreeze" compound in their bloodstream. But now it's spring, and they're coming back to life. And part of their resurrection is their song.

The song itself is rather repetitive—a cross between a click, a call, and a whistle, repeated up to twenty times a minute. Only the male frogs sing; it's their way of attracting females during the spring egg-laying season. As the season progresses, the song does also, increasing in strength, intensity, and speed of repetition. Upon researching this phenomenon further, I was fascinated to discover that the single loud chorus I hear in the spring is composed of hundreds of individual trios—groups of three frogs singing in concert with each other. By knowing its role within its own trio, the frog becomes a perfectly synchronized part of the larger whole.[1]

The science behind the peepers' song is fascinating, but it's the song itself that charms me. I hear it on warm spring nights, when dusk is soaking into the rejuvenating earth. As sunlight dies, the peepers come to life, their song floating over the swampy fields and the greening hills, the sprouting trees and newly built birds' nests. It's a song of life, of renewal. And it gets into my soul somehow, and it releases something there that's been held prisoner all winter long. The song of the peepers, you see, is the song of rebirth.

The peepers' song affects me so strongly that one spring, I became seized with the desire to see a peeper, to meet one of these minuscule musicians face-to-face. Unfortunately, I discovered that was easier said than done. Despite their operatic prowess, they are shy little creatures. A single step toward their bog, I learned, was enough to silence them all as effectively as if an invisible mute button had been pressed. In whatever corners they were tucked—under leaves, amongst the grass, half-buried in the mud—they would wait, revealing no sign of their presence, until I reluctantly backed away. And then the song would begin merrily again, as if nothing had happened.

Yet still, I wouldn't give up. And finally, I thought I had my chance.

It was about mid-March, and I was in the woods behind our house, gathering loads of brush and building them into a massive pile to be burned. Just to the left of the site where I planned my future fire was a marshy area flooded by recent rains. And as night approached, I heard the song of the peepers, right there beside me in that bog.

As I'd done before, I tiptoed toward the site, moving my body an inch at a time, determined to give no sign of my presence. Yet the peepers' mysterious faculty for sensing possible danger prevailed. As I inched closer, the song stopped.

Frustrated, I was about to back away when a new tactic suddenly burst into my mind. What if I crept up to their hiding place and stayed motionless? After a time, wouldn't they begin singing again?

I didn't know, but I resolved to find out.

Slowly, I lowered myself to my hands and knees. The bog was only a few feet away, but with the care I took, I spent several minutes arriving there. I slithered forward an inch at a time, until I was right at the margin of the water and the mud. I crouched forward, focusing on the border of short grass around the water. And I waited.

For several minutes, nothing happened. I remained perfectly motionless. So did the peepers, wherever they were. My position was awkward and mud was slowly soaking the knees of my pants, but I refused to budge.

And then it happened. Just inches in front of me, I saw a tiny flicker of movement. At the same time, the sharp "cheep!" of a peeper rang out.

I concentrated on the spot, and then it came again. The "cheep" and the motion. So quick—so small—but there was something there.

At last, in the lowering dusk, I realized what I was seeing. A tiny frog, the size of my thumb and as brown as the marsh, was peering up from among the grass stems. He was so small—so still—that I would have never seen him if I hadn't been so close. About three or four times a minute, he was singing. And when he did, his throat pouch expanded in a great bubble of song, then collapsed again. That had been the movement I'd seen.

Now that I knew what to look for, I was suddenly conscious of peepers all around me—little frogs on every side, singing in unison. I could see their glistening eyes, their upturned faces, their white throat pouches expanding. I didn't notice the mud any more, or the strain on my wrists, or the fact that my feet were falling asleep. There in the dusk in the mud with the peepers, I felt as if I were a part of their song—as if somehow I too had joined with them, and together we were bringing spring back to the land. Part of me wanted to laugh with glee, because I'd found them, at last! And another part of me wanted to cry, the hushed tears of suddenly finding oneself, without warning, in the middle of a miracle.

Now, when I was brainstorming topics for this devotional, the peepers kept showing up, kept dancing around the edges of my mind. And when I think of the peepers, I think of that special moment. But this is the odd part—I don't have anything profound to say. There's no earth-shattering lesson to be learned here. That experience wasn't a grand epiphany for me or a life-changing event or the spark that ignited a great revelation. Even as I wrote this, I argued with myself: *I knelt in the mud and watched frogs. How is that anything to write about?* But I couldn't shake the sense that it was important for this story to be told.

And the longer I considered it, the more I realized that perhaps the lack of seeming significance is part of what makes it so very important. Nothing amazing happened—and maybe that's just the point.

Maybe the lesson is simply this: things don't have to be big to be meaningful.

It's Kodak moments and gigantic milestones that get all the attention, sure. We assume they'll be life-changing. We pin our hopes on them like medals on a hero. We view them with a certain sense of awe. *My wedding will start a whole new life for me. This promotion has changed everything. Attending that worship conference is going to rekindle my walk with God.*

Certainly, those big things can be meaningful. And there's nothing wrong with having expectations. But you see, God isn't the God of only the big things. He's also the God of the infinitely small. The same God Who created the roaring oceans also lovingly fashioned the tiny peepers. And it is sometimes in those small moments, those moments when we aren't expecting Him, that He unmistakably appears.

My evening with the peepers wasn't a big event. It wasn't a fireworks occasion. But it was intensely meaningful. And it reminded me of something—all around me, all around us, small yet brave and beautiful things are happening. I've been blessed in my lifetime to see a handful of amazing miracles, but I know that there are thousands more that I've simply overlooked.

These small miracles are no less powerful than their major counterparts. They're not as glamorous. They're not as well-attended.

And they're painfully easy to ignore. But when we pause to notice them, they forever change our perspective. That's because in the dry-dust of the ordinary, they are the jewels, glittering in the dirt. They are the meeting place where God's finger touches our lives in a special and irreplaceable way.

So why do we often miss these moments? If they are so valuable, if they are so impactful, then how are we passing them by? It's because of one simple reason: they are special, but they are not spectacular. We're not expecting them. They show up in the strangest of places, and we rush by, intent on our own agenda. We don't have the time, or we can't muster the patience, or we never thought it would be that important anyway. If we truly knew what we were passing by, we'd drop everything to experience the miracle, but we simply don't realize.

I'm reminded of the disciples on the road to Emmaus (Luke 24). As these two followers of Jesus left Jerusalem, they had to be feeling defeated. They were headed home after a heart-wrenching weekend in which their Messiah had been crucified. And as they walk the road, Jesus joins them.

The road from Jerusalem to Emmaus was about seven miles in those days, give or take.[2] We don't know if Jesus traveled the whole distance with His friends or joined them somewhere along the way. But even if He only traveled one mile with them, they should have been able to recognize His Presence. This was Jesus—their Lord, their Savior, their Teacher, their Friend!

Not only that, but He's talking. He's telling them all about Himself, sharing the Old Testament prophecies that point to His death and resurrection. As they accuse Him of being callously unaware of local events, He gently reminds them of the power of God's promises.

By the time they reach their home and invite Him to spend the night with them, we as the readers want to reach through the pages of time and shake these two. What is their problem? Isn't this painfully obvious? Here's Jesus, right beside them, and they don't know!

But before we level judgment—before we roll our eyes and wag our fingers—let's remember how many miracles we've passed by. We've heard a bird song, but had no time to search out the little creature who made it. We've seen our child's face, but we've had no patience with his endless questions. We've felt the tug to pray for a stranger, but isn't that awkward?

We've all walked that road to Emmaus.

I told you I had no life-changing message to relate today, and I still don't. But I believe God does—if we'll just watch for it. So today, let's try to find those tiny miracles. Let's be willing to be patient. To be quiet. To silence ourselves and cover our assumptions with humility. Let's be willing to kneel in the mud, if we have to, and focus on a dusky corner of a swamp. Because God is always speaking. Sometimes He speaks through a frog half the size of my thumb. Sometimes He speaks through a serendipitous patch of sunshine. Or a smile from a friend. Or a beautiful sunset. But His unexpected, undeserved miracles surround us always, as simple yet lovely as the song of the peepers. And when we find them, wonders always await.

THE TRAIL TO NOWHERE

I f you've followed my blog for any length of time, you know that one of my favorite places on the planet is the Great Smoky Mountains of Tennessee. This national park is the crown jewel of the Appalachians—a treasure of patriarchal trees…vistas to the end of the world…enchanting wildlife…the rolling shoulders of mountains draped in the silver mists that inspired the park's name. And the wilderness, as you might guess, is a hiker's paradise—over eight hundred miles of trails replete with the crashing thunder of waterfalls, the shy glimmer of spring wildflowers, the sun-soaked glades and shadowy streams and towering forests that sing the chorus of life in the Smokies.[1]

I can close my eyes and roam in imagination over those beloved routes. Rainbow Falls—The Bullhead—Trillium Gap—Alum Cave Bluffs—each name is a familiar friend, holding the fragrant memories of past adventures as well as the golden promise of future exploration. But when I think about the Smokies, I also remember another trail, my memories of which are not so glorious. In fact, when I compare Middle Prong Trail to the others I've mentioned, the only word that comes to mind is, to be blunt, *boring*.

Named for the river whose banks it follows, Middle Prong was once a logging road, created for timber harvesting in the days before the park was established. The loggers are long gone now, but the roadbed remains and has been converted to a trail—a wide swath of dusty, rocky terrain that marches monotonously at a steep gradient up the mountainside. And for several reasons, it's never been my favorite trail.

For starters, the trail is, to put it simply, downright dull. It begins with the forest on one side and the river on the other, and that dynamic doesn't change for the duration of the hike. There are no sweeping views, no dramatic scenery. The terrain is unimpressive. When we journeyed on this route, even wildlife sightings were rare.

In addition to being dull, the trail is long. The old logging road seems to stretch into infinity. And as a result of the trail's length, there's no real destination. Someone informed us one time that after many miles, the trail would eventually end at a lovely waterfall. However, we never traveled far enough to see any evidence of that. And between the trailhead and the mythical waterfall, there is no other point of interest.

In retrospect, I'm not sure why we hiked this trail, given its monotonous nature. Yet if we needed a "filler" hike—a way to sandwich time in the woods between our other adventures—we usually turned to this trail. We'd plod up the mountainside for a while—however far we wanted to go—and then retrace our steps.

And I found the whole experience maddening. To me, it seemed pointless, utterly devoid of purpose. Why embark on a hike that was so empty? I didn't want to march up the mountain for a random distance—I wanted to reach a destination, a waterfall or an overlook or even just an intersection with another trail. And while I hiked, I often fumed, exasperation writhing within my soul. *I'm wasting my time on a trail that goes nowhere!*

When I recall my frustration with that trail, I realize that trudging along the banks of the Middle Prong isn't the only time I've felt as if I were going nowhere. In fact, in the years since then, I've come to realize that sometimes the journey of our lives, the pageantry that has been so exciting and wild and colorful, begins to lag. The music dwindles to a softer cadence. The colors fade to grey. The scenery loses its sparkle. And before we know it, we're slogging up the trail to nowhere—and the destination we'd longed for is too far away to provide us with even a glimmer of hope.

I've hiked that trail to nowhere in my life, in the times when I've faced debilitating health conditions that have left me frustrated and grasping for answers. I've wept and I've mourned and I've floundered for a way forward. And on days when the pain and fear and anger threatened to submerge my soul, it was all I could do to continue crawling toward the destination I didn't see. And I know I'm not alone in this. The infamous year 2020 held plenty of "trails to nowhere" for all of us, with the coronavirus crisis upending our world and the days of social distancing and mask-wearing seeming to blur together.

So what do we do in these times? When it seems that everyone is making progress except us? When we can only see a weary climb with no end in sight? When our every step feels as if we're moving further and further into the depths of a lonely nowhere? There's one key—not always easy, but always necessary. Simply this: we remember we're not alone. Many in the "great cloud of witnesses" who surround us have felt the exact same way (Hebrews 12:1 KJV).

Just consider Moses. We tend to think of his story in two parts—his tenure in Pharaoh's palace and then his return to Egypt as the deliverer of the Jews. But sandwiched in between is a forty-year stint in the wilderness of Midian. For four decades, Moses did nothing more than herd sheep in what was quite literally the middle of nowhere![2]

Or what about Joseph? If anyone ever had a right to think their life was locked in limbo, it was Joseph. The favored child of his father, Joseph was kidnapped by his own jealous brothers and sold into slavery at the age of seventeen. Then, after he climbed to a position of honor and trust in his Egyptian master's house, he was falsely accused by the man's wife and sent to prison. He remained in prison not a week, or a month, but many years—according to some sources, twelve years! Imagine all those lonely days and desolate nights. Surely Joseph believed that his life had stalled in a never-ending rut.[3]

When we're on a "trail to nowhere," it can be tempting to believe that God's forgotten us. Yet the accounts of these saints clearly show that is far from the case. And if we look closely, there are precious gems of truth glittering from the dusty trenches of even the emptiest days.

First of all, it's important to realize that we don't have to reach a destination. On that Middle Prong Trail, I was always so impatient to "get somewhere." I craved a destination—and I still do today. Long weeks of bland days fill me with unease, as though every day needs to be red-letter. But sometimes, as counterintuitive as it seems, our greatest growing and learning and trusting happen in the emptiest times.

Secondly, there's always beauty around us. Even in the mundane, more glory shimmers than we dare to believe. When I think of Middle Prong, I remember that it was boring. And certainly, compared to the other trails, it was uneventful. But at the same time, it was epically lovely. The rippling stream that danced over the stones, the towering trees that spread their protective arms, the rustling wind that whispered wondrous secrets to every gentle flower—these held a quiet beauty that I didn't appreciate at the time. So today, if you find yourself on a less than spectacular path, look for the beauty even when you don't expect it. I promise you that it will be there.

Thirdly, we must choose to trust the Guide even when we don't see the path. Trails to nowhere make us nervous precisely because they strip away our illusion of control. We're uncomfortable in the present, and we can't see the future—and we realize that there is no way we can command or cajole the scenery to change. It's in these moments that we remember that God has scheduled our trip, and He holds the only copy of the itinerary. We find our strength by relaxing our grip on our lives and remembering that "the mind of man plans his way, but the LORD directs his steps" (Proverbs 16:9 NASB).

And that leads me to what is possibly the most encouraging truth, the one that scatters the light of hope over our paths: sometimes, when we think we're stuck, we're actually moving forward in dramatic ways.

You see, our idea of "progress" is radically different from God's. We see progress as equaling productivity. Miles logged, tasks completed, prizes won, friends impressed, accolades received—these are the yardsticks with which we measure. But where we marvel at fruits, God examines roots…patiently tailoring the events of our lives to mold us and refine us for His service, not our own futile schemes.

Think about Moses and Joseph again. We skip over their boring years—but were those periods truly so "boring"? On his trail to nowhere, Moses developed a relationship with the God of the universe—learning how to labor diligently and remain humble and lead with both strength and grace. And Joseph? As he languished in prison, Joseph was moving toward maturity, developing from a cocky and arrogant teenager into a wise and devout man—the kind of man who would later rescue an entire nation.

My friends, trudging the trail to nowhere isn't a punishment. And guess what? It's not even a life sentence. You see, God won't abandon us in the blahs. He's not luring us into a cul-de-sac or snaring us in a dead end. This current season will end—and when it does, we'll realize with amazement that on the boring trail to nowhere, we never took a single step alone.

So today, if you're stumbling along the trail to nowhere, take heart. Yes, the way might be boring. The destination may seem nonexistent. And the whole journey might seem incredibly futile. But there is good news. You're not being forsaken—you're being formed, shaped into the image of God. Actually, as it turns out, the "trail to nowhere" might just lead to somewhere very special after all—straight into the heart of God and the future He has designed for you.

Hope from a Hummingbird

L isten…do you hear it?

The earth is singing the song of spring—the happy cadence of growth and grace and green, at once as old as the ages and as new as each rosy dawn. Grass is racing along the hillsides, unrolling lush carpets of verdure over every field and forest. Flowers are dancing in the breezes, swelling buds unfolding into living origami. Bees are zigzagging from bloom to bloom, pollen dusting their backs and a murmuring song tangled in their wings. And as I gaze on all these marvels, basking in the smiling sunshine, a shimmering flash, zipping from blossom to bush, alerts me to the return of one of my favorite springtime residents: the hummingbird.

All creatures are wondrous, but the hummingbird seems to have been endowed with a touch of extra magic. More butterfly than bird, it seems, with its elegantly tapered bill and ceaselessly throbbing wings and dizzying array of brilliant colors. Each feather shimmers with a storybook glamor, as if these little creatures were fashioned from the same stuff as rainbows. Like nature's ballerinas, they pirouette from flower to flower and spiral into the sky—darting by spectators like a mirage, leaving nothing more than a sudden blur of color and zipping hum in their wake.

In the public eye, hummingbirds, or "hummers," are viewed as rather delicate creatures. Perhaps that reputation stems from their position as the smallest birds in the world; the familiar Ruby-throated Hummingbird has a diminutive wingspan of about four inches, with an average weight of four grams, less than that of a U.S. nickel.[1] More likely, however, their perceived vulnerability is a result of their exotic beauty. They seem to whirl transiently through our lives, lovely but fragile creatures—like stained-glass windows or ephemeral sunset clouds or rainbow-rolled bubbles on a stream.

But there's another side to the hummingbirds' lives—an aspect of their existence that belies their seeming weakness. What many people don't realize is that these so-called fragile birds undertake a biannual migration journey of colossal proportions—a voyage that requires these tiny creatures to exhibit extra-large courage.

You see, as tropical birds most at home in the endless summer of equatorial regions, hummingbirds can't tolerate winter conditions here in North America. Cold temperatures not only threaten them with hypothermia but also put an end to the insects and nectar that form their favored food sources. Therefore, every fall, hummers relocate to Latin America in a daring voyage that staggers imagination.

In the first place, the journey is long. Depending on the exact starting and ending points, it can be a passage of hundreds or even thousands of miles. Secondly, it's grueling. As they race the onset of winter, hummingbirds complete the entire migration in about two weeks, with only minor rest stops and intense flying schedules each day. Lastly, especially for hummingbirds in the eastern half of the United States, the journey involves a specific hazard that must be faced—crossing the Gulf of Mexico. In an astounding act of courage and stamina, hummingbirds are renowned for flying directly across the Gulf, a five-hundred-mile distance that requires between eighteen and twenty-four hours of nonstop flying! (Can you imagine running for an entire day without ever stopping once?)[2]

It boggles my mind to consider how a creature this tiny can make such a bold journey and display so much strength. The diaphanous character of the hummingbirds that daintily sip from our feeders belies the fact that they have conquered terrific obstacles to arrive with the spring. It's amazing—what many would consider the weakest bird is capable of far greater feats than anyone could imagine.

And knowing this gives me more than just increased respect for the hummers on my feeders. It provides me with hope for myself as well.

You see, we serve a God Who delights in working His ways through things, people, and places that the world views as weak or unworthy or incapable. As Paul reminded the Corinthian church, "God chose things the world considers foolish in order to shame those who think they are wise. And he chose things that are powerless to shame those who are powerful" (1 Corinthians 1:27 NLT). All throughout Scripture, we see this principle in action. For example, Moses was an awkward introvert with a painful stutter, but he led four million people out of Egyptian bondage. David was an overlooked teenager whose closest associates were sheep, yet he became one of Israel's greatest kings. Even God's own Son came to the earth not as a princely monarch or a conquering hero but as a weak and humble infant, born to a frightened teenage girl in a sleepy country hamlet.

Perhaps the best example of this principle is the story of Gideon. At a time when Israel was occupied by foreign invaders, Gideon was commanded by God to liberate the people. And he responded much as we probably would—by planning a strategy and gathering a decent-sized army to carry it out. But then God spoke again with a startling announcement: "You have too many men. I cannot give the Midianites into their hands, or Israel would boast against me, 'My own strength has saved me'" (Judges 7:2a NIV).

We hear the echoes of this refrain again later in Scripture, when Israel was once more outmatched in a military conflict and God provided them with this assurance: "Have you seen all this great multitude? Behold, I will give it into your hand this day, and you shall know that I am the LORD" (1 Kings 20:13 ESV).

These verses provide the answer—the clue to the riddle of why a Deity with every resource at His disposal would still choose to use the weakest instruments to accomplish His purposes. You see, the lightning flash of a miracle is most brilliant when it is seen against the shadows of the impossible. Consider the hummingbirds again. If they were large, powerful birds with fourteen-foot wingspans and streamlined bodies, their flight wouldn't be remarkable; it would only be expected. What makes their feat miraculous is that it's so disproportional to their seeming strength. Likewise, if God only helped us accomplish tasks that were already within the range of our abilities, then the watching world wouldn't see the evidence of His glory. Worse, we ourselves, like Gideon's army, might be lulled into believing that we were strong and capable in our own might. But when God makes power out of weakness, when He uses our frailties and failures to effect events and situations that are clearly outside our own resources, then everyone knows it had to be Him.

And when God works in weakness, that gives us hope as well. The world advocates living by an ego-bolstering narrative of power—crowning ourselves with accolades like "strong" and "successful" and insisting that strength is mined from within, not granted from without. But those of us who have given ourselves more than a sideways glance are soberingly well-acquainted with the feebleness of our spirits. We know our every fear and failure, mistake and misstep, blunder and bluffing. But the good news is that if we feel weak—if we feel inadequate—if we feel totally incapable—then we are exactly whom God is looking for. As author Margaret Feinberg reminds us, "Accepting our powerlessness is a sacred discipline."[3] When we realize that we can't conjure power on our own, that any shred of strength must come from Someone higher than ourselves, the door is open to the extraordinary. And when our humble weakness is struck with the power of the Holy Spirit, miracles begin to flash like fire in our souls.

So does God want to use us? Unquestionably yes. But will we allow Him to do so? Well, that's sometimes another story.

You see, like the hummingbirds, we all have an "ocean" in our lives, and oftentimes God's plan will lead us right to the brink of it. We know the journey is all-or-nothing, do-or-die, and we are simply too scared to launch into the unknown. This is where our weakness seems most insurmountable; we look at the other "birds," and they seem so much larger and stronger and better-prepared. We begin to believe that obedience is impossible if we don't have their wings. And so we hover at the border of our ocean, longing to begin the journey, yearning to obey the voice urging us to make the flight, yet too afraid to move at all.

This is a paralyzing place to be—when we can't quite believe God's promise, when we just can't imagine how His strength could possibly compensate for our glaring weakness, when the ocean is far too big and our wings are much too small. But the answer to this struggle lies once more in the example of the hummingbirds. How do they find the courage to make their flight? One simple reason: they know abundant life is on the other side of the ocean.

Hummingbirds are aware that the seeming safety of the land is actually no safety at all. If they remain on the continent, secure though it may appear, they will freeze to death in the approaching winter or starve from lack of food. Their only way is forward. Their pathway to life plunges straight through the heart of what they must surely fear most. Don't you imagine their hearts flutter faster than their wings when they see the churning waves below? Don't you suppose fear flickers in their minds when they see the shoreline disappearing? I do. But still, they are able to press boldly onward—not because the waves aren't formidable, but because they are focused on what lies beyond the waves.

My friends, the same is true for us as well. When God uses us, our weakness is asked to encounter vast oceans, shaped in the image of what we would most like to avoid. Like Moses facing Pharaoh, or David meeting Goliath, or Gideon taking on the Midianites, we find ourselves face-to-face with enemies that seem fabricated from our darkest nightmares. But in every fear, we are sustained by the knowledge that "it is the Lord Who goes before [us]" (Deuteronomy 31:8 ESV). And when we look forward, beyond the present fear or pain or uncertainty, we see something marvelous: abundant life. We see the joy promised to those who stretch their wings—of whatever size—and soar away from the land, straight into the crash and clamor of the ocean. We see the blessings reserved not for those who hesitate on the shore, but for those who set their sights in the only direction God ever moves—forward.

So are you ready? Is it your time to make the journey? It doesn't matter if you feel inadequate; that's really the point. God isn't looking for super saints with impressive spiritual resumes. Instead, He's searching for trusting hearts that will take the plunge and eyes that will focus on what is ahead. He's not begging you to summon strength; He's only asking that you receive His.

So in these sparkling days, as you admire the darting delight of the hummingbirds, as you marvel at the way the sunlight shimmers across their pulsing wings, remember that these little creatures hold in their tiny bodies a power no one could have predicted. Remember that they are able to live now only because they pushed through the heart of the impossible. And remember that the same God Who guides their wings, the One Who still leads His people across oceans, the One Who uses the weak to humble the mighty, is calling for you and me. Let's fly forward—with Him.

THIN PLACES

> *Is this place really nearer to God?*
> *Is the wall thin between our whispers*
> *And his listening? I only know*
> *The world grows less and less—*
> *Here what matters is conquering the wind,*
> *Coming home dryshod, getting the fire lit.*
> *I am not sure whether there is no time here*
> *Or more time, whether the light is stronger*
> *Or just easier to see. That is why*
> *I keep returning, thirsty, to this place*
> *That is older than my understanding,*
> *Younger than my broken spirit.*
> — *Kenneth Stevens, "Iona"*[1]

When I close my eyes, in my most rapturous daydreams, I'm there.

I'm in a fierce stark wilderness of an untamed country where the air smells like courage and the sun shines freedom. A haven where I feel completely at ease—a rare feeling for someone like me who so often feels like an awkward spectator at a game whose rules I

102

cannot understand. I'm surrounded by a whole world full of towering mountains, glistening snow, bugling elk, warbling birds, endless trails, and enough beauty to burst my heart. This place is my adopted home—Estes Park, Colorado.

I've been blessed with the opportunity to visit Estes several times, but it never loses its appeal for me. I keep returning, over and over, like a bird flying home to its nest. And no matter how glowing my memories of it are, each time I return, I am in awe once more at its sheer glory.

There are many reasons I love Estes so much. First of all, there's the town itself—a quaint western village nestled in a valley, accessible only by a narrow mountain road and full of friendly people, interesting shops, beautiful recreation areas, and a festival for every occasion. Also, there's the scenery. Towering mountains roll their enormous shoulders against the sky, featuring bristly evergreen forests, vistas that stretch to the world's end, and lakes of a particular shade of blue found nowhere else. And let's not forget the opportunities to explore the wilderness. In Colorado, everyone is on the move, and nature is prioritized. Whether you prefer fishing, boating, hiking, running, rock-climbing, skiing, or bicycling, Estes is an outdoor paradise.

Yes, there are many reasons that I love Estes Park, many excuses I can find for making my way back, year after year. But the best part of the town isn't the Western hospitality, or the weekend block parties in Bond Park, or the way the High Peaks glow scarlet in the sunrise. It isn't even the sight of locals obligingly sidestepping a herd of elk strolling down the main street or the whirling whiteness of a surprise September blizzard. Instead, it's the peace—the gentle embrace of God…the glory of His grace.

A journey to Estes isn't a vacation, where I don a tourist persona and stroll the countryside snapping photos. Nor is it an escape, where I insulate myself from practicalities and try to drown out my worries by pure willpower. No, a journey to Estes, for me, is a homecoming—a return to the home of my spirit and the temple of God.

We all want such a place, don't we? We all search for moments of respite, when we feel as though God draws us into His loving arms and holds us so close we can feel His strong heartbeat. Some people, like me, might have a special place that brings them peace—the beach, maybe, or their childhood home, or even a busy street in a well-loved metropolis. Others, however, might find that peace when they pursue a God-given passion, using their talents and gifts for the glory of their Creator. Still others might experience something similar when they gaze into the eyes of their spouse, or hold their newborn child, or admire a beautiful sunset. Wherever and however we find them, though, those moments are priceless beyond words.

We know when we've found one, because time slows ever so slightly. The voices in our head cease. The soul-aches of living each day in so crazy a world throb a little less. We catch our breath and feel a shiver of relief—and our hearts remind us all over again that we are seen, we are known, we are loved.

In the beautifully simple theology of medieval Celtic Christians (the same believers who created the Wild Goose analogy), these moments had a special name—Thin Places. Thin Places were widely discussed among the Celts even before Christianity arrived in Ireland. Believed to be locations where the divine impinged upon human experience, Thin Places, explains author Tracy Balzer, were "where the veil between heaven and earth fluttered aside."[2] After Christian missionaries introduced the Celts to Jesus, the concept of Thin Places wasn't abandoned; instead, it gained even greater power as an indication of the presence of God.

If the idea of a Thin Place sounds fictitious or far-fetched or even downright heretical, consider the story of Jacob from the Bible. When Genesis 28 opens, Jacob has been leading the life of a top-notch con man. He's claimed to be his brother Esau, thus earning himself the dubious notoriety of becoming the world's first recorded identity thief. He's allowed himself to be used as a pawn in a favoritism game by his conniving mother, and he's hoodwinked his situationally unaware father. Finally, he's nabbed his brother's rightful inheritance—along with the paternal blessing. And like any con man, Jacob finds himself forced to leave the area quickly before justice, in the form of a murderously angry Esau, can catch up with him. After traveling all day, he comes to the basically unknown town of Luz and decides to camp out overnight.

But as Jacob sleeps, his spirit awakes. In an amazing dream, he receives a vision of angels traveling between Heaven and earth, as well as the breathtaking promise that God is with him, has architected great plans for him, and will protect him.

Is this a Thin Place? Absolutely. Awaking from his dream, Jacob immediately names the site "Beth-el," meaning literally "House of God." He's been in a Thin Place and watched that veil flutter aside. It's not a magic moment of complete repentance; for years, he'll continue to struggle with his stubborn fleshly tendencies. But God has made the first dent into this man's sinful soul. Jacob can still choose to disobey God, but he can't choose any longer to completely ignore Him.

And this is the essence of a Thin Place. A true Thin Place won't just turn your head; it will turn your heart. It won't only comfort; it may also convict. And it doesn't necessarily bring God closer to you; it brings you closer to God.

This is why visiting Estes Park is a transformative experience for me. It's a journey of healing, when old wounds finally close and stale fears are soothed. It's full of moments of breathless wonder, when I fall to my knees at the sight of the Lord. And it's been the backdrop for some of the most life-changing and profoundly impressive words I have ever received from the Holy Spirit. After a Thin Place, you aren't the same. It's not something you can shrug off or chalk up or walk away from unscathed. It's something that changes you—dangerous, but delirious; risky, but rewarding.

In addition, a true Thin Place won't depend on your behavior. It's nothing you can control, manipulate, or earn. You won't miss it because of past failure or merit it because of good deeds. For proof, just picture Jacob's Thin Place experience. At the time of his arrival at Beth-el, Jacob is far from the strait-laced saint or the clean-handed kid. He's been living his life according to one simple policy: get whatever he wants, however he can, no matter the cost. A simple examination of his life reveals that honoring God with his choices is probably not a priority for him. But God, the Lover of sinful souls, the Master of surprising plot twists, the pursuing One, has a surprise. He reveals Himself to Jacob in an amazing way—a way that is gratuitously generous and overwhelmingly kind. He doesn't visit this scheming man in a dark cloud of judgment or a lightning bolt of fury. He doesn't force Jacob into submission; He woos him tenderly.

Likewise, we never deserve to stand in a Thin Place. And ironically, one of the first emotions associated with a Thin Place experience is usually an awareness of our own inadequacy, our own unworthiness—similar to Simon Peter, who after watching Jesus work an incredible miracle cried out, "Depart from me, for I am a sinful man, O Lord" (Luke 5:8 ESV). However, that's part of the beauty of a Thin Place. We serve a God Who wants to draw near to us, Who wants to make His voice heard and breathe truth into our lives.

And that brings us to the most amazing truth about a Thin Place. A Thin Place can, and is, found anywhere and everywhere.

Certainly there are particular sites—like Estes Park—where the voice of God is louder and the truth is clearer. It's easy to label these Thin Places, and they are. But just because we feel God more strongly in a particular place does not preclude His Presence in another area where His leading seems less certain.

My friends, our God is the God of Thin Places and Thick Places and all places in between. He's the God of the mountains and the God of the valleys, the God of the whirlwind and the God of the calm, the God of the raincloud and the God of the snow. When I stand on the spine of the High Peaks and look across a fathomless abyss to the Never Summer Mountains, God is there. When I perch on a glacial boulder in a filed brimming with violet dusk and listen to the eerie screams of bugling elk, God is there. When I walk the streets of Estes Park, plunge through snow at Lake Haiyaha, and skip stones across the pristine waters of Mills Lake, God is there. But God is also there when I drive east out of Estes Park—out of Colorado. When I drop ten thousand feet in elevation and return to a world that harasses me with worries and regrets and uncertainties, God is there.

And He's there for you too.

He was there for Jacob. Did you notice Jacob's remark in verse 16? Don't miss it. "Surely the LORD is in this place, and I did not know it."

You would think it would be impossible to be side-by-side with the God of the universe and be completely unaware of His presence. But sadly, it's far more common than we realize. We can muddle our way through difficult situations without ever looking up, without ever noticing that God is in the mess with us, helping us.

And Beth-el can be anywhere, my friends. Usually where we don't feel God and never expect to experience His presence. But frequently, the most powerful and life-changing Thin Places are found in the most painful and heart-crushing places. The night when you cry yourself to sleep—the day you learn you didn't pass the course—the moment you receive the terrible phone call—even the afternoon filled with wearying mundanity—all of these are possible Beth-el moments. In the midst of pain, or grief, or fear, or boredom, sometimes you see the glimmer of Jacob's ladder, and you realize the

Lord is still moving. And you cry out with Jacob, "Surely the LORD is in this place…and I did not know it."

So today, find your Thin Places. Seek them out. Bask in their comfort, absorb their joy, and praise the Lord for them. Refresh your spirit in their hidden springs. But when you find yourself in a very Thick Place, where the air grows heavy and dark and fears lurk like rapacious birds of prey, don't forget that Jacob's ladder can always touch earth, and Beth-el is found in the most unusual places.

Yes, I enjoy my sojourns in Estes Park. I'm always beyond thrilled to be in my mountains, to connect with my Creator in a special way unique to my journeys there. But when the time comes for me to return home, I don't leave the Lord behind as well. My God never deserts me. And whether I can see His dear face through the crystal air of a Thin Place, or whether the sorrow of a Thick Place hides Him from my view, it doesn't change the truth—He is with me always.

12,000 FEET

U pward.

It's a direction that's stamped indelibly on our human souls. There is a relentless draw to move upward—both physically and spiritually. In fact, we take journeys in life designed to move us in this direction—designed to take us to a higher plateau.

My own voyages to Estes Park, Colorado, reminds me powerfully of this truth. As I travel westward from Arkansas, I leave my home elevation, a humble 440 feet above sea level. At my overnight stop in Kansas, after the first day's drive, I find myself at just over a thousand feet above sea level—more than double my starting point, but still an insignificant figure compared to what lies ahead.

During the second day of travel, the altitude gain becomes even more intense. When I reach Kanorado, the hybrid-named town on the border between Kansas and Colorado, I have risen to almost four thousand feet. As I enter Denver, I notice colorful signs welcoming me to the "Mile High City," because Denver sits 5,280 feet—exactly one mile—above sea level. Yet even here, where the elevation is so dramatic that adjustments must be made in following

108

recipes and water turns to steam at a temperature ten degrees lower than its standard boiling point, my journey upward is not over.[1] At the city limits of Estes Park, my elevation is a precise 7,522 feet.

If your head is already spinning from the thought of these elevations, buckle your seatbelts. While my "base camp" may be between 7,000 and 8,000 feet, that doesn't take into account the fact that Estes is nestled in a valley—a high one, to be sure, but a valley all the same. During my hiking expeditions, I routinely ascend to over ten thousand feet! And when I travel to the other side of the national park, from Estes Park to the town of Grand Lake, I reach the ultimate apex—Trail Ridge Road.

Trail Ridge Road is the sole route across the national park, a well-loved icon for surrounding residents, and the highest continuous paved road in the United States.[2] Its forty-eight serpentine miles provide a driving experience that is interesting to say the least, because the road has steep grades, sharp turns, and best of all, no guardrails. Closed from late September to late May or early June due to heavy snows, the road requires several weeks of intensive plowing before it can be made available to public use. Trail Ridge, however, is more than just a route to Grand Lake or a scenic jaunt through the mountains or a daredevil driving experience. It's a gateway to another world—the world of twelve thousand feet elevation.

And this is where facts and figures break down. Twelve thousand feet is impossible to understand. It doesn't fit into the framework of our minds, especially if, like me, you live in lower elevations. Twelve thousand is just an abstract number dangling far above our heads...until you've stood on the spine of the Rockies with the world laid out at your feet and felt the glory sweep over you.

Twelve thousand feet. Incredible, right? it's an elevation that can't be matched. Every time I visit Colorado, I never miss my chance to travel across Trail Ridge Road and feel that top-of-the-world dizziness for myself. And all around me on the road will be multitudes of other visitors seeking that same experience. Because in this world, twelve thousand feet is where we all want to be.

No, we don't all flock to Colorado and hang out on the tip-tops of the mountains, but look around you, and you'll see a world obsessed with height. Our culture tells us that life is a collection of Kodak moments, of mountaintop experiences, and that these are the things to be lived for. And as a result, we have become a society enamored of altitude—a people convinced that only in climbing higher and higher can true success be found. Our attention is captivated by the sparkling moments, the Big Events that earn a place in a photo album or a mental milestone in the landscape of our mind. It's easy to see why. These events provide an emotional boost, filling our souls with the taste of victory. But what happens when the moment ends?

Certainly, there's nothing wrong with mountaintop moments. Such milestones as weddings, births, anniversaries, or holidays should be celebrated and honored. Moments of euphoria, of elation over a goal faced and conquered, are beautiful things. The problem arises not when we enjoy these moments, but when we idolize them, or worse, anchor our mindsets to them. If we're not careful, it becomes all too natural to rush from mountaintop to mountaintop, scrambling for the next big thing to give us a jolt of elevation. But with this mindset, we unwittingly choose a shaky foundation for our lives— fickle emotions that must be constantly inflated.

In real life, just as in mountain climbing, we can't simply bungee-jump from peak to peak. Nor would we want to, because it is actually in the valleys that life happens. Sure, the twelve-thousand-foot moments are exciting, but they are the dessert of a life, not the main course. The main course—as uninspiring and drab as it may sound—is the valley. And without the valley, the mountaintop would never be possible.

I discovered this firsthand when, after years of hard work and prayer, I graduated from college. The day of the commencement ceremony when I flipped my tassel and received my diploma was a twelve-thousand-foot experience for me, as exhilarating as any moment on Trail Ridge Road. However, I didn't magically arrive at that destination. There was no shortcut, no quick fix to negate the late nights spent studying, or the tears shed, or the prayers prayed. The mountaintop was glorious, but the journey—the growing, the becoming, the traveling—didn't take place there.

It happened in the valley.

Some people never realize this truth. They struggle to live their entire lives at twelve thousand feet, ignoring the valleys altogether and grabbing at anything to bolster their altitude and provide them with the excitement they crave. Other people wisely recognize the fact that they can't maintain their elevation, but the knowledge provides only despondency. When they compare their quiet lives with the glittering high-altitude tabloids of celebrities (or even their own social media connections), they become convinced that they are somehow failing, and in the troughs of mundanity, they wallow in a restless discontent and even question the validity of their faith. They fail to realize that at times, Christians may not feel happy or successful or victorious or even very spiritual. We are not always standing on the mountaintops. But neither are we supposed to.

That's why it's time for us to step back—or maybe even step down. Time for us to break free from the addiction to the peak that our society emphasizes. Because here's the truth about high altitude—it can kill.

Yes, it's fun to stand at Medicine Bow on Trail Ridge Road and look out over the endless mountain ranges. It's fun to consider how high you are, how far removed from the lower valleys of daily life. But I could never live there. And if I tried, if I dug in my heels at twelve thousand feet and refused to return to the valley, the experiment would be deadly.

Look again at the photo on the first page of this devotional, the one from the tundra region of Trail Ridge. Do you notice something? No trees. Somewhere between 11,000 and 12,000 feet, conditions are too harsh to support a forest environment. As you ascend Trail Ridge Road, the noble giants of the lowland forests turn to dwarfed and shriveled shrubs and finally disappear completely. The soil is usually frozen within a few inches of ground level (a phenomenon known as permafrost), and winds routinely in excess of 80 miles per hour, with gusts to over 170 miles per hour, not only freeze delicate vegetation but also dehydrate the leaves beyond the point of survival. Thus, the botanical roster of the tundra is limited to lichens, mosses, and tiny dwarf plants with special designs to combat these conditions.[3]

Where trees can't live, people can't either. Visitors to the tundra are in danger of many serious conditions, such as extreme sunburns that develop within mere minutes, frostbite even in July, and a dreaded condition known as altitude sickness, in which the body becomes unable to cope with the lack of oxygen in the thinner air, leading to dizziness, nausea, fatigue, weakness, confusion, headaches, and, if left untreated, death.[4]

Yes, the mountaintop is wonderful. It's a special kingdom all its own and an amazing destination to visit. The keyword is just that—*visit*. The tundra is beautiful, but deadly. It's a good place for an afternoon excursion but a terrible site for a permanent abode.

And the same rule applies to the high places in our lives. It's so easy to become addicted to that feeling we get from being at "twelve thousand feet." It's devastatingly simple to become a professional altitude chaser, leaping from platform to platform in an attempt to squeeze a few more drops of power. But that's not how God designed us to live. If we give in to this urge, we'll spend our lives in a frantic search for temporary excitement that will always fizzle out and leave us gasping for air. The mountaintop experiences are glorious, no question, and they're completely necessary for our spiritual health. But they are a means, not an end. The next time you find yourself craving that excitement, stop and remind yourself— twelve thousand feet can be a scary place. Then look around you, and realize the joy and the peace and the blessings that are here, right now, just waiting to be found.

We are not designed to spend our lives living on mountains. Instead, we're designed to hike through the valleys…engaging our muscles, expanding our lungs, growing and maturing and becoming and learning. Every now and then, we reach a crest, and we pause for a well-deserved moment of elation. We scan the treacherous terrain we've already crossed, and we rejoice. But then we look ahead—to the next mountain.

And we leave twelve thousand feet, with its beauty and excitement and its deadly seduction. We plunge downhill, into the valley. Soon we'll be below the tree line, and we'll have to cling by faith, not sight, to those glories we glimpsed from the high place. But we'll stand at twelve feet again. And when we do, when we summit that next mountain before us, we'll be stronger and braver and better.

HOMESICK

(A note to readers: this devotional and the one following it were released on May 1 and May 15 of 2020. Two months into quarantine, facing nauseating realities and the loss of everything familiar, I turned to writing to help me cope. I always strive for my writing to be "evergreen content," meaning that it's not specific to a particular date and could be enjoyed by anyone, in any time or place. In one sense, these releases are far from that. However, it doesn't take a pandemic to shatter our normal and leave us grasping for peace. It's my prayer that these releases, despite their historic specificity, will continue to encourage you in whatever season you find yourself.)

T his isn't the blog I planned for this day. In fact, it's just the opposite.

Those of you who have followed my writings for some time are aware that this is normally an exciting month for me—the month when I return to my beloved Rocky Mountains in Estes Park, Colorado. These first moments of May usually find me packing my belongings, reading through the Estes Park Facebook page, and counting down the hours until departure. For me, May is associated with only good things: receiving blessings, fulfilling dreams, exploring mountains, coming home.

113

In Colorado, I've stood on the slopes of Longs Peak and gazed thousands of feet upwards to its sheer rock face—the Diamond, they call it, and it truly does glint like a jewel on the mountainside. I've hidden in the brush on the edges of a lake and watched a cranky bull moose stomp his clunky hooves in a shallow stream and devour mouthfuls of water-plants. I've been surprised by the season's first snowfall in a mountain gorge and caught the delicate snowflakes on my tongue. I've been awakened at night by the haunting bugles of the elk calling their herds. I've smelled the hypnotizing aroma of the blue spruce, and I've raced in the shadow of the eagles skimming over Lake Estes, and I've climbed to the hidden mirror of Lake Haiyaha and seen the ice fields of Andrews Glacier, stubborn remnant from the Ice Age, glistening in the sun.

I love these grand adventures. Each one makes me more keenly aware of the heartbeat of God. And I love sharing what I learn with all of you. Many of you have told me how you look forward to my mountain posts, how reading my words transports you to the High Peaks right alongside me. The posts and photos from Estes Park are some of my most popular articles, and for good reason. It's my privilege to be able to give you a glimpse of Colorado—and of how the majesty of God echoes from every mountain.

But Colorado doesn't just bring me smiles or give me good stories to tell or permit me to indulge my passion for wilderness. Colorado, you see, brings me home.

I may have been born in the modest valleys of Arkansas, but my heart-home is Colorado, where the mountains scrape the clouds from the sky. As we drive west across the Great Plains, I hail every town along our route as an old friend, a stepping-stone to an awesome destination. Even now, I can say the towns in my sleep: *Broken Arrow… Sand Springs… Tulsa… Salina… Russell… Kanorado… Burlington… Denver… Longmont… Lyons…* I record our progress and count down the miles and invariably feel the prick of rapturous tears when, somewhere near Denver, I catch my first glimpse of the mountains, etched along the horizon line.

"I don't know why or how I love the Rockies so much, but I do know that I can't live without them," I once wrote in my journal. Perhaps the words sound melodramatic, but believe me when I say they are true in a way I can't frame in neatly structured prose. When I am in Colorado, I'm the best version of myself—the closest I ever am to my true self. I feel at peace—no white-knuckle worries to field, no expectations to meet, no questions to answer. I feel brave—

somehow, breathing the wild, sharp High Country air reminds me that I'll live forever. I feel hopeful—during my darkest seasons, it's been my travels to Estes Park that have soothed me, silenced me, and quite literally saved me. And I carry the sparks of that fire with me, and in terror or trials, the courage I learned in the mountains rings in my soul. So back in Arkansas, even when I'm chained with fear, or tormented by uncertainty, or harassed with doubts and questions— when I'm sick or sad or lonely or lost—I face the western horizon, picturing the glorious mountains that are still there, even when we're apart. And I remind myself: *May is coming. I'm going home to the mountains. I will be brave; I can make it just a moment longer.*

But this May, the promise of the mountains has been shattered.

There's no need for me to wax eloquent on the evils of coronavirus or the restrictions of social distancing or the limitations of quarantine. This isn't a news story or a political commentary or a science article, and so I simply state that for now, the mountains are off-limits to me. We will not be loading into our RV, we will not be crossing state lines, and we will not be traveling to Colorado this May.

Please understand—I'm well aware that this is far, so far, from the worst consequence of this outbreak. We're reeling from a damaged economy—many people, including myself, have lost work. We're faced with frightening disease—illness and death seem to be lurking around every corner. We've been shut off from our neighbors and trapped in our houses, we're dealing with shortages and hysteria, we're rearranging our plans and lamenting weddings that weren't and clinging to the conflicting opinions of government officials. In the midst of such desolation, I feel almost guilty for bemoaning canceled travel plans. But you see, I'm not whining over a pleasure deferred. I'm grieving a hope destroyed. I cannot be in my homeland this May. I don't know when I can be again. And in the meantime, I look around with tear-filled eyes and think, "No...this is not home."

And that brings me to the purpose for this blog. I'm not writing to vent my personal feelings over my homesickness; I'm writing because today, we're all homesick. Some, like me, may be hungering for places—the house of relatives you're not allowed to visit, the place of your former employment, the restaurant where you always met friends. Others are homesick for less tangible things—the sense of safety you once cherished, the trust you felt for authorities, the ease with which you took for granted the ability to go grocery shopping without fear. Not everyone longs to see mountains; some just want to see friends, or fellow church members, or the café on the corner. Not everyone wants to go hiking; some want to go back to work, play in the band again, commute to a classroom, or sit in a cubicle. But mark my words—no matter what we yearn for today, we are all homesick.

I understand. I do. This pandemic has raised questions we thought we'd never have to answer and stirred fears that lay dormant in the depths of our souls. It's stolen chunks of our security and left the rest spider-veined with crumbling cracks. It's gouged out the rhythm of daily life—there were so many things, such little things, that we didn't realize formed the bedrock of our existence, and now they've been suddenly, irreparably, ripped away. With me, you're probably thinking, "No...this is not home."

That's why today, I don't want to deliver a profound lesson I've learned or relate a powerful anecdote from nature. Today, I just want to sit with you, wherever you are, and experience the homesickness. Because this feeling of incompleteness is uncomfortable—but it holds both a reminder and a promise.

The reminder? This is not our home.

The promise? We do have one.

"This world is not my home/I'm just a-passing through."[1] We sing this old song with gusto. Yes, we know we're not here permanently. Yes, we understand that nothing here lasts. Yet at the same time, we too often fall into the trap of living as if we're here to stay. Our plans become our focal point. Our accomplishments become our idols. We gaze with pride and anticipation down the corridors of our lives. C. S. Lewis insightfully addressed this reality: "Prosperity knits a man to the world. He feels that he is finding his place in it, while really it is finding its place in him."[2] This world becomes the end-all in our minds, and Heaven is relegated to nothing more than a hazy blot on the far horizon.

But then a reminder comes. Sometimes it's in the form of a tragic illness. Sometimes it's a sense of sadness we can't shake. Sometimes it's the loss of a friend or an act of terrorism or a terrible news report. Or sometimes it's COVID-19, which combines elements of all the above. The reminder, however it comes, is sharp. It probes the depths of our convictions, it divides our muddled loyalties, and it pierces the hot-air balloon of our apathetic satisfaction. It comes on a tidal wave of pain and grief and uncertainty, yet it's one of God's greatest tools. Because He likes to

116

watch us writhe in agony? No. Because it sends our eyes upward toward Him as nothing else can. Like people waking up in an unfamiliar room, we immediately know: we don't belong here. This is not right. This is not home.

And that's where the promise comes in.

"But as it is, they [the people of God] desire a better country, that is, a heavenly one. Therefore God is not ashamed to be called their God, for he has prepared for them a city" (Hebrews 11:16 ESV). A heavenly country. Doesn't that sound good right now? A place where death is banished? A place without sin or sickness? A place where we can forget our fears, demolish our doubts, and bask in the presence of Jesus? I can close my eyes and envision the splendor of the Rockies, but I can't begin to imagine the glory of Heaven!

The Bible is a bit reticent on the details of our coming country. (Apparently, God felt it was more important for people to know how to get to Heaven than what to expect when they did.) We know it's a perfect place, restored to the image of how God intended life to be. We know it's inhabited only by those who love God. And we know it's a place where God's will is enacted in its fullest extent. But while we may clamor for more details like tourists wanting a travel guide, what more do we need to know? An eternity without fear or limitations, spent in the personal Presence of Love Himself! Whatever the specifics, that's more than enough to whet our anticipation.

"In My Father's house are many dwelling places; if it were not so, I would have told you; for I go to prepare a place for you. If I go and prepare a place for you, I will come again and receive you to Myself, that where I am, there you may be also" (John 14:2-3 NASB). Right now, we hold this promise: Jesus is preparing a place for us. But more importantly, He is preparing us for the place. What if that's what He's doing—right now? What if all this heartache and homesickness is loosening our grip on earth, teaching us to find our fulfillment in only Him? What if this crisis was required to open our eyes to our own weakness, strip us of our feeble defenses, and bring us to our knees?

I can't solve the virus. I can't resurrect the economy. I'm not a scientist or an immunologist or a prophet with a trumpet-toned message from on high. I'm just a girl who misses my mountains—but I know I'm going there someday. And although I know this is not my home, I have a destination beyond my wildest dreams, a more sure hope than Estes Park ever could be. So for now, yes, we're homesick. But instead of using this time to bemoan what isn't, let's renew our joy in what will be. When we leave this groaning world behind, we'll be ushered into the presence of the Lamb Who died for us, and we'll spend eternity in our splendid home. What glorious love!

Slow Stroll

(Those of you who read my last devotional, "Homesick," are aware that this is the second installment in a two-part series originally released in May 2020, discussing the lessons I've learned from the fallout of COVID-19.)

G ive me five seconds, and I'll give you twice that many complaints about quarantine.

Confession time: when I first heard about the stay-at-home order, it didn't sound so bad. In fact, it seemed downright halcyon on the surface. No work. No commuting. No finagling out of social events (you know, the ones you don't want to attend but can't politely decline either). No schedules to keep, deadlines to meet, people to please, or problems to solve.

Alluring (and, I now realize, completely unrealistic) visions came to mind of leisurely sipping tea (which, by the way, I don't drink) and perusing novels. Or indulging in long hikes over the mountains, gleaning blog inspiration. Or enjoying fun-filled evenings with my family—movies, board games, jigsaw puzzles? (I think we've all discovered that you can, in fact, have *too* much quality time with loved ones.) After all, with all my free time, shouldn't this seem almost like a vacation?

I have now been in quarantine for exactly sixty-three days (not that I'm counting or anything), and this is my emphatic statement to my naïve self of two months ago: *You fool.*

Quarantine, you see, is not a jubilee. It's a jail. And it's filled with enough pitfalls and perils to make my head spin. However, I'm still learning some hard yet valuable lessons through all of this. Here are just a few of the things COVID-19 has taught me:

1. It is possible to shop by proxy. My father is especially fond of going to get groceries and then FaceTiming my mother and me to show us the selection available. I don't know if he's soliciting our advice on what to buy or rubbing in the fact that he is in a real, actual store. I hold that phone and drink in the sight of the aisles behind him as though he's standing on a white sand beach in Aruba.

2. The American public apparently will sacrifice their lives, their fortunes, and their sacred honor for a handful of essentials. From our family's experience, these essentials seem to be the incongruous combination of toilet paper, fresh meat, cat food, and car batteries.

3. God left off the Eleventh Commandment, but it is worthy of being included in the canon: Thou Shalt Not Hoard. *Please. There are about three billion other people out here too.*

4. People frequently complain about the news, but in the midst of a crisis, it takes on a mollifying role akin to a pacifier. Also, the media seems more than ok with that.

5. My house is a lot smaller than I thought it was.

Obviously, these lessons are tongue-in-cheek. But behind the laughs, the general truth remains for me, as it does for you as well: our lives have been detonated. Humor, for me, is just one way of attempting to deal with the fallout.

Because there is a lot of fallout. This virus dances in a strange dichotomy. On one hand, things feel incredibly urgent. We're all living on what seems like the border of Armageddon, teetering on the verge of a New World Order unlike what we've seen before. We're assaulted with an hourly flood of bad news and constantly ambushed by panic. Yet on the other hand, the situation is unbearably boring. We're trudging through weeks in which the days run together, days in which time seems fluid, months of our lives spent in a state of hibernation.

Because of that, quarantine (all jokes about it aside) feels most like a flat and dreary holding state—as if I'm alive but without a life, free-floating in time and place. And so, in the desperate need to retain some semblance of sanity, to keep the frayed edges of my nerves intact, I've become addicted to a new activity—outdoor walks.

Rest assured, I still go for my daily run, chasing solitude for four miles down a deserted country road. But later in the afternoon, my family and I take our dogs and begin an unhurried ramble.

Our route varies but usually encompasses the expansive cow pastures near our house, where birds sing from the bushes and the cattle show a peaceful apathy to world events. We move from there to a nearby lake, waters ruffled from a gentle breeze and frogs singing melodically from the banks. In the evening twilight, we can watch purple martins zipping over the waters, their shrill whistles zinging in the air. Lastly, we find ourselves in a stately forest, trees arching over the path like paternal guardians bending to whisper secrets.

These walks restore my soul in a way I didn't understand until recently. I knew that I could leave for a walk irritated, weary, or downright distraught and return calm, happy, and filled with an indefinable sense of security. However, I didn't know why. Then one evening, my mom and I were discussing the ramble we'd had that day. Like me, she credited the walks with helping her maintain equilibrium. But then she went on to explain why.

"You know," she mused, "The walks are nice because they're restful. We're used to working when we're outside."

I didn't understand, so she explained: "Running, hiking—those are fun, and we love them, but they're still work. But the walks are just rest."

She was right. Immediately I realized what the walks held for me that hiking or running didn't. It was the element of grace—the permission to not strive, but simply thrive.

Oh, I love hiking, and I couldn't live without my running. But each carries a certain set of expectations—an unseen judgment regarding how far or fast I should go. I'm enjoying the experience, but I'm also pushing myself to beat a time or climb a mountain or reach a goal. But the walks? I'm just wandering—no need to measure distance. And who cares how long it takes? Since I pause frequently to admire birds or take in the view, I'm neither setting records nor aiming to do so.

In a way, it's a poignant metaphor. At one time, my life was most comparable to a run or a hike—a specific journey, with a single purpose, accomplished at an efficient rate of speed. Now, it's been reduced to a walk—a leisurely, lingering stroll, devoid of destination.

The pace is far slower than it was, but I'm finding to my astonishment that it's filled with beauty—beauty that perhaps I didn't notice or appreciate before.

I can't ignore the questions: before COVID pushed pause on my life, was I so focused on *living* that I forgot about simply *being*? And what if maybe, just maybe, this whole situation is a way for God to grind the brakes on our hectic velocity and give us a rest? What if, when we're used to running and hiking, He wants us to walk with Him?

These questions are sobering, because we are trained to live at a frenetic pace. Our phones run on 5G; website loading time has been shaved to fractions of a second. Our microwaves cook a frozen chunk of meat in less than a minute. Our businesses feature express checkouts and automatic doors and drive-thru windows. Our roads, even with ever-rising speed limits, have passing lanes to oblige impatient drivers. The pace we maintain is killing us, but even as we pant with exhaustion, we constantly search for ways to raise the tempo yet further.

But now, things are different. Our world hasn't just been slowed; it's been completely stalled. We can't complain about traffic because we're not driving. We can't mutter about long lines at the stores because they're closed. We can't even sneak a glance at our watch during our pastor's sermon; churches are empty. God slammed a gate across the track and called off the race. And suddenly, the world that was loud and demanding, the world that was beeping phones and honking horns and impatient voices, is completely empty.

And in this emptiness, what voice will we heed?

We have two options. The first one is the one I followed during the initial few weeks of quarantine, and I suspect it's familiar to many of you as well. This choice is to frantically search for ways to stuff the silence. Compulsively check news reports. Fret over postponed plans. Wander aimlessly around the house and groan as we imagine how "far behind" (by whose standard?) we're falling. We're *wasting time*! We need to be *doing* something!

But then there's the second choice.

This one is hard to accept, because it completely goes against all our human tendencies. This one is to accept the silence. Now, I'm not suggesting that we assume a laissez-faire attitude and passively become a victim of circumstances. What I'm saying is that we stop our own striving and open ourselves to the possibility that even here, even now, God could be speaking.

And if God is speaking, then what does He say? What He has always said: "In quietness and in confidence shall be your strength" (Isaiah 30:15 KJV).

In quietness.

I don't know about you, but I've noticed a lot of quiet lately. Quiet in stores…in streets…even in churches. And quiet is unfamiliar to us, even downright threatening.

Yet God says that quiet is our strength. And if so, then that means that we can choose to wait for Him in this time. Our inclination is always to cram tasks into our fragile days like a tourist jamming a week's worth of belongings into a tiny carry-on. But in this time, we've been given a bittersweet gift—the gift to be empty so that He can fill us. The gift to be silent so He can speak to us. The gift to walk instead of run.

But there's dualism in this verse: "In *quietness* and in *confidence* will be your strength" (emphasis mine). Quietness—allowing God space to speak. And confidence. In what? In ourselves? Certainly not. In our elected officials? I don't recommend it. In the latest timetable for when we can all get back to "normal"? Probably not. This is confidence in none other than the God of all the universe.

You see, these two have to dance hand-in-hand. One cannot be divorced from the other. Quietness before God produces trust in God. And trust in God—that He is working, that He is present, that He will not abandon us—gives us the serenity we need to embrace quiet.

The rest we've been offered through this situation isn't embodied in an apathetic attitude. It isn't encapsulated by wearing pajamas all day or vegging out on TV or neglecting basic chores. Instead, it's once again best exemplified by my daily walks. During my walks, I don't strain to reach a destination or analyze my route or weep because I'm not running. I tune my soul to the slower cadence, and I walk hand-in-hand with God. I talk with my family, I admire the beauty of the green and growing world, and I occasionally spot a beautiful bird singing from the treetops. I can't cover as much ground as I can when I am running, but that's ok. There's enough glory here for me.

I wander along the margin of the lake, watching the sun sprinkle the water with glitter, and I'm reminded of Jeremiah 29. In this passage, the Israelites are begging for an explanation. They've been uprooted from their promised homeland, dumped in a strange land, and subdued by a powerful nation. Like us, they are asking for answers, for deliverance, for a tangible action they can take that will turn things around. Yet God's answer returns with a surprisingly anticlimactic twist: *Go on with your daily lives. I have good plans, but you can't see them—not yet. Invest in the present moment. When the time is right, I promise I'll bring a change.*

Do I know what God's doing? Do I have a mirror to His mind? Of course not. But while we wait, let's approach this with quietness and confidence. I know I'm hearing Him—especially in the evenings when I look over the gentle swells of the lake and once again offer my soul to a God Who invites me to walk with Him beside the still waters.

LOST AND FOUND

One of the easiest things on earth is getting lost in the woods.

Trust me; I've spent my life roving meadows and mountains, and along the way, I've become lost a time or two (or a dozen). It's shockingly, frighteningly easy. For starters, the trees all look the same—endless ranks of faceless soldiers marching across identical hillsides. In addition, the sorts of obvious landmarks that abound in urban areas—that gas station on the corner, the house with the red swing in the yard, the restaurant that always smells of sausage—are missing in the woods. With few exceptions, the forest holds no identifying sounds, smells, or sights to jog our memories. And as if all that weren't enough, false paths abound. Some are what are known as game trails—the narrow tracks worn into the landscape by the habitual meanderings of deer and other animals. Other pseudo-trails include shallow ravines or cracks among boulders or even just the gaps between trees. Whatever their origin, all these paths convincingly mimic real trails. Especially when trying to navigate little-used pathways (the kind that have a habit of disappearing right when they're needed most), I've often been vexed by the dozens of look-alikes, frustrated at my inability to distinguish between an angle of the rightful trail and the beckoning allure of an imitation that will only lead into emptiness.

And part of what makes getting lost in the woods so concerning is the fact that misdirection multiplies. A single step in the wrong direction compounds itself. Veering a mere degree or two off course unleashes enormous consequences. Pilots refer to an axiom known as the "1 in 60 rule"; this means that a plane swerving off course by just one degree will be one mile removed from its planned destination for every sixty miles it flies.[1] For hikers, this rule is no less dramatic on a smaller scale.

So yes, getting lost in the woods is a snare into which it is easy to step. And over the years, I've come to realize that there are three primary factors that lead hikers (myself included) into the trap. The first is cockiness. The individuals who make this mistake arrogantly tramp through the brush without bothering to check a map; they're sure they know which course to take, until they don't. The next is distraction. Folks become occupied in admiring the scenery or chattering with their friends or daydreaming about their options for dinner, and in so doing, they forget to attend to their direction. The third reason is disaster. People often become lost when they're overtaken by adverse environmental conditions, like storms, snow, extreme heat or cold, or even darkness. Maybe they derail their course to seek shelter, or maybe the conditions leave them disoriented and unable to follow the route.

Whatever the cause, getting lost in the woods is a serious matter. I know the emotional progression well—the slithering uncertainty about the route, the falsely reassuring bravado, the climax of stark realization. No matter how calm or collected one might be, it's nearly impossible to avoid at least a moment of raw terror when your gaze is met with a forest where every tree looks familiar and unfamiliar at the same time, where directions seem to have been completely scrambled. No matter how beautiful the environment, it's difficult to shake the uneasy sense that it has turned on you—as if the forest is grimly glad at your unease and waiting to appraise your next move. I've stood there, baffled in the branches, and I've tasted that

126

sour certainty-of-uncertainty—*I'm far from where I want to be, and I don't know how to get back. I don't even know how I ended up here!*

On movies and television specials, getting lost is often featured as the ultimate doom, a hopeless predicament impossible to solve (complete with haunting music and a gripping plot twist). I'm certainly not denying that there are few things that can so effectually coil fear around a hiker's heart. However, in reality, getting lost doesn't have to be as dramatic as some might believe. There are actually plenty of clues that will help you recover your way—if you know what to look for.

In the instinct of self-preservation, I've collected many of these strategies over the years (and have had the occasion to practice them more than once). One of the most valuable tips I've ever heard is to move to an open area; a meadow is ideal, but if none are available, a small clearing or even a ridgeline will do. At the very least, you'll have a better view and new perspective, and you might even be able to recognize familiar landmarks. Another helpful clue is to note the position of the sun. if you know to what point of the compass you should be heading, remembering that the sun sets in the west and rises in the east will help you find your bearings. You can even make more precise estimates by taking into account the sun's seasonal slant (northward in summer; southward in winter). If you need another directional hint, check for the presence of moss on nearby trees. While the folklore about moss growing only on the north sides of trees isn't a hard and fast rule, it's certainly true that northern hillsides and tree trunks will tend to be wetter, cooler, and thus mossier than sunnier, drier, south-facing slopes. If all else fails, head downhill. You'll not only save energy but also have a better chance of locating a river or stream. Walking alongside a waterway gives you a clear route to parallel, and because cities often lie along rivers, following a stream long enough will likely lead to discovering civilization. In all my woodland wanderings, I rehearse these strategies in my mind— because I know that getting lost is so very effortless.

My friends, as simple as it is to get lost in the woods, it's even easier to lose our way in life. Like the forest, life often poses as a trackless wilderness—full of potential pitfalls, feigned trails, vanishing landmarks, and confusing terrain.

And the same issues that underlie getting lost in the woods also lead to misdirection in life. We puff with pride, certain that we know where we're going. We dabble in distraction, drifting aimlessly and forgetting to watch our route until it's too late. We're derailed by disaster, when catastrophes like sickness or loss or divorce or unemployment leave us reeling. But regardless of the initial impetus that dragged us off trail, the end result is the same: we're miles off course, stumbling through a life we don't recognize, desperate to find our way back to the familiar forest we once called home.

If that's you today, I understand. I've ended up in unfamiliar terrain in my life before. Paths that I thought were reliable snaked instead into the depths of desolation. Landmarks I'd depended on vanished before my eyes. I know how bleak that feels, how terrifying. But take heart, because I have some good news. Yes, there are many ways to be lost in life...but thankfully, just as in the woods, there are also many ways to be found.

The first strategy is listening to our conscience—the initial line of defense to help us orient ourselves. This gift is more general, providing mainly black-or-white, yes-or-no guidance, but it's still a good starting place for making course corrections. It's similar to judging the sun's position in the sky; it won't give us a specific trail, but it can point us in a general direction.

Once we have our bearings, the next step is to look for landmarks. And that can best be accomplished by seeking wise counsel from godly friends, relatives, and mentors. Note that worthy advice must come not from social media slogans or trendy Google headlines but from people who heed the Spirit and value our hearts. There's something freeing in admitting how far off course we've wandered and in hearing the fresh perspective and compassionate wisdom of a trusted friend.

Our conscience can point us in the right direction, and the advice of others can help to narrow our route. But to truly find our trail, we have to keep going to the next step—looking to the map, God's Word. Some believers lament that the Bible doesn't give us enough detail to be of value in our specific situations. After all, there are no personalized verses directing us to go to that college or try that career or date that person. But although the Bible doesn't prescribe our steps, it does outline the trail—toward never-failing virtues like hope and joy and self-sacrifice—the big-picture points of our lives that are actually far more important than the daily decisions over which we agonize.

The final step in fine-tuning our route is to pay attention to direct signs from God. It's ironic—this is the method we request the most and the one God utilizes the least. Apparently, the God of grit and grace prefers to work not through sparkly pyrotechnic displays but the bread-and-butter stuff of everyday life. But while He's not likely to scrawl an answer across the sky or thunder His message in an audible voice, He will frequently reinforce our decisions with confirmation. As author Stephanie May Wilson points out, "God isn't shy when it comes to making his will known."[2] His confirmation may come through the most creative and commonplace things: song lyrics or sunshine, a line in a movie or book, a billboard we see or a comment from a friend or a feeling of freedom in our hearts.

These, then, are the steps to take...the redemptive road to follow to get ourselves back on track when we're lost. Yet there's a final decision to be made: choose to not become lost again.

A skilled hiker, after he finds the trail again, will carefully evaluate how he left it. Did he mistakenly follow a game trail? Did he change his route to evade an obstacle? Did impending darkness or inclement weather blur his vision? He'll analyze the experience and then use it to keep him from repeating the same mistakes.

We'd do well to follow that pattern in life too—viewing our times of lostness not as an embarrassment to be hastily forgotten but as an opportunity to learn from our blunders. And if nothing else, the experience of having been lost reminds us of our own frail humanness...of the instability of our plans, the limitation of our scope of control, and the need to continually hold the hand of our Guide and not let our eyes drift from the map He's provided us in His Word.

My friends, God is in the business of reaching out to wandering souls. As we've just seen, He's provided us with a myriad of ways to help us find our path. But as wonderful as those blessings are and as vital as they can be in our lives, He's gifted us with something even better—Himself.

You see, even if we truly can't find our path, if after every attempt we're still left grappling for direction—even then, God never, never leaves us lost. He's the Good Shepherd—the stalwart Defender, the eternal Rescuer, the caring Father Who leaves the security of the sheepfold to search for the missing lamb. In every ravine of regret or forest of fear or stream of sadness, He comes calling our name. And no matter how far off course we feel we've strayed, He longs not to chastise us but to restore us. We are never lost to His love.

WHEN THE TREES FALL

A t the edge of the property where I grew up, and still live today, there is a ridge of mountains. Actually, these are more like steep hills, and while they certainly can't compare to the high country of Colorado, they are still a comforting presence.

These mountains are part of a gigantic tract of land, a small area in the holdings of a family who is seldom involved with the property. The hills are completely wooded and have been virtually undisturbed for several decades. They are devoid of houses and feature no sign of human activity, except for an old railroad bed abandoned by the Union Pacific since before I was born. It still harbors the occasional rusted iron spike or train-car coupler and features a concrete bridge with the date "1936" stamped on the side.

These mountains don't legally belong to me, but they are still part of my home. I've spent many hours roaming their slopes (with permission from the owners). These are the mountains where I first learned to use a compass. Where I learned the rudiments of tracking wild animals and discovered that moss truly does grow on the north side of trees. Where my beloved dog Angel, years ago, chased a mountain lion and inadvertently led it back to me (but that's another story!).

Perhaps, in the familiarity of the mountains, I took them too much for granted. To me, they seemed like an unspoken guarantee, a knowledge that tomorrow and tomorrow and tomorrow they would still be standing there. They seemed anything but fragile. But one summer, my mountains were destroyed.

For the better part of a month, I awakened each morning and lived each day to the sound of saws. The crews arrived at dawn in the morning and stayed nearly twelve hours—sometimes longer. They were busy clearing the mountains, they said—clearing my memories, my background, my life away as surely as they removed the trees.

They widened that lonely railroad bed, grading it and converting it into a dirt road for their log trucks. They cleared scarred swathes through the woods, tearing down trees in enormous, barren sections. They parked equipment just over our property line, spilling diesel, leaving litter, hacking, chopping, destroying.

For them, it was just a job, but for me, it was like a slow-motion horror film, like watching a piece of myself be stolen every day. In the evenings, I walked across what was once a verdant mountaintop, and there was not a tree left—only twisted shreds of bark and branches crushed on the ground, only powdery dust that billowed with my every step. It felt like walking across a world after Armageddon. The air smelled unfamiliar, and I required a compass to maneuver these once-familiar mountains, because all my old landmarks were unrecognizable. I saw the deer trembling on the edges of the devastation, exhausted, anxious, and I pictured the fate of all wild things—cornered into an ever-shrinking box by the relentless push of people. And I watched the fireflies glimmer in the sparse corners of forest that still remained, and I wondered—if I have children one day, will I have to explain to them what fireflies were, because humans will have erased their habitat entirely?

Devastation. Destruction. It always hurts. And as I watched this personal destruction unfold, one truth tapped me on the shoulder—it is always easier, in this twisted world, to destroy rather than create.

Those forests have grown for years, without haste or interference. A typical tree grows about 1-2 feet a year, depending on the species.[1] Many of the trees on those mountains had stood like sentinels for well over a century. Yet in a matter of a few brutal moments, they were gone—chopped down, sawed up, carted off to lumber mills.

Yes, it's easy to destroy. We see that in the world around us…and in our own lives. It takes a lifetime of good decisions to build noble character, but only one poor choice to send it tumbling down. A friendship of years can be wrecked with one small lie. A marriage that has weathered many storms can be destroyed by a forbidden decision. Nothing in this world is ever invulnerable. We are all only one choice from destruction.

Just consider the life of King David—a man after God's own heart, he's called. As we watch him fight Israel's enemies, accept the coronation as king, defeat Goliath, and pen hundreds of cherished psalms, the title seems appropriate, well-deserved. However, one day, this righteous man makes a terrible choice—the harmless-seeming decision to stay home during a battle and allow his armies to do his fighting for him. Alone in his palace, he walks up to the roof; and "he saw from the roof a woman bathing; and the woman was very beautiful" (2 Samuel 11:2 ESV).

And now the poor choices begin to accumulate rapidly, faster than David can handle. He doesn't stop with observing the woman; he then begins inquiring about her, seeking details he doesn't need to know. Next, she's in his palace, and then, she's reporting a pregnancy. In the blink of an eye, David is guilty of lust, deception, seduction, adultery, and finally, the elaborate murder of her husband. All that he has sought to build—the trust of his nation, the respect of his family, his character before God—has been shattered in a single destructive moment.

Perhaps you've stood in David's shoes. Perhaps you've watched the trees fall and seen the landscape of your life be irrevocably altered. And now, all around you, what was once a beautiful forest is simply a barren waste. Your life is beyond recognition.

When destruction visits a life, it always hurts. It makes us feel angry—*why is this happening?* It makes us feel vulnerable—*this could happen again.* It makes us feel disoriented—*where am I now?* But most of all, it makes us feel hopeless—*what can I do?*

Some of us, like David, can point to a litany of bad decisions that began the destruction. We can look back over a pattern of poor choices—or even just one catastrophic decision. However, others have no such point of reference.

Consider the case of Job. His children dead, his wife estranged, his possessions gone, his health ruined—Job's formerly tree-filled life is now dust and ashes. But despite his friends' stubborn insistence to the contrary, Job isn't responsible for his own sufferings, and he's not harboring secret sin. "My face is red with weeping, and on my eyelids is deep darkness, although there is no violence in my hands, and my prayer is pure" (Job 16:16-17 ESV).

Destruction without explanation is one of the most disempowering experiences in the human condition. We work hard to maintain a good life, one of peace and joy, centered on the people and callings that mean the most to us and surrendered to the will of the Father. Yet, in a moment—one phone call from the doctor, one pink slip from an employer, one drunk driver on a highway, one natural disaster—that life vanishes. The fabric of our existence is forever changed, and we lack not only the capacity to salvage it but also the ability to explain why it has been destroyed.

In such moments, what do we do? What *can* we do?

When sin has bred suffering, the answer is obvious, if not easy. Restoring a right relationship with God is the only first step to removing the shrapnel of the fallout from your life. But when destruction is not caused by wrong choices—when it is sudden, unexpected, and terrifyingly random—the path to recovery is less clear-cut.

I can't offer you a magic formula or a five-step process to managing pain, although I desperately wish that I could. I can't even give you that golden gift that people in unexpected pain crave more than anything else—an explanation. I can only tell you these truths.

First, *the ways of God are higher than ours.* A wise friend once instructed me to view my life from the perspective of the end. In other words, we must not look at our future through the lens of our present pain but look at our present pain through the lens of the future. As Paul reminds us in Romans 8:28, "For those who love God all things work together for good" (ESV). Is this a guarantee that we will be free from pain? Absolutely not. But it does mean that eternal lessons and blessings are being shaped from the raw material of your suffering.

Secondly, *there is no substitute for faith.* In times of trial, many people abandon their faith—some in anger, because they feel that God has mistreated them. Others become fearful of His seeming capriciousness and cower in the shadows. Still others are driven away by the well-meaning but simplistic didacticism of other Christians. "Though He slay me," Job declared in the midst of his grief, "I will hope in Him"—even when he believed God was responsible for his anguish, he stubbornly clung to his faith (Job 13:15 ESV). Instead of allowing your fear, or guilt, or anger, or confusion to stand between you and God, bring it to Him. Honestly confess your emotions, and then determine to continue your pursuit of His presence.

Lastly, *trees will grow again.* This is perhaps the most comforting, amazing, and hope-filled truth available. When you feel completely robbed of any reason to hope, remember that God is in the business of radical restoration. It's the way His world is designed to work. After a terrible plague, God assured the nation of Israel, "And I will restore to you the years that the locust hath eaten"—this promise included not only physical renewal but spiritual restoration as well (Joel 2:25 KJV). Even as I stood on the barren landscape and looked at the dusty deadness, I knew that in that dirt were the seeds—the seeds of the trees that once rose there. And when the work crews retreated, and the land was left to itself, it began to gradually recover. The world of God—and the people of God— possess a resiliency unlike anything else on earth.

So yes. Destruction is painful. I felt its stabbing wound as the growl of heavy equipment filled my ears, as I helplessly watched the skyline of the mountains changing right before my eyes. It's always easier to tear down than build up. But if you have been torn down, if the life you once knew has been altered beyond description, I have hope for you today. Seeds are being sown, even if you don't realize it. Press through the pain. Trust God in the shadows. And I promise, I promise, that one day, trees will grow again.

Midsummer Miracle

It's the one night that exemplifies summer. And it's almost here.

At my home in Arkansas, we are currently experiencing just two minutes shy of a full fifteen hours of sunlight each day. Nightfall is delayed a bit further every week, and even the late time of 8:00 or 8:15 finds me still able to enjoy outdoor activities without a flashlight.

It's remarkable—this stretching of the sun. And in just a few more sunrises, we'll welcome the summer solstice—the longest day of the entire year.

The science behind this phenomenon is fascinating. Because the earth is tilted as it orbits the sun, different areas of the globe receive the most direct rays at different times of the year, creating our seasons. For the Northern Hemisphere, the summer solstice is the day when the North Pole is angled closest to the sun, making the sun appear its farthest north in the sky today. After the summer solstice, the earth's orbit makes the sun begin appearing progressively farther south in the sky, until we reach the winter solstice, when the sun is focused instead on the Southern Hemisphere.[1]

Even knowing the logical explanation for the solstice, people today are still awed by it; solstice celebrations occur around the world

135

every year on this day. So imagine how intriguing it must have been for ancient cultures with no knowledge of the whys and hows. Perhaps that's why the practice of celebrating the solstice is such a time-honored one, with roots dating back over four thousand years—right after the dispersal from the Tower of Babel. And it's not a local phenomenon, either; observances are a staple of such cultures as diverse as China, England, Norway, India, Iran, Sweden, Russia, and America, just to name a few.

Most of these celebrations were startlingly similar. Fire was one such common element. People greeted Midsummer with torches, candles, and huge bonfires—in fact, leaping over the burning piles was a popular (if reckless) sport. Water was another priority—streams and rivers played an important ceremonial role. And lastly, midsummer practices were interlaced with a good dose of superstition and magic.[2] On this night, the ancients claimed, the line between the mundane everyday world and the mysterious spiritual one was blurred. Mythical creatures such as dragons and fairies were believed to roam the earth after nightfall on this evening. And because of that, anything was possible—from a heightened possibility for romance to unexplained mystical phenomena.[3]

One might have supposed that our modern scientific advancements would have squelched this sense of mystery, stifled the legends, and dimmed the ardor of humans for celebrating this event. However, the thousands of popular solstice events that occur every year prove that is far from the case. The romance lives on…because no cut-and-dried explanations can begin to encapsulate the mysticism of this time.

The wonder is found, after all, in the name; our word *solstice* comes from two Latin roots and literally translates as "sun stand still," because at Midsummer, the sun seems to poise directly overhead.[4] The whole of the growing season, from the first shy tulip buds in spring to the more recent arrival of the fireflies, has led to this day. And so I stand outdoors on the afternoon of the solstice, and I marvel at the sun swinging so low above my head. The world seems hushed, somehow—synchronized with the slow-sifting moment. And sometimes it seems I can feel the tilt of the axis, and the thrill of awe that gripped the ancients shivers along my spine. For in a world that is so often chaotic and unpredictable is a sun that has faithfully followed its footsteps since the first day its Creator spun it into motion.

But one of the most powerful parts of midsummer is its strange duality. On one hand, this is an occasion for rejoicing. After all, summer is at its height. The melody of growth and birth and life, of birds and grass and blooms, has reached a crescendo. And this exciting occasion will be punctuated by the longest day—an opportunity for light to far outweigh the darkness.

Yet on the other hand, even as we marvel at the solstice sunshine, we're keenly aware of a less bright fact—tomorrow there will be a little less daylight than there is today. The days will shrink just a bit each week. The sun will swing back southerly in the sky, retreating from its northward advancement. The energy of the growing season will decelerate to the languor of July and finally the slumber of September. On the solstice, summer will be winning. But the day after, we will begin an unmistakable and irrevocable trajectory that will take us without fail to the depths of winter. The bookend to the riot of midsummer is the silence of midwinter.

So is this an occasion for smiles or tears? Do we rejoice at the sun's advance or mourn its slow retreat? I wrestled with this question as I prepared for this blog. And finally, the answer came in a moment of clarity—*we do both*.

You see, it's my belief that our culture trains us to think of emotions in more streamlined terms than is truly feasible. We are either happy *or* sad. We love someone *or* we are disappointed in them. We are excited for the new job *or* we cry when we clean out our old cubicle. But in truth, the human heart is much less clear-cut. It's not desirable—or even possible!—for us to experience only one emotion at a time.

In olden times, this complexity was understood far better than it is now. As hard as it is for us to believe, ancient people lived in a world far more unpredictable even than our own. The narrow line between life and death was a tightrope they walked daily. Yet while there's ample evidence to demonstrate that their lives were rigorous, dangerous, and often abruptly curtailed, there's also proof that they were by no means colorless or joyless. Compared to modern observances, ancient rituals were deeply reflective, and it appears that these people could willingly assimilate joy and pain into one ceremony—not dismissing the more painful aspects but considering them as equally valid.

For an example, just look at the rites performed in solstice celebrations. The burning of fires and torches was believed to give life to the sun, in turn making it shine brighter and longer. However, many solstice celebrations also included lighting a wheel of brush and rolling it down a hill to be extinguished in a river at the bottom. This action symbolized the surrender of the sun to the darkness as the days shortened. Both aspects of solstice—the one long day and the shorter ones to follow—were thus honored, without preference or judgment.

And this is why midsummer still speaks to people today. Yes, the celebrations are fun, and the science is interesting. But more importantly, midsummer forces us to confront the mixedness of human emotion and experience. It brings us face-to-face with something we avoid if at all possible—change.

You probably won't be terrified by a dragon prowling after dark, and you might not see fairies dancing in your garden (although if you do come across any mythical beings, be sure to let me know!). But change? That's a creature you're certain to encounter—and not just at the summer solstice either.

Our lives are never stagnant; indeed, tectonic shifts are continually shuddering through our circumstances in a thousand ways. We get the new job. We fall in love. We have a child. We lose a family member.

Just as the sun is constantly shifting position in the sky, our lives never stall in the same place for very long. Sometimes, change comes in a jolt—a sudden wrenching of everything we thought we believed. Other times, change is more gradual—like the progressive lengthening and shortening of the days, we may not even notice it at first. But regardless of whether the change is expected or unforeseen, inconspicuous or obvious, temporary or permanent, it still requires a stretch in our souls, and learning to adapt to it can still lay all our vulnerabilities bare.

Change is a sensitive issue for us precisely because we have a love-hate relationship with it. On one hand, we don't want our lives to remain stagnant, and new adventures can make us eager for a fresh work of God. Yet at the same time, we innately cling to what we know, preferring the security of our well-worn grooves to the possible options on the horizon. And even if those alternatives are intriguing, they require us to leave behind a part of ourselves.

These days leading to Midsummer are perhaps the embodiment of change. The daylight is shifting, the earth is leaning, the sun is migrating across the sky. Indeed, this is in many ways the astronomical fulcrum of the entire year. So this moment as the sun hovers overhead is the perfect opportunity for us to pause and consider some valuable truths regarding change.

The first step to handling change with grace is to acknowledge its value. The act of change, while discomfiting at times, is innately natural and healthy; as Solomon reminded us, "For everything there is a season, and a time for every matter under heaven" (Ecclesiastes 3:1 ESV). If you don't believe me, just think back to the weeks of quarantine we underwent in the wake of COVID-19; months of identically empty days profoundly convinced me of the value of change! In all seriousness, though, without change, our spiritual growth would be stagnated.

This understanding can be less than helpful, though, when we feel as if the foundations of our lives are being shaken. And that's when the second truth gives us comfort: even in change, there are still constants to which we can cling. Need proof? Just look at the solstice. The sun might be shifting position—but it still rises every morning. The season might change—but the annual rhythm doesn't stumble. The days may begin to shorten—but they don't grind to a halt. In times of change, it's soothing to identify and recognize our anchors: the comfort of family, the support of friends, the beauty of the seasons, and of course, the love of the God Who is "the same yesterday and today and forever" (Hebrews 13:8 ESV).

Lastly, celebrate the change! Now, I'm certainly not recommending that we stifle our emotions and force a happy façade. Acknowledging our feelings about a change—both positive and negative—is instead a key ingredient in truly celebrating. Opposing emotional responses shouldn't force us to choose a side. In the Presence of God, we can be completely honest about it all. After all, as Midsummer proves, it's possible to hail the longest day and grieve a declining season—all in one night.

Midsummer. It's a strange and poignant time—a shining coin whose two sides are joy and pain. Sounds a lot like our lives, doesn't it? So on this holy day, step outside for a moment to admire the blaze of the Midsummer sun. And then look beyond the shining rays—to the One Who holds us throughout our lives, in midsummer and midwinter and every hour in between.

LIGHTS IN THE NIGHT

D o you want to see a miracle?

Then do me a favor. This evening, in that subdued time just when day and darkness have collided, walk outside. A forested place, perhaps with running water, would be best. As you stand there, you'll hear the rhythm of the cicadas and smell the fresh scents of plants growing and blooming. If you glance upwards, you'll see the first pinpricks of stars emerging, twinkling in the dusk. And then, if you look down at the grass, you'll see the miracle—stars rising upwards to meet their friends in the sky.

Now, despite all appearances, the little lights aren't true stars. They're actually tiny insects: displaying lightning bugs, also known as fireflies. However, when we consider these little creatures, and their powerful message, what we find is no less miraculous than stars floating up from earth.

First, some background. Fireflies (which are neither flies nor true bugs) are one of only eight kinds of land-dwelling animals able to produce light. This delicate phenomenon is called *bioluminescence*, which means "living light." Fireflies are able to glow thanks to a complex series of chemical reactions that take place in specially-designed organs on their lower abdomen.[1] One of the enzymes

140

involved in these reactions, luciferase, is actually used in medical research to develop new cancer protocols, tag cellular malformations, and highlight brain abnormalities.[2]

To make matters even more impressive, the chemical reaction is extremely efficient. Consider a normal incandescent light bulb. After it's been turned on for a while, it becomes extremely hot to the touch; in fact, an ordinary light bulb expends 90% of the energy it produces as heat and only 10% as light. If fireflies operated with that same light-to-heat ratio, the effects could be disastrous. However, their reactions are so efficient that a full 100% of the energy produced is used for light. A firefly will not become hot from its own light-producing reaction.[3]

You may be wondering if this devotional is only going to provide a (hopefully) interesting yet ultimately irrelevant science lesson on the lifestyles of lightning bugs. That's definitely not the case. The point of relating all this information is to emphasize a very important and very relevant truth—one that I'm reminded of each time I see a firefly glow. That truth is this: *God didn't have to.*

We serve a God Who didn't have to do any of this. There was no external force pressuring Him to produce a galaxy. He wasn't compelled to create the mountains or the rivers or the fireflies—or you and me. So why? If not necessity, what motivated Him to perform such acts? In Revelation 4:11, the elders worshipping in Heaven's throne room give us the answer, "For thy pleasure [all things] are and were created" (KJV).

For His pleasure. The world we see around us—in its sweeping grandeur and its tiny intricacies—is the product of the boundless imagination and creative delight of our Lord. Like an artist pouring loving detail into his painting, God has richly endowed His world with beauty beyond belief—and a few fun surprises. After all, if God didn't even have to create the whole universe, He certainly didn't have to create a little bug that lights up at night! Who besides our great God would have thought of that? Would we? If God had asked our advice on a new insect species, would we have ever hinted that we'd like a light-up one? Of course not. But God's imagination is so boundless that He lovingly fashioned a creature that flies around in the summer flashing its built-in light—a light that is safe, cool, efficient, and even valuable for medical research. And He did this because He takes pleasure in it.

And that raises another even more amazing idea. If God's creation gives Him pleasure—if He admires the stars and smiles at little light-up bugs—wouldn't He be even more pleased by light-up humans? Of course, we don't have the bioluminescent capability to actually make our bodies glow (though wouldn't that be interesting?). Instead, God created us to be light in a spiritual sense—to glow with His power and love and to project that light into a world stumbling in darkness. Just as fireflies beautify even the blackest, gloomiest night, God has chosen us to shine for Him in a fallen world.

"You are the light of the world. A city set on a hill cannot be hidden. Nor do people light a lamp and put it under a basket, but on a stand, and it gives light to all in the house. In the same way, let your light shine before others, so that they may see your good works and give glory to your Father who is in heaven" (Matthew 5:14-16 ESV). These verses clearly identify that God's plan for Christians is for us to be His lightning bugs. And why? "So that they may see your good works, and give glory to your Father who is in Heaven." When we shed our light on the people, the places, and most of all, the situations around us, others sit up and take notice. They watch us and wonder what's different. Then, people who are tired of walking in darkness are drawn toward our light, which ultimately points them toward Jesus, the true Light of the world (John 8:12).

There's only one slight problem. Although fireflies are bright for their size, they are exceedingly tiny compared to all the darkness around them. In fact, it is said that in a totally dark room you would need about forty fireflies glowing simultaneously and continuously to read a book![4]

Isn't that how we feel at times? Small. Ineffective. Even insignificant. We hear God's command to shine forth into the world, and we do our best to glow as brightly as we can. At first, we are excited, ready to make a difference. But then we look all around us at nothing but cavernous darkness, and our excitement dims as we slowly come to believe that nothing we could possibly do would lift the blackness around us even slightly.

The prophet Elijah certainly knew that feeling. No one can doubt that he was a shining light—he delivered God's words to wicked kings, raised people from the dead, and even called down fire from Heaven—but with an evil queen seeking his life and an apathetic audience who clung stubbornly to evil, he sank into a mire of discouragement. Alone in the desert, he cried out to God, "It is enough; now, O LORD, take away my life, for I am no better than my fathers....I, even I only, am left, and they seek my life, to take it away" (1 Kings 19:4, 10 ESV).

142

Here was a man who had ceased to believe his light could affect anyone, and when we look at the darkness of our world, it's easy for us to sink into Elijah's hopeless attitude. But this is when we need another important lesson from fireflies.

To understand this, it's necessary to head to the Great Smoky Mountains National Park in the Blue Ridge Mountains of eastern Tennessee and western North Carolina. For a two-week window in late May and early June, fireflies in this area begin blinking, just as all other fireflies do. However, there's a special twist to these displays—a bonus so unique that researchers, naturalists, and ordinary tourists converge on the mountains from all over the world just to witness one of these rare lightshows. These fireflies are synchronous fireflies—meaning they all light up at once! The resulting bright light pulses on and off as the fireflies time their lighting exactly to be in unison with each other. Having witnessed one of these displays for myself, I assure you that it is a stunning experience that its viewers never forget. Researcher still aren't certain why the fireflies behave in this way, but one theory, according to park rangers, is to be noticed more readily.[5]

Look again at 1 Kings 19. Don't miss God's answer to Elijah's despair, because His every word is stitched with hope. "Go, return on your way…And Jehu the son of Nimshi you shall anoint to be king over Israel, and Elisha the son of Shaphat of Abel-meholah you shall anoint to be prophet in your place….Yet I will leave seven thousand in Israel, all the knees that have not bowed to Baal, and every mouth that has not kissed him" (v. 15a-16, 18). In other words, God assures Elijah that he's not alone, and then he instructs him to find these fellow believers—Jehu, Elisha—and unite with them. Elijah doesn't have to be the lone ranger. Instead, he can join with the other worshippers of God—the ones he didn't even know existed!—and create a far more powerful effect.

If you feel like a tiny firefly whose light is lost in the thick darkness around you, find a friend. Maybe two, or three, or ten. Together, shine for God. Before you know it, you'll be making a huge difference. As park rangers say, you'll be noticed more readily. As Jesus says, "A city set on a hill cannot be hidden."

The early Christians knew this secret. In the book of Acts, Luke explains that they were "synchronous fireflies" of sorts. These believers were united in fellowship, with a striking result: the Holy Spirit descended upon them, making possible the salvation of thousands of people![6] Nor is this an isolated incident. The Book of

143

Acts alone records half a dozen times in which the disciples are specifically mentioned as being in absolute agreement and many other references in which it is implied that they were. With this harmony, they did more than just make some light—as Paul reminded his readers, "Their voice has gone out to all the earth, and their words to the ends of the world" (Romans 10:18 ESV).

God never intended His people to be a conglomeration of independent lights, disconnected from each other and barely more than a pinprick in the distance. Instead, He planned for us to be synchronous fireflies—working together to create a display that would draw people from all over the world to our light and by extension to His. One firefly alone can make a difference, of course. But add several, all united with the same goal and shining to honor the same God, and the world is awed with a sensational, unmistakable, amazing display of God's glory and goodness!

So, if you want to see a miracle, go outside tonight. Wait quietly in the dusk until the shining beacons of fireflies begin swirling in the air around you. Marvel at the overwhelming love and imagination of the Creator, Who designed all things for His pleasure. But if you want to not only see a miracle but also be an even greater one, gather some fellow believers and commit to radiating God's light into the dark corners of this world.

TOADS ON THE ROADS

W hat is more calming than a summer night?

The heat of the day has dissipated, leaving behind a gentle breeze that whispers in the trees and ruffles the bodies of water. As dusk deepens, the fireflies begin emerging, at first cautiously, in pockets of two or three, and then in full force until the trees are bejeweled wonders. And around and behind and over all else is the ceaseless music of the little creatures tucked away in the trees: cicadas, katydids, crickets, tree frogs.

It's a relaxing state, a chance to unwind after a long, hot day and absorb some of the evening's peace. It's also one of the few times when it is not dangerous to take my heat-intolerant dogs outside. They enjoy going for leisurely walks at this time of day, trotting down the road and exploring their surroundings as evening falls.

Yet during these walks, I've begun to notice something strange, something that is unexpected and a bit disturbing. As we traverse our asphalt course, we frequently find frogs and toads squatting on the road.

Over the course of a summer, I see all kinds. There are the smooth, slick water frogs, moist bodies glistening. Some of these frogs feature beautiful yellow stripes along their back and legs, and all have webbed feet for swimming. The opposite of these large frogs are the tiny spring peepers. These minuscule creatures, most less than an inch in length, spend their winters burrowed under the mud in roadside ponds or bogs. With the advent of spring, they rise to the surface and sing their hearts out all summer long. The most abundant species I see seems to be the toads. They can be differentiated from frogs by their habitat—toads live on land, while frogs require water— and their appearance. Toads are chubbier than frogs, lack webbed feet, are usually a monotone beige color, and have a rough, bumpy skin.

Yes, I see a full menagerie of amphibian species each summer—not in a pond, or in a field, but on the road. To them, sitting on the highway makes sense. Both toads and frogs are cold-blooded animals. Whereas humans and mammals are warm-blooded, manufacturing our own body heat through internal processes, amphibians like toads and frogs can't produce heat on their own. Instead, they must absorb it through their skin from an external source—the same way we might supplement our body's warm-bloodedness with a heated blanket in the winter. Cooler temperatures not only cause discomfort for these animals; they also decelerate their body processes, like digestion, heart rate, and cognitive function (yes, there is actually activity happening inside a frog's head!).[1] During the day, the heat of an Arkansas summer keeps these creatures fully energized, but at night, the temperature gradient sends them looking for a substitute. And they choose…the road.

On one hand, it's a smart choice and one that shows how God designed animals with the ability to adjust their lifestyle to accommodate human development. The black asphalt soaks up more heat during the day than almost any other surface; thus, it retains that heat well after everything else has cooled. For these amphibians, basking on the road is like lying on a giant heating pad. However, on the other hand, this is a terrible decision…one that makes me concerned for these small creatures. The reason, of course, is that while the road may be warm, it is by no means safe.

Huddled on the heated blacktop, the frogs and toads seem to let their guard down and become less-than-alert to their surroundings. They're also extremely resistant to leave the warmth that feels so nice. Thus, when a car comes roaring through the night, the creatures don't even flinch at the headlights—and as you can imagine, the results are disastrous. Even beyond the cars, other serious dangers await. A main predator of frogs and toads is snakes. And guess what? Snakes are also cold-blooded and seeking the warmth of the road. Any intelligent snake quickly learns that the road provides both heat *and* food—and the frogs and toads continue to fall into this trap. Even if they manage to dodge the cars and the snakes, sitting on the road makes them vulnerable to being trampled by pedestrians, and of course, my dogs take a heightened interest in these creatures and would probably snack on some without my intervention.

Even worse, sitting on the road takes frogs and toads to a place where their main defenses don't work. You see a toad has been equipped by God with two primary ways to protect itself—swell up and play dead to discourage predators, or use the sharp spurs on its hind legs to dig into the ground for safety. Obviously, snakes and cars alike are unfazed by swollen toads, and it would take far more power than an amphibian has to tunnel through asphalt. At the moment these creatures feel the best, they are actually in the greatest danger.

Doesn't that sound familiar? It's one of the errors for which we as humans are famous. No, we don't huddle in the middle of dark roadways (hopefully!), but we run to other things just as dangerous. All is fine during the daytime, when the sun shines brightly and our spirits are warm. But when night falls, things change. Darkness envelops our worlds—maybe in the form of a phone call from a doctor, an overdue bill that can't be paid, a rebellious child or a distant spouse or a traitorous friend. The cold isn't just around us; it's inside our souls. And we become desperate to ward off the chill, desperate to find some way to feel whole and safe again. But that desperation can take us to some scary places.

And the real problem is that we don't know they're unsafe. We might have reservations, at least at first, but we can quickly brush those aside because *it feels so right!* It can't be bad, because it makes us feel good. It numbs the pain, warms the chill, and disguises the ache. How can that be wrong? And so we relax on what feels like a warm, comforting surface, while in actuality, it's a death trap.

The Israelites did this. The book of Judges is a sad story—the tale of a nation that slipped from a lofty position as a true theocracy to a scattered collection of territorial tribes, descended into the filthiest kinds of sin. What caused such chaos? At the end of the book, the answer is provided: "In those days there was no king in Israel. Every man did what was right in his own eyes" (Judges 21:25 ESV). It's a sobering exhibition of the consequences of seeking pleasure at any cost. There was no leader because the people had rejected their own true King—God Himself. Their "god" became their own sinful appetites. The need to numb pain and satisfy desire was the only law they followed.

Yet notice something interesting. The verse doesn't say, "Every man did what was pleasing in his own eyes." It doesn't say, "Every man did what was necessary in his own eyes." It doesn't even say, "Every man did what made sense in his own eyes." It says, "Every man did what was RIGHT in his own eyes." As frightening as this thought is, it appears that the Israelites didn't view themselves as the rebellious, ungodly people they were. This verse makes it obvious that they thought all was well. They believed that by doing what felt good, they were doing what was "right" for them. How quickly our emotions can become our compass…and what a fickle compass it is.

What happened in Israel happens to us: the "roadways" we run to are dangerous because our judgment becomes clouded. However, there's a second deadly consequence: our resistance becomes misdirected.

To illustrate this point, let's return to the story of the frogs and toads. As someone who has been known to cry over the death of a beetle, I can't bear to leave these creatures on the road to accept their fate. So I stop my walk and try to gently move them to the ditches, where they'll find safety. It's not a good idea to pick up an amphibian, because touching their skin can disturb its special protective coating as well as irritate human flesh. However, I gently nudge them toward the margin of the road with my foot. The idea is that they will take this cue and begin hopping off the road of their own volition.

Unfortunately, that's not usually what happens.

Instead, the frog or toad will immediately inflate itself into a puffball of indignation and cling even more persistently to the warm pavement. If I continue to nudge it, it might close its eyes and refuse to budge, or even roll onto its back in a display of mock death so that I will leave it alone and allow it to remain on the road. Instead of welcoming my concern and being grateful that I am saving it from almost certain death, it acts as if my intervention is an intrusion. I am generally forced to resort to shoving the amphibian off the road while it resists the entire time.

148

It's an ironic twist; the toad or frog views me as a threat to its warm, secure location. But actually, I am its savior, rescuing it from that very place it finds so appealing. That is what I mean when I say that our resistance becomes misdirected. Instead of using our energy and resources to resist the temptation to crawl onto the road in the first place, our priorities become completely flip-flopped. We channel all our fight—and animosity—toward anyone or anything that would remove us from the environment—even God.

Consider the story of Saul. After the chaos of the era of judges, Israel decided that civic order needed to be restored. However, they believed the way to do that was not to return to God, but to instate a human king. Saul, the first monarch of Israel, provided some political stability but not much spiritual reform. Instead, he found the moral relativism of the culture to be quite enticing. Although at the beginning of his tenure he habitually consulted the prophet Samuel to receive God's guidance, he ultimately began taking more and more into his own hands. Finally, when he offered an unauthorized sacrifice to God, he had arrived at the place where his punishment was sure and the collapse of his reign imminent, and even though Saul had insulted and shunned Samuel, the prophet returned to warn Him. Wouldn't you think Saul would be grateful, overwhelmed to know how close he had come to destruction? Instead, he offered up excuses, rationalized his behavior, continued to shift the blame, and directed his anger at Samuel (1 Samuel 15).

How tragic! Saul was the one disobeying, the one running to a "warm road" to inflate his own pride. Yet the thing that made him feel so good—holding power in his own hands—was the thing that would destroy him. And since Samuel's warning collided with Saul's inclinations, he directed his resistance not toward his own evil tendencies, but toward the one who loved him enough to correct him.

We all experience that temptation to run to warm roads. The nights get cold on this earth, and the pavement looks like just the thing to warm us up and give us life again. But don't be fooled. It may look good, and it may feel good, but it is deadly. Don't believe the lie that you can find fulfillment there. And if you see someone else on the asphalt, don't ignore them. They may not appreciate your warning at first, but you will have done what God requires of us: "If you warn the righteous person not to sin, and he does not sin, he shall surely live, because he took warning, and you will have delivered your soul" (Ezekiel 3:20-21 ESV).

FLOWERS IN THE DITCH

I'm grateful for more reasons than I can count to be living in a rural area. But one of the most wonderful benefits is the fact that just half a mile from my house is the intersection for one of the few old-fashioned country roads remaining. Unlike interstate highways or other major thoroughfares, this road doesn't blaze from one destination to another, bludgeoning its way through the landscape—it meanders, weaving gently through hills and curves, basking in patches of sunlight and splashing through rustic streams.

There's hardly a day of my life that I'm not on this road—running, or heading to town, or just walking through the evening quiet. I love this old road as a faithful friend, and I know every bump and curve as well as I know the layout of my home. Despite my familiarity with it, though, I noticed one summer that I had overlooked something surprising.

The scenery along this road makes an excursion down it a relaxing journey for the soul and a field trip for the eyes. Beginning near a beautiful lake, the road winds up a mountainous ridge, bristling with trees, then swoops down into a pleasant, spacious valley, full of sprawling farmhouses and pastures dotted with sleek cows, framed by the ripples of rolling hills. So, when I travel this road, I'm generally

151

looking at the profile of the hills, or the cloud shadows on the pastures, or the noble horses trotting through a field. I focus on the treetops, hoping to spot birds; scan the forests, noticing deer; or even smile at the church camp located at the end of the road, where I can often see kids enjoying themselves in the great outdoors. There's only one place on this road that doesn't grab my attention—the ditch.

It's not surprising. Few people are drawn to the ditch. Google defines it quite simply as "a narrow channel dug in the ground, typically used for drainage alongside a road or the edge of a field."[1] That's it. It's not put there for conservation purposes, or aesthetic appeal, or recreational use. It won't be featured on the front of advertising brochures or filmed for a television special. It's nothing more than a trench to direct muddy runoff to a place where it won't impede traffic.

That's uninspiring at best and repulsive at worst. For one thing, all that dirt-filled water can coalesce into some serious mud. (My Jack Russell terrier, Gailey, once stepped casually into the ditch during an evening walk and immediately found himself securely lodged in goo up to his belly. Extricating him was a very *interesting* experience.) In summer, the ditch becomes weedy and overgrown, clogged with rambunctious vegetation. In winter, the water forms sad puddles of discolored ice. And at all seasons, the ditch is unfortunately randomly scattered with rubbish—decomposing tree branches and toadstools as well as the empty Styrofoam cups, shattered beer bottles, paper bags, and candy wrappers discarded by a thoughtless crowd.

So it's no wonder that I overlook the ditch. It's not a shock that I don't feast my eyes on it or make a special effort to notice it. The beauty of the road is found elsewhere—in the forests, the ridges, the lovely farms, the shy deer, the scenic valleys.

Right?

That's what I believed. Until one summer—when I saw something that changed my mind forever.

I don't know when it started, and I'm not sure why it took me so long to notice. But one day, while I was running, I saw a beautiful patch of black-eyed Susans. Their shiny yellow petals waved proudly from their bushy dark centers. I paused to admire them. And guess what? They were growing in the ditch.

Later, I noticed something else. Some plant akin to a morning glory had spread soft tendrils through one section of the ditch. Each day, I was treated to more of its flowers—full white blooms, cupped to catch the sun, with breathtaking violet hearts. And this beauty was growing in the ditch.

Next came some triangular flowers, pointed like paper hats and electric-blue. Then the misty white ones, like so many tiny stars. Then some like little yellow buttons, stiff and proud on their stalks. Even several patches of thistles joined the fun; their snaggle-toothed leaves and spiky purple flowers brought a smile to my face.

How had this happened? Before I could blink, before I could realize what was occurring, the flowers had taken over the ditch— reclaiming something barren, normal, even ugly and turning it into pure loveliness.

Almost without thinking, I began noticing the ditch. I began watching for the flowers, examining them, marveling over each new variety that appeared. I began counting the kinds I saw, rejoicing in new blooms, even taking photos of them. The ditch that had never received a moment of my attention (except when I was freeing an irate Jack Russell) had now become a spectacular part of the landscape. The ordinary had been transformed into something very extraordinary.

My friends, I made a dramatic misjudgment—one that is very common but very deadly all the same. The assumption is that beauty is absent in the everyday. Beauty, so says the world, is found in the dazzling moments, the jaw-dropping *wow!* times. And with this mindset, we categorize our world. Over *here* is the beauty—the moments of heartfelt worship, the days of personal triumph, weddings and graduations and anniversaries and holidays and big-picture occasions. Over *there* is everything else—the "normal" world, of balancing checkbooks and brushing our teeth, eating lunch and cleaning up Cheerios and vacuuming the car. Sometimes we create a whole separate mythological existence—the life we dream of, the life that, in our heart of hearts, we perhaps feel that we deserve. It's the "someday" we're imagining when we talk of our dreams and hopes, the ethereal "tomorrow" behind every boring today. It's these—the hoped-for futures, the Kodak moments—that get our attention. But maybe—just maybe—what lies between these isn't as meaningless as we think.

You see, we become accustomed to our everyday. Like the ditch, it's ever-present, a well-worn groove always running alongside our journey. And sometimes we miss the beauty in it precisely because we're not expecting it. We look so high up the mountains of anticipation or so far down the road of future goals that we miss what's right under our very noses—the beautiful gift of today.

Our everyday, though, is where we live. Don't misunderstand me: the big moments are fun, and plans for the future are valuable, but nothing can replace the day-to-day pattern of our lives. It's the fabric of our existence. And by far the vast majority of our time on this planet is spent in mundanity. That sounds distasteful, but it's true. However, just because every day isn't a far-flung adventure doesn't mean that you can't plant some flowers in your ditch.

Your "ditch"—your everyday existence—will either be a mindless rut or a meaningful path. And the wonderful news is *you get to choose*. If we rush through our days half-awake, gaze fixed on a to-do list and mind harassed by worries, then our "ditch" is guaranteed to be unappealing. But there's another way—a secret, found in a simple attitude shift. "Whatever you do, do it all to the glory of God" (1 Corinthians 10:31 ESV). Does that mean mowing the yard, cleaning the countertops, and grocery shopping are all acts of worship? Absolutely. And they're the things that ground us, that give us a chance to connect with the rhythm of life—to look around and smile and think, "Yes, this is where I live. This is who I am. Maybe someday it will be different, but for now, this is my today. I embrace it."

Perhaps the "trendy" nature of modern Christianity is partly to blame for the lack of interest in the normal. We're trained to continually look for the next Big Thing—the next church conference, the next Christian concert, the next spiritual high. But in the flurry of novelty, we've lost sight of the truth that ancient believers, living in a far more patient time, knew and understood: we either choose to walk hand-in-hand with God down a long path of normal, uneventful days, seeking Him humbly for daily grace, or we don't walk with Him at all. God didn't ask us to run ourselves ragged chasing sporadic tastes of His Presence. He's the God of the big days, the sad days, the happy days, the red-letter days, yes. But most importantly, He's the God of the ordinary days. He's the God of the ditch.

If you don't believe me, just look at the Gospels. We might miss this fact, but most of Jesus's miracles were performed on very ordinary days, during very ordinary occasions, among very ordinary people. He went to a routine synagogue service, and He healed a man with a palsied hand. He noticed a blind man beside the road, and He restored his sight. He was quietly praying on a hillside, and then He calmed the sea. The miracles of Jesus were starbursts in the middle of an otherwise uneventful day. And let's not forget that the public ministry of Jesus—His baptism, teaching, healing, ministering, discipling, His crucifixion, His burial, His resurrection and ascension—was crammed into the space of three short years. That's less than ten percent of His entire time on this globe. Imagine how many ordinary days He experienced—days of working with Joseph in the carpentry shop, helping Mary around the house, playing with His brothers and attending school and celebrating the family milestones. Does God notice the ordinary days? Absolutely. He lived through thirty years of them before He ever began His public ministry—thirty years that prepared Him, even though He was God, for the great work He did in three.

If Jesus was intentional about His everyday, it's doubly important for us. Treat each day like an act of worship—a loan from God that you return to Him, loaded with the interest of love and service. In her book *One Thousand Gifts*, author and philosopher Ann Voskamp speaks of how her life changed when she remembered that "God is in the details; God is in the moment. God is in all that blurs by in a life."[2] At the same time, she acknowledged how "frustratingly common" the search for God is on the days "with laundry and kids and dishes in sink," the days full of "insulting ordinariness."[3] But in the end, she concludes that encounters with God are near, and that "surging magnificence…cascades over our every day here."[4]

"Surging magnificence." Yes, we're not stuck in our everyday. We're placed there—placed there by a God Who knows exactly what we need, Who spills beauty over our lives with the gratuitous exuberance of confetti at a party. So today, take a closer look at your ditch. There could be flowers growing there—the love of a family member, a smile from a friend, a walk with a pet, a job you enjoy, a glimpse of sunset fire in the west, the swinging sling of the crescent moon. At first the flowers might be harder to find, but then you'll notice one. And another. And then another. And soon you'll see the beauty of your ditch. It may be messy at times. It may be boring at times. It may be wild at times. That's ok. It's your life—and from the very mundanity that feels so dead, from the dry-dust ordinariness of the everyday, spring the beautiful flowers God has planted.

SONG OF SUMMERTIME

C onfession time: I don't particularly care for summer. In fact, I have to admit that it's my least favorite season.

For starters, it's hot. And I mean *hot*. Here in July, the heat feels unbearable, but I know there are many more weeks of suffering ahead. As the days drag forward into August, the temperature will routinely rise above a hundred degrees. Just stepping outside makes me feel as if I'm roasting.

And if the heat weren't torture enough by itself, it's coupled with famous Arkansas humidity. Now, maybe you think you have humidity where you live, but let me assure you that only those of us who endure summers south of the Mason-Dixon line know what true humidity is. Our humidity is consistently 70% or higher; at such times, I feel as if I'm drowning on dry land. My hair turns curly, book pages ruffle, and my clothes become soaked with sweat.

So summer has negative connotations for me. It signals a curtailment of outdoor activities, an influx of sticky weather, the invasion of mosquitoes, and lethargic afternoons when the sun seems to be baking the very ground. But you know something? Just when I think summer has no redeeming features—when I'm disgusted with the heat and sweat and languor of the day—night comes. And everything changes.

You see, summer nights are somehow a peace offering. As if the season is trying hard to atone for its brutal days, it boasts some of the most beautiful nights imaginable. Dreamy…relaxed…softened…soporific.

As the sunlight drains from the afternoon, the heat dissipates with it, sinking into the ground now fresh with dew. The scorching sun dies in embers on the horizon, and a gentle breeze begins to whisper around the corners of the trees—a cool, fresh breeze unlike the furnace-blast of the afternoon. Gathering shadows spin cobwebs of twilight all around the brushy bits of forest where the lightning bugs glitter. If I watch closely, I can catch the moment when the evening star first lights its beacon near the swinging crescent of moon. And overhead, between earth and stars, is the squeaking and flitting and zigzagging dizziness of bats in flight.

All these are the magic of sheer loveliness. Yet the most unforgettable aspect of a summer night is not the sights, but the sounds.

When I walk outdoors on a summer night, admiring the stars and feeling the tension of the day release into the forgiving darkness, I am surrounded by a canopy of sounds. Hundreds of thousands of little creatures all around me are singing, each in their own voice, doing their part to celebrate the season of life and birth and growing.

First of all, there are the frogs. Over twenty species of frogs make their home in Arkansas, and each has its own special call.[1] Spring peepers cheep from the warm, wet bogs just down the road. Gray tree frogs are another common species. They generally cling to trees or leaves, but I've seen them perched on doorframes or even windows, gripping with their oversized feet and trilling their call. Beneath these high-pitched frog species can be heard the grumbling baritone of the bullfrogs, their voices rumbling like bass drums from every lake and pond.

The insects are another layer of the summer symphony. For example, there are the cicadas. Now, these aren't the ones that emerge and wreak havoc every seventeen years. They're instead a far more innocuous variety, and if you've ever seen one up close, you know that they're surprisingly beautiful—glistening ruby eyes, shining shell of body, filigree-like wings folded daintily. And if you've walked underneath the trees that harbor them, you've heard their shrill, incessant song. According to researchers, it can sometimes reach 100 decibels—the volume of a lawnmower![2]

I've only scratched the surface of the creatures that grace our summer nights, and there are so many other sounds I could mention—the whirring of June bugs, the soft flutter of moths, the shrill whine of crickets, the clacking of katydids. I've grown up on these sounds, and they never fail to bring a smile to my face. They lull me to sleep and help me relax and transport me to all the woodland places I've ever loved. Despite all my complaints about summer, I tolerate the less-than-ideal components because I love this soundscape.

And until last summer, I assumed everyone shared my affection for this nighttime serenade—but then I had a startling conversation.

I was in Colorado, visiting my beloved Estes Park, browsing a local artisans' fair. As I admired the pottery crafts at one booth, the lady who had created them began chatting with me, the usual small talk: weather, how I enjoyed hiking, where I was from (apparently my southern accent is obvious to everyone except me and thwarts all my attempts to pass as a native Coloradan).

"Arkansas," I replied.

"Arkansas?" She frowned. "You people have some really loud bugs there."

I was taken aback, primarily because the volume of local insects isn't usually my first thought when hearing someone's place of residence. However, I attempted to remain polite. "Well, we do have lots of bugs…"

"No, I mean *loud* bugs," she insisted. She went on to relate a dramatic story of how she had once been forced to take a trip to Arkansas for a few days right in the middle of summer and had heard the sounds of the summer night. To my complete surprise, the same insects that were so soothing to me were downright painful to her. "And at night—ugh! I couldn't even sleep. They were so loud, all the time." She grimaced. "They sounded like a chainsaw."

Like a chainsaw? My beloved chorus of insect voices was being compared to a chainsaw? Granted, the song could be repetitive, and yes, it could get noisy—but a *chainsaw?* I retreated to the relative safety of a lukewarm answer: "Yeah, well, they can be a little loud." (Even this noncommittal reply left me feeling as if I were betraying all my little nighttime friends.)

158

The woman just shook her head and laughed. "I don't know how you can stand it. I'm just thankful we don't have loud bugs like that here."

Even days after our conversation, I caught myself thinking about her comment…not because I was suddenly concerned that our insect population was ruining out-of-state tourism, or because I feared that I would one day go deaf from listening to cicadas at night, but because I was simply amazed by the woman's attitude. It had never occurred to me that someone could be annoyed by something that was, to me, so very beautiful.

I heard a song; this woman heard a saw. I reveled in the noise; she reviled it. What struck me as fascinating was that we had been exposed to the same circumstance…yet we'd responded in dramatically different ways.

But isn't that always how it is?

We're accustomed to judging circumstances as good or bad, positive or negative, fortunate or downright "unlucky." We see the events and situations around us as black-and-white representations that force us to adapt to them. But circumstances can't truly have the weight we assign to them, because two people can be in the exact same circumstances and yet respond in completely opposite ways.

So why is it? Why do some people with a disability overcome against all odds and inspire the world, while others allow that label to define them and sour in defeat? Why do some who survive abuse or neglect develop hearts of fathomless compassion, but others weaponize their pain and lash out at those around them? Why is it that when faced with marital strife, rebellious children, difficult diagnoses, or a demanding employer, some people emerge from trials stronger and more mature, but others swell in bitterness and close their hearts?

The secret is in one small but powerful word: *attitude*.

As we all know, we cannot choose our circumstances. We can't bypass the pain, the trial, the setback any more than we can manipulate the victory, the blessing, the triumph. Life happens, and the events unfold, and despite our most frantic grappling for control, we can't narrate our own story.

So does this mean that we should assume a fatalistic position? Absolutely not—because while we cannot choose our situations, we can choose something far more meaningful—our responses. You see, we are accustomed to viewing the events around us as shaping our destiny, but if we could see from God's perspective, I'm sure we'd be amazed to realize that our responses create a much deeper footprint. Our external actions flow from one internal decision—the choice to gaze through the lens of Heaven or squint with our own human vision. We'll be looking at the same circumstances…but we'll see two very different images.

Consider the account in Mark 3:1-6—Jesus healing the man with the withered hand. Here is a man who has struggled with a horrible disability, and he's been made whole! As we watch the celebration in this passage, we can see how beautiful this moment is. Heaven has come to earth.

Yet the religious leaders have a different viewpoint: Jesus has broken Mosaic law by healing on the Sabbath. We want to reach through the pages of time and shake the rabbis by their clerical collars. This man has received his life back, felt the touch of Jesus, and all they can do is haggle over Rule #345,971? They've just witnessed the God of the universe perform a miracle, and they're already looking for the problem? It's maddening, it's tragic, but most of all—it's convicting. Because before we blame the religious leaders too harshly, I think we've all done the same thing.

We'd like to believe that we would never respond to a miracle in such a way. But haven't we all reacted with soured attitudes? Haven't we all overlooked the good in a situation to focus on the flaws? And haven't we all loudly complained about events, people, circumstances—only to later realize that they were exactly, miraculously, positioned in God's good plan for us?

Humans love to fault-find. A bad attitude is something of an art form for us—who knows why. Perhaps it's pride—*I am wise enough to see the flaw here!* Perhaps it's fear—*If I constantly anticipate bad things happening, I'll never be caught off guard.* Perhaps it's distrust—*How do I know God's plans are good?* Perhaps it's our own insecurities—*If I can't be perfect myself, at least I can try to make everything perfect around me.* But regardless of our motives, we end up in the same situation: blind and deaf to the beauty. Pointing out the flaw instead of gasping at the glory. Hearing the summer sounds as irritating noise instead of a marvelous symphony. And when we respond this way, we not only miss the moment we're facing; we close ourselves off a little more to seeing the beauty in all the moments that follow.

That's why today, I'm challenging you to a different approach. This is the approach that unlocks the gates we build around our spirits, that sets us free to marvel instead of complain. The secret is gratitude.

"In everything give thanks" (1 Thessalonians 5:18 KJV). And this isn't meant to be conditional: *I'll thank You when You do what I want!* Or grudging: *I'm saying "thank you" for this terrible thing, but know that I'm doing it under protest!* Instead, I'm convinced that what Paul is referring to here is less of an action and more of a position—not just mouthing words, but truly opening our hearts to experience and revel in the goodness of God. If we live each day from an outlook of gratitude, so much is transformed:

I have to... becomes *I get to...*

I wish I had... becomes *I'm glad I have...*

Give me more... becomes *Make me more...*

There's a problem with this... becomes *There's a miracle in this...*

Why does God request our thanks? Not to stroke His ego or buy His favor, but to open our own eyes. You see, God isn't a God of long faces and rigid rules, as some would have us believe. Far from it! He's a God Who delights in the splendor and wonder and mystery, Who would have His children share His glee in the story He tells. When we practice gratitude—when we change our attitude—we open ourselves to seeing things a little more from His expanded heavenly perspective than from our narrow earthly one. We notice ways that we ourselves can respond in gracious, loving, faith-filled ways. And when we do that, the Kingdom comes a little bit more—in our world, and in our hearts.

There will always be a reason to complain. We'll never be free of problems to scrutinize. But there will always, always, be much grander and larger and wilder reasons to burst with gratitude.

I don't write this from a place of perfection...far from it. I've grumbled about the "bugs" a time or two (thousand). When my ego is bruised, my will threatened, or my convenience overlooked, then I find it embarrassingly easy to fixate on all the complaints I have. Sometimes I even begin loudly airing them to God.

But then I remember.

I don't ever want to take anything for granted about this life. I don't want to behave like a spoiled brat, turning up my nose at the gifts He lavishes upon me while simultaneously demanding others. Instead, I want to be the one who finds the miracle, the one who finds a reason to choose joy and render worship.

And so on these peaceful summer nights, I step outside, and I let my praise join the song of the crickets and cicadas. Because somehow, I think they sing to Him too.

A ll around me, the world is drying up.

We've finally reached the true apex of summer here in Arkansas, and the defining characteristic of this time of year is blistering heat. Almost before the sun can clear the horizon, it's already evaporated the morning freshness. By mid-afternoon, its direct rays seem laser-focused on our corner of the world, and our temperatures soar well over ninety degrees with a heat index that can be ten or fifteen degrees higher. Even the nights are uncomfortable—warm and muggy, without clouds or wind.

This is the time of year when the weather finally begins to take its toll on the natural world as well. When I step outside, I notice the changes. Heat drifts in shimmering waves above the ground, and the grass that was rank and verdant has withered into crispy stalks that crumble into dust under my feet. The sky, so impossibly blue in early spring, now seems to have faded as well, as if bleached by the sun. Although autumn is far away, yellowed leaves are dropping from some of the trees—a survival tactic to conserve precious water. Even the animals are more subdued—the birds seek the shade of the forest, the deer linger in the deep woods, and the squirrels stretch themselves on shady tree limbs, hoping for a reprieve from the heat.

All of these signs tell me that the summer is turning stale, that the promise of the growing season has dwindled to the sweltering monotony of these gasping summer days. But the most obvious indicator—the true barometer of when summer's full power has arrived—is found behind my house…where Ten Mile Creek is drying up.

This stream runs through our property, a silver thread in the tapestry of natural beauty that surrounds us. And for most of the year, it's an unmistakable presence. In fact, when rainfall is frequent in the spring and fall, the creek often floods in dramatic ways. I've watched its turgid currents rip through our backyard—carving gouges in the landscape, carrying full-grown trees downstream, and once even knocking my father off his feet and sweeping him some distance before he was able to maneuver to the bank. Even when it's not flooding, the creek is still a significant feature in the area—moderating the climate, nourishing the sycamores and birches that throng its banks, and providing a place of rest and refreshment for wildlife.

But at this time of year, the combination of heat and lack of rainfall is merciless. And as a result, the creek that is so robust and boisterous most of the year condenses to a tired trickle. Its bed is merely clammy mud in spots, its waters lukewarm and stagnant. Even though I see this sight every summer, it's still disconcerting when I stand on its ever-widening banks and see the inches-deep stream dragging itself along. It's an undeniable image of just how serious the summer dryness is. And it reminds me of another stream that dried up—one described in the Bible as the hiding place of the prophet Elijah.

The story is fascinating. Living in a horribly chaotic and dark part of Israel's history, Elijah was commissioned by God to deliver a message of judgment to wicked King Ahab: "As the Lord, the God of Israel, lives, before whom I stand, there shall be neither dew nor rain these years, except by my word" (1 Kings 17:1 ESV). Immediately afterward, Elijah found himself in need of a refuge (possibly because of Ahab's revenge), and God gave him one. "[H]ide yourself by the brook Cherith" (1 Kings 17:3 ESV).

This chapter of Elijah's life is a showcase of God's miraculous providence. He was completely alone in the wilderness, sleeping under the stars, with no possessions, distractions, or friends—yet he was never forgotten or abandoned by the Lord. With infinite loving care, God provided a brook to give Elijah fresh water and even commissioned ravens to bring him food twice a day!

The Bible doesn't specify how long this lasted. We don't know if Elijah lived in the wilderness for a week, a month, six months, or a year. But what we do know is this: as the foretold drought intensified, one day the brook dried up.

Imagine how Elijah must have felt. After all, Israel is a very arid country, and he was far removed from civilization. His key to survival in the dry, parched wilderness was this one brook—likely the only source of water for many miles. Imagine how anxiously he must have watched it, how desperately he must have prayed. And then envision the morning he awoke to find that the last thin trickle had congealed into sluggish mud. The brook—the symbol of God's care for him—was gone.

I can understand his pain. And I think you probably can too. Because let's face it—we've all had times when the brook dried up. We prayed that the very worst thing would not happen—and it did. We depended on our job to feed our family—and we were fired. We needed that hope—and it was squelched. We reached out to our friends—and they turned away. We took care of our bodies—and we were rewarded with ill health. We sought God—and He seemed to have disappeared. Like Elijah, we've all mourned the mud and wept on the banks of a dried-up stream.

And in these moments, what's worse than the immediate pain, or loss, or suffering, is the confusion, the doubt, the distrust. After all, we're here at God's command. We thought we had witnessed miracles, but now we begin to wonder. We believed we were in His will, but now doubt slithers inside our souls. We wrestle with the problem of pain and the science of suffering, but all we really want to know is why—why God would lavish gifts of grace on us and then suddenly, capriciously, unexpectedly, yank them away.

The bank of a dried stream is no place for platitudes. When you're left staring at the withered husks of your faith, you don't need Sunday-school soundbites or neatly packaged pseudo-answers. So today, it's with great compassion and humility that I share with you, not tidy answers, but the grains of truth I've learned firsthand from standing on the banks of my own dry streams.

First of all, please hear this: God hasn't abandoned you. This is neither His punishment nor His neglect. Just as part of living in Arkansas is hot summers that make my creek disappear, part of living in this world is experiencing spiritual dry spells. So when your stream dries up—when the provision disappears, the prayers seem to go unheard, and the promise lingers unfulfilled—remember that "whoever would draw near to God must believe that he exists and that he rewards those who seek him" (Hebrews 11:6b ESV). These are the two touchstones of belief—first, that God exists in sovereignty and omnipotence, and second, that He does not turn away from His children. No matter what streams have dried up in your life, God is still God, and God is still good. This is the essence of faith.

So then what is the explanation? If God hasn't turned away—if He is still God and still good—why is this happening? It's counterintuitive, but often, God allows dry spells for a profound reason—to move us into the middle of a miracle. If you don't believe me, look again at the story of Elijah. His tale doesn't end with a discouraged man staring at a dried-up stream. Instead, God told him to go to a widow in the town of Zarephath. To tell the rest of the story would make this devotional far too long (although I encourage you to read it for yourself in 1 Kings 17), but suffice it to say that this woman was at the end of her hope, and through Elijah, God restored her faith. Not only did she shelter him for the remainder of the drought, but he provided a tangible blessing from God during some of the worst storms of her life. The miraculous working of God was far more manifest than it ever was next to the brook Cherith.

My friends, when one door of opportunity or provision closes, you're not being retired. You're being reassigned! And sometimes the only way God can push us forward into the next assignment He has for us is to remove other options—to "bust up your earthly nest," in the memorable phrase of preacher Jentezen Franklin.[1] Think of it this way: if the creek hadn't dried up, Elijah might have been strongly tempted to linger there for years or even for the rest of his life, enjoying the solitude and sustenance. At the very least, it would have been a struggle to put aside his complacency and heed the calling of God. But by drying up the brook, by "tearing up the nest," God jolted the prophet from his apathy, and He made sure there was no retreating. Thus, what seemed like an act of cruelty or neglect on His part was actually a loving gesture—a gentle nudge in the direction of destiny. And that is so often true for us as well.

That brings us to the final promise to cling to: the dry spell will end. Even as I stare at the ruins of Ten Mile Creek now, I know that the creek will flow again. Sometime in September, the equinoctial rains will drench my land, and the creek will be imitating the muddy Mississippi once more. The same is true in our lives; God promises that no drought lasts forever. The driest and most unpromising circumstances can still be resurrected in His hands. And even if He chooses not to restore this particular "brook," He will lead you to a new one—a new source of His grace, a new place of growth in Him.

Seasons of drought are painful. When we wander the banks of the dried-up creek, we're pelted with questions about everything we thought we believed. I know; I've been there. But today, I'm encouraging you to never let what you see change what you know. Dare to have a faith in God that hangs on even in spite of emotion, or circumstances, or appearances. Dare to grip His grace with both hands and believe that even when it looks as if He's turned away, He hasn't. And then watch Him work—because sometimes, a dried-up streambed is actually a trail to a miracle.

LESSON FROM A LIZARD

There are dinosaurs in my yard.

Ok, perhaps not the lumbering giants of *Jurassic Park* fame, or the winged reptiles that once screeched through the sky. I have to grudgingly admit that true dinosaurs are folded in the pages of the past. Yet every summer, I'm blessed to be visited by a very special creature—one that is linked to dinosaurs not only in appearance but also in family ties. I'm referring to the unobtrusive yet unforgettable denizen of sunny days—the lizard.

Lizards are one of those quirky animals that only a God of unlimited creativity could have devised, and their very uniqueness has always fascinated me. Oh, I'm aware that not everyone shares my enthusiasm for these reptiles. My father disgustedly refers to them as "snakes with legs"—considering them a subset of the creatures he loathes more than any other. Nor is his attitude uncommon: plenty of people dismiss lizards without a backwards glance. Lizards are rather humble creatures, after all, and they seem to simply scurry around the corners of our lives. They're not flashy or flamboyant, and as a result, the wildlife spotlight rarely falls on them.

167

But far from being mere nonentities, lizards are actually amazing creatures. If you're fortunate enough during these long and languid days to glimpse one sunning on a stone or scrabbling along a vine or clinging to the bark of a tree, don't simply dismiss it. Take a closer look. Observe their amazing features—from the intricacy of their scaly skin, to their streamlined physique, to the rapid fluttering of their sides as they pant in the summertime heat. Most of all, notice the signature facial expression—an oddly ancient demeanor, like the gaze of a storybook dragon guarding a priceless secret that will never be divulged.

We have thirteen different species and subspecies of lizards in Arkansas.[1] But my favorite lizard, and arguably the most remarkable species in my home state, is the green anole. In the lineup of lizards, anoles stand out precisely because they don't—their camouflage abilities are legendary.

With their lithe forms and diminutive size, anoles have the ability to hide in nooks and crevices that conceal their whereabouts from predators. In addition, they feature a pattern on their backs designed to imitate vegetation; in the treetops, they can pass for nothing more than a shadow on the leaves. But most impressive of all, anoles take camouflage one step further: they actually change colors.

You see, an anole can appear in hues of either vivid lime green and earthy rust brown—or any subtle shade on the spectrum between these—and they can switch from one tone to another whenever they choose. Scientists are still unsure of exactly why anoles change colors. Theories include territorial displays, temperature regulation, or even emotional distress.[2] Evidently, anoles don't always use this ability to hide; in fact, sometimes, such as during territorial displays, they intentionally select a color at variance with their background in order to flaunt their presence. However, it's indisputable that at other times, having the power to change their hue provides the anole with options for camouflage that few other animals can boast.

For example, a vivid chartreuse anole stretched along a grass stem would be indistinguishable from the vegetation. But if that same anole were crawling across a stone wall, brown might be better suited to match the colors of the rocks. And an anole can select either of these options at will.

The science behind this is incredible. When an anole makes the decision to change color, a specialized hormone is released from its pituitary gland. Complex cells embedded in the anole's skin respond immediately by producing a flood of melanin (the pigment that leads to dark coloration in skin, feathers, and hair).[3] As a result, the anole is a quick-change artist, completing the process of a color swap in less than a minute.[4]

How good of God to give this otherwise defenseless creature such a marvelous ability! Although the functions of this talent are quite varied, certainly camouflage is likely among them—after all, having the option to be either brown or green gives the anole more flexibility than either color alone would. And for anoles, changing their color is a remarkable strategy. But the problem is that we humans change our colors too—and it doesn't work so well for us.

We're constantly trying to blend in, aren't we? Consider the boy in the locker room who pretends to laugh at his friends' raunchy jokes even though he's uncomfortable. Or the woman who hides her cross necklace at work. These are just a few examples of what C. S. Lewis called the "subtle play of looks and tones and laughs by which a [human] can imply that he is of the same party as those to whom he is speaking." Lewis went on to give this sobering verdict: "That is the kind of betrayal [the devil] should specially encourage, because the man does not fully realize it himself."[5] Sometimes our colors fade before we even notice.

And like the anole, our color change is motivated by many factors. Maybe it's for safety—to preserve our job or our relationship or our reputation for being "cool." Maybe it's for confidence—sometimes we change our colors to feel more like who we wish we were. Maybe it's for nothing more than convenience—because we feel doing so can momentarily help us escape a particular problem, evade an inquiry, or dodge a tough conversation.

But regardless of our reasons for doing so, changing our colors is one of the most detrimental actions we can take. For one thing, it's frustrating to everyone around us. Trust can't be built without consistency, so as people watch us play the continual chameleon, they're left unsure of our true convictions and skeptical about our intentions. Also, it's confusing to ourselves—as we shuffle through roles, like a kid playing dress-up, we can easily begin to forget who we really are. Lastly, it's pitifully futile. We can't hide our true colors from the God Who sees our hearts. The One Whose opinion of us matters most cannot be fooled by our finagling. And in God's plan, we are called not to blend in but to stand out.

You see, conformity never has been and never will be God's will for His people. Just look at His design for the nation of Israel: "I will make you as a light for the nations, that My salvation may reach to the end of the earth" (Isaiah 49:6 ESV). In the New Testament, the theme continued. Jesus compared His disciples to fairly conspicuous things—the strong flavor of salt or the brightness of a beacon on a dark night (Matthew 5:13-14). Peter reminded his readers that they were "a chosen race, a royal priesthood, a holy nation, a people for [God's] own possession" (1 Peter 2:9 ESV). These few examples are enough to remind us that in every instance in Scripture, the people of God were never told to keep their heads down or remain inconspicuous but were specifically called to appear radically different from their surroundings.

For an example of this, just look at the story of Daniel. When we think of Daniel, we imagine the lions' den, or perhaps his mysterious dreams and prophecies. But many casual Bible readers miss the backstory. You see, Daniel was a very young man—probably still a boy—when King Nebuchadnezzar of Babylon besieged and ransacked Jerusalem. In accordance with Babylonian custom, intelligent and high-ranking Jews were transported to Babylon as captives, Daniel among them. As soon as these new captives arrived, they were immersed in a three-year program designed to completely eradicate all traces of their former existence and conform them totally to Babylonian culture, language, ideals, and religion.

If ever there was a time when someone was tempted to change colors, this must have been it. After all, Daniel was uprooted from his home, separated from his family, and drowned in a tidal wave of propaganda. Who could have blamed him for conforming? Yet in Daniel 1:8, we see Daniel entering this program of complete self-realignment with a single confidence expressed in this simple phrase: "Daniel purposed in his heart" (KJV). And what did this teenager purpose? To remain true to who he was on the inside— something that no outside change could efface.

Did you know that when Daniel arrived in Babylon, he was given a new name: Belteshazzar?[6] It was an idolatrous title designed to negate his allegiance to God and instead designate him as a servant of the Babylonian sun deity. Yet here's the beautiful thing: we never see him referred to as such throughout the book of Daniel. Even when the kings and rulers addressed him, they used his own name— the name of a man who refused to change his colors.

Centuries later, Daniel's example was echoed by Paul's advice to the Roman church: "Do not be conformed to this world, but be transformed by the renewal of your mind" (Romans 12:2a ESV). The syntax of this verse clearly declares that there are only two choices. We can be conformed to the pattern of the world around us, or we can choose to let the Holy Spirit transform us. This is the fulcrum—the fork in the road between two radically different routes.

But why is this so important? Let's face it—no matter how devoted we are, no matter how firm our convictions, we all have moments when we'd prefer to change color like the anole and blend seamlessly into our surroundings. Why is it so crucial that we resist this temptation? For a very important reason: transformed people transform the world.

Look at Daniel again. He was the advisor to at least eight rulers, surviving the political upheavals of three different empires. He served in government roles for many decades, charting affairs for some of the most powerful dynasties the world has ever known.[7] He was, according to Daniel 5:29, the third most powerful man in the whole empire. If ever a follower of God exerted transformative influence on a culture, it was Daniel. And it was only possible because he refused to blend in.

Just consider this: Daniel was only one Jewish import among thousands. Yet he and his three friends are the only captives mentioned in the Book of Daniel. Apparently the others accepted their new names and assumed their new identities and blended seamlessly into Babylonian culture. Like the anole, they registered the "color difference" between Jerusalem and Babylon and altered themselves to match. Rather than remaining true to their internal compass, they changed their colors to fit every backdrop.

In contrast, Daniel chose transformation over conformation. He chose to invite the Holy Spirit to work in his life in a way that couldn't be hidden. As a result, God used him to quite literally change the world. And when we read his account, we feel hope—that maybe, just maybe, the God Who worked through Daniel can work through us as well.

My friend, perhaps you can identify with the anole today. Maybe you've mastered the art of changing your colors to fit every situation—but you're feeling a bit lost in the process. If that's you, remember something: we were not made in the image of Google, or the image of Instagram, or the image of our coworkers, or the image of that popular magazine model. Instead, we were made in the image of God—the fingerprints of the Creator imprinted on our souls, the breath of the Spirit in our lungs. We're masterpieces—designed and purposed to give glory to our Maker. And when we embrace this truth—when we remain faithful to the calling God has placed on our lives—when we show our true hue and refuse to fit the world's color scheme—then we are free to live our stories with the power, passion, and purpose that radically change our world.

ITCHY ISSUES

"One mosquito can keep me 'awaker' than a bad conscience."
– *L. M. Montgomery,* Anne of Windy Poplars[1]

T his humorous declaration may make us chuckle, but it's also a very real reminder of one of summer's least attractive qualities: the presence, in every location and at every time, of innumerable biting insects.

I'm not talking about the lovely creatures of the summer nights—the cicadas, the crickets, the katydids. I'm also not referencing the delicate butterflies, the glass-winged dragonflies, or the feathery moths. No, my complaint is instead with those insects that (at least from my limited human perspective) seem entirely unnecessary.

Perhaps you live in an area of the country where these insects are annoying, yet not overpowering. Better still, perhaps you find yourself in the far north or in the mountainous regions, where they are a rarity even in the middle of the summer. If so, I congratulate you (while also experiencing a tsunami of envy). For me, in the middle of a sunburnt, humidity-soaked Arkansas summer, irritating bugs are not just present—they're unstoppable.

There are the gnats, for one—tiny winged creatures that hover perpetually around one's face and seem to have no other goal in life beyond entering the eyes, ears, and noses of human beings. There are the ants—one grain of spilled sugar, even in the remotest corner of the kitchen, will summon an army of at least two hundred. And there are the wasps—like fighter pilots, they dive-bomb my head as soon as I cautiously step out the back door. But although the insects we see all around us can be irritating or downright painful, they're not nearly as menacing as the ones we *can't* see.

These bloodthirsty bugs are too small to be seen with the naked eye, yet their destructive power rivals that of many much larger insects. They cling to the tips of grass blades, just waiting for an unwary victim to brush through the vegetation. Then, they burrow under the skin of their unwilling "host," creating welts that blister, swell, and itch until the host loses all will to live and enters a state of temporary insanity that lasts for the duration of the itch. (Trust me, it's true.) In Arkansas, we refer to these creatures by the entertaining yet terrifying name of "chiggers," but other regions of the country have their own versions of these frightening foes. In Florida, for example, the diminutive sandfly, which functions much like a chigger, is dubbed a "no-see-um" because, well…you don't see 'em.

Because I was cursed at birth (no, not really, but it's as good an explanation as any), I seem to be remarkably attractive to these invisible vampires. I can walk over the same territory with a group of friends, and they will emerge unscathed while I wake up the next morning writhing with half a hundred chigger bites clustered around my ankles. I do my best to discourage them—using essential oils, developing a paranoia about grassy areas, even wearing long pants on hundred-degree days—but despite my best efforts, the chiggers keep coming. In fact, from April through September (the duration of an Arkansas summer!), I have to be aware that a week of itching is the price to pay for walking across nearly any grassy area. Most amazing of all, chiggers seem to be particularly attracted to me whenever I have momentous upcoming events, so I have not-so-fond memories of squirming at my music recital or staying awake the night before an important exam scratching frantically.

Perhaps you understand why I believe Genesis 3:17-18, in which God describes the curse that resulted from man's sin, should have read this way: "Cursed is the ground because of you…; thorns and thistles *and chiggers* it shall bring forth for you."

It's incredible, isn't it? An insect too small to see can cause a week of agony.

Sometimes I imagine describing a chigger to someone completely unfamiliar with their biting power. My concern would sound absurd, wouldn't it? It would seem ludicrous to cower in fear of such a tiny creature. Perhaps that's because we humans tend to dismiss the tiny things. The small issues are too easy to sweep under the rug or stuff in a corner or brush from our minds entirely. But often, those seemingly insignificant issues can prove to have the most devastating and destructive consequences.

When we think of catastrophe, we think of big problems—things like a depressed family member, a bankruptcy file, a faltering friendship or a rebelling teen or a flailing marriage. What we don't realize, though, is that each of those massive issues started with tiny, but no less tragic, problems…problems that slowly swelled and grew until a mountain of misery was staring us in the face.

And that's the frightening thing about tiny choices—the thing that makes them so devastating, so deadly. They're very difficult to see.

Think back to the facts about chiggers. Supposedly, chiggers resemble bright-red spiders.[2] But they're so microscopic that however much I strain my eyes, I can't see them. If I could, wouldn't they lose a great deal of their power? If I could walk through a grassy patch and then immediately see scarlet chiggers dotting my legs, I'd brush them away before they had time to dig into my skin. The chances of my ever being bitten would be extremely low. But because I can't see them—because I'm not aware of their presence—I can't react until it's too late.

Small choices carry the same danger. They're so easy to ignore, or even to overlook altogether. And we don't react until it's too late. Perhaps the husband and wife didn't realize their bickering was that big of a deal—until the walls went up, the emotions shut down, and the divorce proceedings were underway. And sure, the rebelling teen had started hanging out with some less-than-desirable friends, but his parents didn't correct him, not until he was openly defying them and experimenting with drugs. The credit card debt was easily manageable, but it was too tempting to keep postponing the payments, and suddenly bankruptcy was the only option.

I'm reminded of a verse in Song of Solomon—an epic love poem written by the world's wisest man, King Solomon. The book is a collection of poetic tributes to his beloved, an enigmatic allegory about Christ's love for His church, and a source of pithy gems of relationship wisdom. One of these is found in Song of Solomon 2:15, where Solomon beseeches the couple's friends to "catch the foxes for us, the little foxes that spoil the vineyards, for our vineyards are in blossom" (ESV).

At first, this seems like a strange request, a bizarre moment unrelated to the love story. We might wonder if Solomon enjoyed hunting or kept a zoo or simply was asking for a weird wedding present! Actually, though, this is a metaphor—somewhat like a miniature parable—drawing from a scenario that would have been relatable to anyone in Old Testament times. The arid climate of Israel was very well suited for grapes, and vineyards were a popular source of livelihood for many. One of the biggest pests for vineyard owners was foxes. These seemingly innocent creatures would steal under the fences and gobble up the crop. According to the commentary of the *Life Application Study Bible*, Solomon is using this as an analogy: "The 'little foxes' are an example of the kinds of problems that can disturb or destroy a relationship....Often the 'little foxes' cause the biggest problems in marriage. These irritations must not be minimized or ignored, but identified so that, together, the couple can deal with them."[3]

A little fox can spoil a vineyard, a little chigger can drive you mad, and a little issue can quickly snowball. Consider the story of Rebekah, the wife of Abraham's son Isaac. Apparently both she and Isaac engaged in favoritism, highlighting different sons in a way that caused some excessive sibling rivalry and domestic discord. The ensuing fraternal squabbles led to a lifelong split in the family unit, with one son angry enough to kill the other, and the rift wasn't mended for over twenty years![4] Or how about the case of Saul? His problem started in a small way, as a lack of security in his own abilities and a bit of envy over the growing popularity of his servant David. However, Saul's jealousy grew into a monster of animosity that led him to plot the death not only of David but also of his own son![5] These are just a few examples of overwhelming disasters that began as tiny issues left unchecked—deceptively small problems with massive consequences.

176

And if we're honest, we know issues such as these are present in all our lives. If you come to Arkansas in the summer, you can prepare for an attack from chiggers. But no matter where you live or how you spend your time or how much money you have or what kind of car you drive, you can never escape the spiritual "chiggers." In every life, friction is created by the small problems, the little issues that get between the wheels of living and sometimes make the going rough. However, the good news is that we are not held captive by this fact. God has given us a choice—a choice between dealing with these "little foxes" now, when they are small and easier to rout, or allowing them to grow until the fallout becomes too widespread to manage.

"For who has despised the day of small things?" This question, in Zechariah 4:10 (NASB), was an encouragement from God to the children of Israel, who were mourning their less-than-impressive attempt to rebuild the glorious Temple of Solomon. However, this verse's reminder that small beginnings grow into massive results is also an admonition to us to not ignore our "chiggers." Whether it's a "little white lie," a barely imperceptible shift in attitude, or a seemingly innocuous habit, *small* does not equal *harmless*.

So each summer when I begin to feel that familiar itching around my ankles, I marvel that a creature smaller than a grain of sand can create so much distress for me. However, the power of chiggers lies in that seeming harmlessness. Similarly, those supposedly insignificant problems in our daily lives can spawn the most devastating consequences. That's why it's so important to examine ourselves for the presence of any spiritual "chiggers"—not only because they cause irritation now, but because the raw material of our choices today builds the future we inhabit tomorrow.

THE MIRACLE OF THE MOTH

"If your studying science and the elements has ever led you to feel that things just happen, kind of evolve by chance, as it were, this sight [the development of a moth] will be good for you....[I]t takes the wisdom of the Almighty God to devise the wing of a moth. If there ever was a miracle, this whole process is one....I feel as if the Almighty were so real, and so near, that I could reach out and touch Him, as I could this wonderful work of His, if I dared....Almighty God, make me bigger, make me broader!"
– Gene Stratton-Porter, A Girl of the Limberlost[1]

S tand near a bright light on a summer evening, and I guarantee you'll see at least one. They're the nocturnal counterpart to butterflies, little feathery creatures that seem to float through the sky. I'm talking, of course, about moths.

Now, I'll admit that most of us don't consider these insects to be particularly extraordinary. They're not as flashy as butterflies.

They're not as glamorized by artists. They're quiet and humble and incredibly easy to overlook. But one summer, I realized just how wondrous a moth truly is—because God gave me a front-row seat to a miracle.

It happened in the Smoky Mountains of Tennessee. My parents and I were traveling a popular hiking trail in a wooded area, a place where a gentle forest spread protective arms around a creek that slipped and skipped over smooth stones. As we walked through this pristine setting, my mom suddenly paused to examine something on the ground. "Wait…what's this?"

As I peered at her find, I was uncertain at first. Then I realized that it was something about which I'd read, but never seen—a developing moth.

You see, when moths initially hatch from eggs, they are in the form of caterpillars, worm-like wrigglers that munch on vegetation and scoot along the ground. Then they enter what is technically called the pupal phase. During this life stage, they burrow underground and build a hard case, called a cocoon, around themselves and quietly transform into their familiar winged versions.[2]

But when they first emerge from the cocoon, they're not yet complete—they're wet, awkward, and still underdeveloped. Their wings are limp tatters, their bodies slimy with the fluid from the cocoon. This one we found certainly gave no clue that it would soon be a splendid creature as it dragged itself across the dirt of the trail. It was candy-striped green and white, its body about the size of my thumb, with frilly antennae and a tiny shred of yellow like a collar around its neck. Yet still, I knew that despite its comical appearance, it was a miracle—a miracle that was about to unfold right in front of us.

Our primary obligation was to move it out of the hiking trail and to a place where it could begin its drying process free from the perils of careless feet. We gently scooped it onto a stick and carried it to the edge of the woods. There, it at first seemed to bumble around helplessly, but soon it made its way to a tree and began crawling up the rough trunk. About two feet from the ground, it paused, anchored its feet to the crevices of bark, and arched its back with an evident sense of purpose. It was time for those tiny shreds of yellow to become wings—and as the first hint of green crept into their already-elongating folds, I recognized this little creature as one of the most amazing and gorgeous of the moths—a Luna moth.

If I could, I'd whisk you away with me to that afternoon in the little cluster of woodland, and we'd stand in silence together and watch the miracle unfold. I'm grasping for descriptions, fumbling for adjectives, but all my words seem too clumsy, too inadequate. How can I explain what we felt as, our hike forgotten, my parents and I stood silently in the oblique gold of a late summer afternoon and gazed at the enfolding splendor?

Slowly the puffy body narrowed and tapered into elegance. Slowly those puny rags lost their wet, fragile look. Yet quickly, too— so quickly we could almost see the movement—the papery yellow appendages were spreading into beautiful pearlescent wings, the lemon-yellow color being subtly replaced by the ethereal chartreuse of the adult Luna moth. It was a prayer to see the lower wings emerge, the veining pattern appear, the frail curl that I had lamented as a tear in the wing unfold into the gorgeous tails of the Luna. The little "worm" that had looked so pathetic, deformed, even absurd, was now a graceful Luna, adjusting to the weight of its newfound wings. And there in the early evening, the trees like a cathedral overhead, the sun's last song bathing the moth in glory, we felt sure that God Himself was hovering over the moth, and we couldn't be anything besides amazed and worshipful. The wonder sank into every inch of my being, and my tears overflowed with my praises to the God Who made such miracles.

It's strange, really. I've had so many awe-inspiring experiences in nature. I've watched dozens of bison shamble across the prairies, heavy heads swinging, wise eyes glinting. I've stood in early-evening meadows when the shadows seeped down the mountainsides and heard the yipping of the coyotes begin along the forest edge. I've climbed to the roof of Yosemite, among the mighty granite peaks, and looked over the world as I stood in the drenching spray of a waterfall. And yet I can say with certainty that one of the most profoundly significant experiences I've had in nature was standing in the lazy July afternoon, sweat running down my back and hair curling from the humidity, watching a clownishly striped worm soak in grace and unfold into the majesty of a moth. I think that, perhaps, this encounter was so significant to me because I can identify with that moth. And maybe you can too.

You see, just like this moth, we are all in the process of becoming. From the moment when we first put our hands in God's, when we first decide to follow His way and not ours, we undertake a great challenge—to learn how to live as children of the Most High.

Just as children mature into adults, so we are unfolding into the people God calls us to be. And this growth is not encapsulated in a trendy self-help book or a five-step Bible study or a handful of catchy life hacks. Instead, it's a process—slow, deliberate, ongoing.

And this process can be less than pleasant. After all, sometimes God asks us to undertake challenges that yank us out of our comfort zones or examine areas of our hearts we'd rather ignore. Other times, we become bored by the mundanity of the process—longing for "big" assignments and losing sight of the whisper of grace in day-to-day life. And at still other times, we sink in discouragement over the tiny increments of our growth. Perhaps we don't feel that we're progressing as fast as we "should" be, or we writhe in humiliation when we compare our character to that of other Christians, or reading the Gospels leaves us feeling as if we'll never measure up.

I know I've been there—groaning in the growing. And I suspect you may have too. So today, I'm pointing you to that tree with that clinging moth and offering some encouragement.

First of all, remember that God is patiently working on us. That means He's working on the big days, the days when we reach a mountaintop of progress and look back with exhilaration on the milestones we've conquered. But that also means that He's working on the quiet days, the sad days, the less-than days when we wish we could pray more eloquently, or perform more perfectly, or love more selflessly. I'm reminded of how quietly the moth grew, how its transformation was so utterly without fanfare. Dare to believe that even in the moments that seem devoid of purpose and barren of opportunity, we can relax into the knowledge that God is gently molding us into His image. And better still, we're guaranteed that He won't leave us as works in progress. Writing to the Philippian church, Paul assured the new converts that "He who began a good work in you will bring it to completion at the day of Jesus Christ" (Philippians 1:6 ESV). God never abandons a project or scraps an idea. He doesn't get bored and capriciously hop to the next challenge. He keeps working on people until He brings them to completion. And what is "completion" for us? It's the day we're presented blameless to God as the chosen ones of Christ. What an amazing reward that will be!

And while God works on us, what is our role? Think again about the moth. What was it doing to further its own growth? Was it vigorously straining its tiny wings, trying to force them to open? Was it impatiently shifting position, wondering why it wasn't ready to fly yet? Was it fretting that it possibly wasn't "good enough" for its wings to develop? Of course not. It was simply resting, clinging trustingly to the rough bark of the tree and allowing time and grace to take their course. And that's what we're called to do. We hold fast to Christ as our anchor, and then we allow His work in our lives to develop and be made manifest.

Now, does this mean we have absolutely no role to play in our own growth? Does this mean we can neglect our spiritual health and scoff at the consequences? Absolutely not. There's a huge difference between *waiting* and *wasting*. An attitude of wasting refuses to adopt healthy practices, using God's direction of growth as an excuse for apathy and disregarding whether growth even happens at all. Waiting, however, is trusting God to produce fruit in us while we day by day obey Him in tiny steps. You see, we continue to align ourselves more and more with His character—but we don't push ourselves mercilessly and then sink into despair when we stumble. Growth should always emerge from a place of rest and trust, not a feverish squeeze of work and white-knuckle effort. Remember, "it is God Who works in you, both to will and to work for His good pleasure" (Philippians 2:13 ESV).

This leads to the final lesson, one I've often struggled to accept: we are as complete in Christ the moment we trust Him as we are after we've been growing in Him for decades. To understand this, picture that moth's transformation again. It was so beautiful when it was fully changed. Yet it was still 100% Luna moth when it was merely a funny-looking worm wiggling along the ground. Its essence was always that of a gorgeous moth—even when its appearance was less than breathtaking. Its identity didn't change depending on whether its wings were completely open, or halfway open, or still little wet shreds.

My friends, right now, God sees us as complete in Him. He sees us from the point of view of eternity—safe in His arms, the people He designed us to be. He sees us as clothed in Christ—our shortcomings filled with grace, our sins blanketed by righteousness. Do we still have growing to do? Of course—we'll never be finished this side of Heaven. But does our growth determine our standing with Him? Does it dictate who He says we are? Can our successes or failures alter His promises? Absolutely not. Relax in the knowledge that growth does not determine your standing. You are forever His chosen child, and nothing you could ever do would shake that identity.

Growth. Transformation. Becoming. Those words will always remind me of a still afternoon in the Tennessee mountains watching God shape one of His most delicate creations. Seeing the glory unfold was a miracle—I'll never doubt that. But you know what? The greater miracle is when God pours His glory into the life of a person. It's a quiet miracle, and it takes some time. But we are His, and we are becoming, if we will only wait and trust Him. Like the moth, let's cling tightly to our truest Anchor and wait for our wings to expand—knowing that the Lord of all will tell us when to fly.

THE BEAUTY OF BATS

I t's a summer evening, and I'm waiting to see them. Any minute now.

This is their time to appear—the magical margin between light and dark. Twilight, like fairy dust, is settling in the shadows. The last fiery streaks of the sunset are fading, the undersides of the clouds tinged with the misty purple of dusk. All around me, I hear the chorus of nighttime creatures lifting their praise. A tiny star winks at the swinging silver crescent of the moon.

Yes, this is a good time. And this is a good place—near the glow of the outdoor light in my front yard. Its beams attract a plethora of insects each evening, thereby creating a smorgasbord for the creatures for whom I wait.

The wind stirs, its whisper all around me, and a few more stars peek from behind the velvet curtain of the evening sky. And then I see the first visitor—a frantically fluttering creature, cartoonishly pointed wings, zipping and bobbing and wildly zigzagging through the sky.

The visitor swoops directly overhead, and as it soars above me, I can hear its unique chittering, squeaking noises. It rushes upward, and now I see others, all just as frenetic in their activity, darker shapes against the darkening sky.

Bats. They're a common sight in the summer nights, and they're one of the most fascinating creatures on the planet. To many people, bats are somewhat frightening, even foreboding. They've been maligned as vampiric threats, carriers of disease, or creepy omens. Yet these labels are undeserved; far from being malicious or sinister, bats are actually incredible creatures.

First of all, they make very good neighbors. They're a natural form of pest control; an ordinary bat can consume as many as eight thousand insects every single night! Because of that, bats are a great asset to farmers, reducing the need for costly and potentially harmful pesticides. Furthermore, these creatures are excellent pollinators; over 450 commercial products and 80 medicines are made possible by the pollination efforts of fruit bats. In fact, through their seed-dispersal role, bats are responsible for over 95% of rainforest regrowth![1]

There are so many more amazing attributes of these flying wonders that I could point out. For example, how many other animals enjoy hanging upside-down? Yet bats find it quite comfortable—sleeping, roosting, and even giving birth in that position![2] Also, bats are one of a handful of animals that communicate through echolocation—basically the emitting of high-pitched sounds, most of which are above a human's auditory range, and then using the reflection of those sounds to determine the proximity, whereabouts, and even density of nearby objects.[3] How impressive is that?

However, the most fascinating aspect of bats is not their usefulness, or their uniqueness, or their capabilities. It is simply their identity.

You see, scientists have divided the animal kingdom into neat categories for classification: mammals, birds, reptiles, amphibians, invertebrates, fish. But bats? Well, they just don't fit neatly in any of these boxes.

Technically, bats are considered mammals. After all, they have hair on their bodies, they are warm-blooded, and they give birth to and nurse live young. However, they're different from other mammals in many ways, the most obvious being that they are the only mammals capable of flight. They're so unique that they have their own order—*Chiroptera* (literally "hand-wing").[4]

Because of these disparities, some believe that bats are more like birds. The argument for this point of view maintains that a bird with fur is no more preposterous than a mammal that flies. Even the Bible classes bats with birds in Leviticus 11:13-19 (although this could have been merely a way of avoiding confusion in that culture).

So, mammal or bird? The answer is that bats have some characteristics of both, and they don't align perfectly with either class. And their contradictory nature baffles scientists, students, and nature lovers alike.

So on summer nights, I'm left watching the bats, seeing them wheel at the edges of dusk, the gray space between day and night, between mammal and bird. They're odd little creatures—quirky and complicated and defiant of all attempts to neatly pigeonhole them. And when I watch them, I feel a sympathy with them. Because I understand what it's like to not fit the mold.

This is a devotional, not a diary, so it's not the place for me to relate how true this has been throughout my life. But I can say that more times than not, I've stood with a foot in two worlds. I was born on the blurry line between generations—too late to be a true millennial, but too soon to feel a kinship with Generation Z. During my childhood, I didn't share the same interests as most of my peers, and forging connections was difficult. As an employee of the college I attended, I juggled the roles of both student and staff. I always seemed to hover on the edges of social cliques, feeling a little bit awkward and a lot unsure.

And I bet you've also felt the way I have—unsure of where you fit. Perhaps, like me, you've gazed with longing on the world, where everyone seems to click nicely into their assigned roles with comforting ease. But you know what? The longer I watched that world, the more I realized that I'd never fit in—and I didn't even want to.

You see, as Christians, we're called to be counter-cultural. Like the bats, we belong to two worlds. First, there's this earthly sphere—the place we live, the school we attend, the job we have, the life we know. But our higher allegiance belongs to another world. Because "our citizenship is in Heaven" (Philippians 3:20 ESV), we feel the tugging in our spirits for a place far beyond this world. That's why we're urged to "not be conformed to this world, but be transformed by the renewal of [our] mind[s]" (Romans 12:2 ESV). As Jesus promised, we are in the world—but we are not of it (John 15:19).

We don't fit the pattern, and we weren't even intended to—but that doesn't stop us from trying, does it? We make every effort to force ourselves into the world's prescribed system. But just as trying to categorize bats is frustrating, pigeonholing ourselves is tragically counterproductive.

First of all, we can't be reduced to a stereotype because we are uniquely designed by God. It's a truth that's drummed into our heads often enough—church, Sunday school, inspirational wall art, even catchy bumper stickers and cleverly worded T-shirts. But what if we let that truth permeate not just our heads, but our hearts? That's why David cried out in Psalm 139, "[Y]ou knitted me together in my mother's womb. I praise you, for I am fearfully and wonderfully made. Wonderful are your works; my soul knows it very well" (v. 13b-14 ESV). Do you realize the impact these words carry? God didn't mass-produce you from a mold or slap you together on an assembly line. He painstakingly, lovingly, attended to every detail of your body, mind, and spirit—all the traits and trademarks, all the flaws and features, that are you. What's more, each of these details was handpicked to equip you for the life He has planned for you to live.

And because you weren't designed to fit in a box, you shouldn't try to squeeze yourself into someone else's. We all have people we want to emulate—maybe we covet that model's appearance, or that coworker's confidence, or that friend's level of physical fitness. But God's not interested in creating clones; He's designed us to live as a community of individuals, each as unique as a snowflake. "For just as the body is one and has many members, and all the members of the body, though many, are one body, so it is with Christ. If all were a single member, where would the body be? As it is, there are many parts, yet one body" (1 Corinthians 12:12, 19-20 ESV). What a powerful image! Without my role, small though it is, the entire body would be incomplete. Your role and mine work in harmony together; neither of us would be effective alone. It's only when we embrace our differences—not comparing or coveting—that we are able to work in unison to share the message of Christ to the world.

We've been lovingly created. We've been freed from comparison. And lastly, we've been given an awesome calling. Because God Himself is our designer and our Lord, we don't have to abide by any expectations besides His.

Paul knew this truth. Now, if anyone ever had a right to feel as if they didn't fit in, it was Paul. A former Pharisee, he was renounced by his previous associates once he followed Christ.[5] But as an erstwhile persecutor, he was sometimes viewed with suspicion by the church.[6] Even some of the apostles disapproved of his ministry.[7] As if all that weren't enough, his character and motives were frequently under attack from false teachers who sought to mislead new converts and undermine his teachings.[8] In fact, Paul wrote the book of Galatians to rebut the arguments against himself and the gospel.

Yet notice how Paul introduces himself in what must have been a very controversial book: "Paul, an apostle—not from men nor through man, but through Jesus Christ and God the Father, who raised him from the dead" (Galatians 1:1 ESV). Isn't this remarkable? He doesn't flaunt his credentials. He doesn't seek to establish his allegiance to any particular faction. He makes no effort to classify himself; indeed, he takes special pains to note that his credibility isn't based in this world. Instead, he points to Jesus Christ—the Source of his authority. Devotional writer Christina Patterson muses about the ramifications for us: "The work [Paul] would do for the Kingdom of God…was confirmed not because of what others thought of Paul but because God called him….If God is the one who calls you, what others say or don't say does not define you."[9] Undefined by the world. What if we lived that way?

My friends, like the bats, we're complex creatures. We're all uniquely designed—works of art in a gallery, not rows of data on a spreadsheet. And because of that, none of us will ever fit into one of the oversimplified boxes into which society would love to cram us. But the liberating truth is this: we don't need to. Rather than chase the false ideal of conformity, let's be comfortable embracing our uniqueness. And instead of comparing ourselves with someone else, let's celebrate how God has designed us. Because our identity is found in Christ and in who He has called us to be—not in the labels we can slap on ourselves.

So…are bats birds, or mammals? The real answer is—it doesn't matter. A bat is simply a bat, specifically designed and gloriously prepared for the life it leads. Wedging itself into a preprogrammed set of expectations doesn't seem to be a priority for a bat. So maybe, just maybe, it shouldn't be for us either.

TRAPPED IN A PUDDLE

It was a scorching summer day—the kind for which Arkansas is famous. The weather was so oppressive that I could almost see the waves of heat rising from the ground. Humidity fogged the air, and even the faint breeze felt lukewarm at best.

And it was only 10:00 in the morning! I had hoped that going for my daily run at this time would allow me to escape the worst effects of the heat, but after a particularly sunny stretch of road, I couldn't imagine things being much worse. With my clothes drenched and my eyes smarting from sweat, I paused for a moment in a rare patch of shade.

Here, I was near the calm waters of Spring Lake, a gorgeous body of water not too far from my house. On this day, the lake looked especially inviting. Stately shade trees leaned over its shores while purple martins skimmed the surface of the water, the ripples twinkling in the sunlight.

Mindful of the Bible verse "Lead us not into temptation" (Matthew 6:13 ESV), I averted my eyes so that I would not succumb to the impulse to leap into the lake fully clothed and escape what felt like a giant furnace. Instead, I glanced down to the side of the road—and I noticed something very unusual.

It was a shallow stream, more like a trickle, actually—a miniature ravine carved by water runoff. Just over the edge of the road, it had formed a small pool. The "pool" had muddy sides and rather stagnant-looking water, and I quickly saw why. In the heat of summer, the water level had dropped, and the ravine was clogged at that point with leaves and sticks. The "dam" had, therefore, created this pool.

It was a sad-looking place, barely worth a mention, and a far cry from the crystal waters of Spring Lake. But to my astonishment, I noticed a flicker in the murky water. Tiny fish—probably minnows—were slowly circling the inside of the pool, the sunlight dancing off their scaly backs. The water was too shallow to provide any relief from the heat, so some of them were burrowing under stones on the bottom, seeking the coolness of shade.

As I watched, I realized what a tragedy this was for these fish. Here they were, confined in a tiny, dirty pool full of warm water, with probably a limited food supply as well. Meanwhile, just a stone's throw away was Spring Lake. I imagined these fish encountering the lake, and I considered what a paradise it would seem to them, with crystalline waters, plenty of food, a huge expanse to explore, and cool, shady depths in which to take refuge. The contrast could not have been more striking.

So why? Why would these fish stay in their cramped, miserable pool when Spring Lake beckoned to them half a minute away? Why would they choose the ravine over the beautiful lake?

The answer, of course, is simple. The fish weren't staying in the ravine because they wanted to. I don't know much about the cognitive or sensory processes of fish (does anyone?), but if they were aware that the lake was just around the corner, I suspect they tried everything to escape their prison. But they couldn't.

These fish couldn't swim to the lake, because there was no water route; and even if there were, they wouldn't know how to navigate it. They couldn't call for help. They couldn't summon an Uber or hop on a plane. They couldn't even get out of their pool and walk across the grass to the lake. They were entirely helpless to free themselves.

And at the sight of those fish drifting around the pool, I couldn't help but feel sadness for them…because I've been them. I've never been trapped in a muddy puddle, but I've been snared by other situations. I've been the person who raced round and round my prison, frantically searching for a way out. And just like these fish, I've gradually come to the realization that I'm powerless to help myself.

It's funny; we humans think we're smart, strong, capable, and confident, and in some ways, I suppose we are. We can invent gadgets and build skyscrapers, paint impressive pictures and sail across the oceans. But in light of the vast immensity of the spiritual world, these accomplishments are no more impressive than a kindergartner's finger painting. And when we face the great struggles of life, we are tragically powerless. We can't match forces with death, outrun depression, grapple with relationship problems. And most of all, we can't escape ourselves.

Everyone who has ever been born has come into this world with a huge problem—the life-or-death issue of eternity. And as sinful people living in a fallen world, we are powerless to secure our own salvation. We can't be good enough to climb a ladder to Heaven. We can't be holy enough to satisfy the demands of divine justice. When it comes to escaping eternal punishment, we are all the fish in that puddle, trapped with time running out. Indeed, in Romans 5:10, we are described as God's enemies!

But even those of us who are saved, who have had our sins washed away, still find ourselves in traps. In this world, we face a dichotomy, one Jesus spoke of in John 10:10: "The thief comes only to steal and kill and destroy. I came that they may have life and have it abundantly." And every day, in every way, our lives swing toward the thief or toward the Lord. On one hand is the abundant life Jesus promised—a life full of rich rewards, dense with purpose, where every day has meaning and we walk in showers of peace and mercy. This life is saturated with enough grace to last infinite lifetimes, enough grace to transform us and ultimately our world.

It's close. We can see it. We can feel it. Sometimes, we can even taste it. But we can't reach it.

Because on the flip side of the dichotomy, we're trapped. Instead of swimming in the lake, we're slopping in the mud. And that can keep us living in the stagnant half of the story, the side of the coin that represents only emptiness and brokenness.

This is what it means to be trapped—to be held back from the life God wants for His people. The chains we wear come in all different shapes. Maybe you're a worrier who can't seem to trust God with today, let alone tomorrow. Maybe you find yourself constantly on edge; you despise the angry outbursts, but you can't control them anymore. Perhaps you've felt the grip of addiction; you want to quit, but the pain is too great.

It's not important how we become trapped, because the result is the same. We're disgusted with ourselves, disconnected from our lives, and distanced from God. Instead of swimming in the lake, we're circling a mud puddle, gasping for grace.

Does it surprise you to know that even a revered apostle who wrote half of the New Testament knew this feeling? Just listen to this passage from the book of Romans. The despair of these words is agonizingly familiar to us.

"I do not understand my own actions. For I do not do what I want, but I do the very thing I hate....For I have the desire to do what is right, but not the ability to carry it out. For I do not do the good I want, but the evil I do not want is what I keep on doing....So I find it to be a law that when I want to do right, evil lies close at hand. For I delight in the law of God, in my inner being, but I see in my [body] another law waging war against the law of my mind and making me captive to the law of sin that dwells in my [body]. Wretched man that I am! Who will deliver me from this body of death?" (Romans 7:15-16, 18-19, 21-24 ESV)

"Wretched man that I am!" We've all felt that way.

I'm a horrible person!
Why can't I stop?
I'll never be a good parent!
I can't keep my temper.
How did I end up here?
I'll never beat this thing.

Paul's honest confession resonates with mud-puddle dwellers. Quite honestly, though, it also delivers a sobering message—there's nothing that we can do to rescue ourselves. This passage highlights the futility of three common "remedies."

The first of these is *knowledge*. It's so easy to believe that if we study the issue a little longer, if we educate ourselves on the morals involved, things will magically improve. But if anyone knew right from wrong, it was Paul. Prior to his conversion, he'd trained under the renowned scholar Gamaliel, being groomed to become a member of an elite Pharisaical sect (Acts 22:3). He described himself as "circumcised on the eighth day, of the people of Israel, of the tribe of Benjamin, a Hebrew of Hebrews; as to the law, a Pharisee; as to zeal, a persecutor of the church; as to righteousness under the law, blameless" (Philippians 3:5-6 ESV). Certainly, Paul's credentials were impressive and would have been considered by his culture as more than sufficient to obtain God's approval. Yet he concludes his résumé with this simple phrase: "But whatever gain I had, I counted as loss for the sake of Christ" (Philippians 3:7 ESV). Paul had ample knowledge and a veneer of religiosity to accompany it—but it didn't change his life.

Another false hope is found in *willpower*. We can't summon enough inner strength or personal potential to free ourselves. The effort is as hopeless and defeating as ordering those fish in the puddle to sprout legs and walk to Spring Lake. It's not only improbable; it's impossible.

The final member in this parade of human desperation is *planning*. This is the lie of "I'll do better next time." A tendency to downward spirals is hardwired into human nature. We may have good intentions, but that's not enough to effect change.

And when we've tried every shot in our locker, when we're exhausted and spent from the effort, when our last manmade hopes lie dead around us, this is when it becomes terrifying. Because we're so close—*so close*—to the abundant life. We can see it from the heat of our puddle. But we can't get there on our own.

But wait! Don't miss Paul's last line. Because this, my friends, is the sentence that changes everything. "Thanks be to God through Jesus Christ our Lord!" (Romans 7:25 ESV)

Through Jesus Christ.

It's impossible for us to rescue ourselves spiritually. And that's why it's so easy to despair when we find ourselves caught in our own traps. We instinctively know that there is no way out. We forget, however, that God loves us radically. His mercy is unfathomable. "God shows His love for us in that while we were still sinners, Christ died for us" (Romans 5:8 ESV). We can't bridge the gap between a stolen life and a sacred life. However, Jesus can—and the best news is, He is more than happy to do it.

We've probably never gasped from a mud puddle, but we've struggled with addiction, fled from anxiety, and white-knuckle wrestled our innate sinfulness. Yes, as humans, we know all about traps. But as Christians, we also know about a God greater than our traps—a God Who breaks every chain, opens every prison door, and rescues every oppressed soul.

Dark Sky

*"If the stars should appear one night in a thousand years, how would men believe
and adore; and preserve for many generations the remembrance of the city of God
which had been shown! But every night come out these envoys of beauty, and light
the universe with their admonishing smile."*
— *Ralph Waldo Emerson,* Nature[1]

Although Emerson harbored some erroneous
theological viewpoints, this quotation is still a
poetically moving tribute to the delight man has
always found from gazing into the heavens. It also highlights a
regrettably accurate paradox: the very fact that we can view these
heavenly beings every night makes us unlikely to notice them at all.

Sometimes, on warm summer nights, I change that. I go
outside just before sunset to watch the world fade and the first
pinprick stars begin to twinkle. And I'm treated to one of the most
artistic displays in all creation.

First, the sun dwindles away in a bed of golden coals on the
horizon. A resplendent palette of purple and scarlet and rose pink
yields to a faint wash of color in the west. The air thickens and
deepens with the hint of dusk, and the song of the night insects
begins its rhythmic melody—quietly at first, then rising to a
crescendo. All around are the subtle messengers of the night—the

white moth rising from the dew-drenched grass—the bat swooping dizzily overhead—the lonely sigh of the whippoorwill.

I search the pale sky carefully, for this is the moment, the fleeting instant, when Day kisses Night and the stars are born. And suddenly I see one—a tiny glimmer, small and easy to overlook. I fix my eyes on it, admiring the way it seems to glisten, like a precious stone—until I notice another one, not far from the first one. And then another one. And another. And another!

In only a few short minutes, the sky becomes sprinkled with stars, and as the last light trickles out of the worn-out day, the whole cast of characters that tell the stories of the stars appear in all their glory—Orion, the mighty hunter; Sagittarius, the powerful archer; Cassiopeia, the beautiful queen; Libra, the divine scales; Draco, the stealthy dragon; Gemini, the devoted twins. The night is here, and the stars are out, and once more I am left standing on the curve of the earth, a mere mortal, staring slack-jawed at the worlds hanging just over my head.

Yes, I love the stars. They're enigmatic, they're majestic, and they're downright fascinating. Did you know, for example, that the average star has a diameter 109 times greater than that of Earth?[2] Or that the number of stars is said to be infinite—and still increasing daily?[3] Or that when you look at the stars, the light you see is crossing such an enormous distance that it began its journey to you at least four years ago?[4]

Perhaps the most intriguing fact about the stars, however, is one that most people don't realize. After all, the fallacy is bred into the fabric of our language: we speak of stars "coming out" in the evening or "going in" for the day. However, much like the idea of a "rising" or "setting" sun (when it is in fact the earth that it moving), that terminology isn't quite correct—because the stars are always there.

Stars don't drop a sky-blue curtain and disappear backstage when the sun rises. Nor is there a magical celestial switch that's flipped each evening to produce their light. The stars shine with the same brightness and consistency twenty-four hours a day. As is usually the case in our sin-feebled world, it's our perception that's skewed. The bright light of the sun drowns out the lesser stars. They can't compete and thus become invisible during the day.

Moreover, in our world today, the stars—and the privilege of viewing them—are in danger. As humans contrive more and more ways to stretch the daylight thin, we are unconsciously stealing the stars' best chance to wow us. All the accumulated light of civilization—airports, shopping malls, gas stations, car headlights, factories, security lamps, even household porch lights—isn't just staving off the darkness. It's also dimming the stars, or at least our view of them.

Once, not so long ago, I could stand in my backyard and have a view of the stars as unobstructed as possible. The main threats to my viewing were trees and mountains, not light pollution. On many nights, I could even view the pink flickers on the horizon known as "airglow"—the mystical colors born of friction in the outer atmospheric layers, similar to the auroras. Now, however, the city continues to creep closer to my home with a gradual but relentless stride. Now, when I look to the west, I can see a glow on the far horizon that has nothing to do with natural processes and everything to do with a burgeoning city not too many miles away. This scenario is being repeated worldwide as mankind literally steals the show from the stars.

In an effort to halt the progression, conservationists have established pockets of designated "Dark Sky Areas." Spearheaded by the International Dark Sky Association, the program seeks to salvage a dwindling and often unappreciated resource: the presence of unvitiated night. An explanation on the society's website laments what is lost when too much artificial light infiltrates the environment: "Plants and animals depend on Earth's daily cycle of light and dark rhythm to govern life-sustaining behaviors such as reproduction, nourishment, sleep and protection from predators. Scientific evidence suggests that artificial light at night has negative and deadly effects on many creatures including amphibians, birds, mammals, insects and plants."[5]

As of now, the foundation has created over 115 Dark Sky Places worldwide. In a beautiful paradox, these places preserve darkness—but reveal light. In designated Dark Sky Places, the sheer volume and brightness of the stars is nothing short of breathtaking. Without the artificial lights of the city, the stars can glow with a beauty that exceeds our wildest dreams.

My friends, there's a lesson for us here. When God made the stars, He spoke a single sentence, and all the trillions and trillions of them, innumerable, unimaginable, leaped into the skies. He flung them across the vast expanses of space with this command: "Let there be lights in the expanse of the heavens to separate the day from the night, and let them be for signs and for seasons and for days and years" (Genesis 1:14 NASB).

There's one part of this statement that grips my attention when I read it. *To separate the day from the night.*

In purely astronomical terms, the presence of stars in the sky provides a distinction between day and night. However, in spiritual terms, the stars bring light into darkness.

Doesn't that sound like our job as Christians?

When God made the stars, He was providing a way to still shine light even into the domain of darkness. And when God ordained us to be His children, He was doing the same thing. "All this is from God, who through Christ reconciled us to himself and gave us the ministry of reconciliation" (2 Corinthians 5:18 ESV). In the dark night of this world, we are His "stars," fulfilling the job of giving light.

How exactly do we accomplish this task? Our job in this world is trifold.

First, we divide truth from falsehood. On a dark night, it is easy to stumble or be unaware of approaching danger. However, starlight helps us watch for potential pitfalls and avoid obstacles. In this world, we as Christians are called to illuminate the people, the places, and the situations in which we find ourselves. Because light exposes sin, sometimes our efforts are met with resistance, as Jesus declared: "The light has come into the world, and people loved the darkness rather than the light because their works were evil" (John 3:19 ESV).

Secondly, we provide guidance. Since the earliest times, stars have served as guides to man. The resounding accuracy of the North Star has faithfully led many to their destination, from the ships of New World explorers to the fugitive slaves of Civil War days. Even the Magi were directed to the infant Christ by a star (Matthew 2:1-2, 9-10). Just like the stars, we provide guidance to the world—a blueprint for how humans are designed to act, speak, think, and live. In a world full of people who are morally confused and spiritually lost, the church provides the map back to God.

Lastly, and most importantly, we glorify God. Yes, we are to expose wrongdoing. Yes, we are to guide others. However, in the final analysis, our primary role is simply to glorify God through the expression of our love for Him. If "the heavens declare the glory of God, and the sky above proclaims His handiwork" (Psalm 19:1 ESV), surely we as the redeemed of the Lord have even more of a reason to shout His praises from the rooftops!

My friends, we are not designed to live insignificant lives, swallowed in the darkness of our culture. Instead, we were created to bring glory to our Creator through the light we produce. But sometimes, shining can seem very difficult. When our marriage is thriving and our family is healthy, when there's money in the bank and a car in the driveway, it's not hard to radiate light. But when darkness engulfs our world—when the spouse is distant, the loved one is ailing, the child is rebellious, or the bank account is dry—then shining seems like a bitter mockery. In the blackness of our own "Dark Sky Area"—with the "artificial lights" we've used to numb our pain removed—we cry out in despair. Like small children huddled in bed, we dread the darkness—whether it be the moral depravity of our society, the haunting evil of our own sin nature, or the cold night of a circumstance that seems to negate everything we once believed.

However, in the marvelous grace of God, the dark times aren't reason to tremble. Instead, they're a reason to rejoice.

Does this sound crazy? Glance back at the photo at the beginning of this devotional—a photo of a Dark Sky Place. Do the stars seem intimidated by all the blackness? Do they look to be cowering in fear? Does all that dark swallow up their light? Far from it! The greater darkness of their environment only provides a greater contrast, making their light even more awe-inspiring. To the stars, darkness doesn't extinguish; it extends.

And the same holds true for God's people. Consider the story of Paul and Silas. A mission trip in Philippi ends in a very "black night" for these two men—confronted by a demoniac, unjustly accused, pummeled by a mob, whipped by the authorities, and then thrown into a torturous prison environment. If ever there was a dark situation, this was surely it, as the two men of God nursed their wounds as they languished in chains at midnight in a foreign jail. However, instead of succumbing to despair, they began praising God by "praying and singing hymns, and the prisoners were listening to them" (Acts 16:25 ESV). God used their testimony and witness to bring salvation to the jailor and his household as well as to impact the lives of the convicts around them! The darkness didn't squelch their light; it only amplified it.

So tonight, clear your calendar for a half-hour around dusk. Head outside and watch the world fade as the lanterns of Heaven begin swinging from the sky. And as you watch, remember that God has given us the ultimate example of how to shine brightly. Like the stars, He is constant, unmoved by time or space. Like the stars, His light traveled an enormous distance to reach us—all the way from the Heaven He inhabits to the lowest depths of the hells we so often create. Like the stars, His light irradiates our lives—comforting, convicting, guiding, and providing endless beauty. We who have been "created after the likeness of God" (Ephesians 4:24 ESV) must follow His example, using our dark times not as an excuse to hide our light but as an opportunity to shine even brighter, in a way that dazzles the whole world.

THE MISSING MARTINS

S ummer is ending.

We've flipped the calendar—the brightness of August fading into the more mellow September. There aren't too many visible indicators of this new season yet. The flowers are still blooming, the grass is still lush and verdant, and the days are still unhurried. However, I know the end of summer is at hand, because of a poignant experience I had a couple of weeks ago.

I was running by Spring Lake, a beautiful area that lies along my daily exercise route, and I noticed that something was missing. Somehow, things were not as they had been all summer. I paused for a moment and scanned the grounds. At first, everything looked normal—the trees still scattered shadow, the winds still ruffled the waters. But finally I realized where the difference lay—the sky.

All summer long, the sky above Spring Lake has been filled with a cheerful, chattering flock of purple martins. These birds, members of the swallow family, arrive in early spring and take up residence in the martin houses Spring Lake has provided for them. During the warm months, they enjoy an ideal environment—the security of nest boxes to raise their young, the privacy of the secluded

201

area, and the throngs of insects that congregate above the waters of the lake. Each time I've passed, I've seen them swirling through the sky on their iridescent purple wings, as if chasing the clouds, and I've heard their distinctive bubbling songs.

But on this day, the skies were empty. No whirl of royal wings, no chorus of whistling calls, no peep from the nest boxes or familiar silhouette in the treetops. The dragonflies hovered undisturbed over the grass, and the martin houses stood like lonely sentinels, silent and abandoned.

I knew why my martin friends had disappeared. It's time for the shift of the seasonal cadence—their southward migration. I stood by the quiet martin houses, under the empty sky, and I pictured the lovely birds flitting south, racing ahead of the winter to come. And I felt it in my soul—an indefinable shift—the end of summer.

I always wonder how the martins decide to leave. Of course, I realize that much of the seasonal rhythm to their lives is based on the length of day and night. However, when they begin their migration— one of the earliest of Arkansas species[1]—autumn has not yet arrived. In fact, by all appearances, summer continues to reign.

Yet on a still-hot, still-sunshiny afternoon, the martins spread their pointy wings and rise in the gregarious flocks for which they're known. They leave behind the green fields and calm waters of Spring Lake, and they fly swift and sure to the south—crossing the beaches of the American coast, skimming the Gulf of Mexico or following the spine of Central America. In about a month, they'll arrive at their tropical destination—the uncharted rainforests along Brazil's Amazon basin. Hidden in this vibrant ecosystem, they'll remain safely through the winter, until spring returns and Arkansas calls again.[2]

Imagine what an observer who knew nothing about the changing of seasons would think as he saw the martins leave. Their conduct would seem bizarre to him. Why would these birds simply pull up stakes and head to South America, especially when it seems as if summer will go on forever? In the eyes of this imaginary observer, the birds' preparation for winter would seem totally absurd.

But in reality, the journey of the martins is far from unnecessary or ill-judged. Instead, it's a wise decision, a defense mechanism that protects these birds from a brutal winter. You see, the signs of the coming autumn may not have manifested yet, but the birds don't require external indicators to bolster their internal faith. Because they know that autumn is on the way, they act accordingly

202

even in the absence of obvious signs, trading Arkansas's mountains and forests for tropical jungles.

My friends, there's a lesson for us here. It may seem sometimes that this earth's current season will last forever. All around us, we hear the world echoing the mocking question related in 2 Peter 3:4: "Where is the promise of his [Christ's] coming? For ever since the fathers fell asleep, all things are continuing as they were from the beginning of creation" (ESV).

But we as believers are aware that regardless of how circumstances appear to us, the change is coming. Christ will return to claim His church and put an end to Satan and his current regime.

Granted, the outward indicators of this coming victory may be hard to see. "For as were the days of Noah, so will be the coming of the Son of Man. For as in those days before the flood they were eating and drinking, marrying and giving in marriage, until the day when Noah entered the ark, and they were unaware until the flood came and swept them all away, so will be the coming of the Son of Man" (Matthew 24:37-39 ESV). The world is characteristically deaf and blind to impending works of God.

However, we as the church are aware of what is to come. And like the martins, we plan ahead. How? By living in light of the coming change even when it's not yet apparent. Just as the martins prepare for the future season, we're called to prepare for Christ's return—not by flying south to the tropics, but by living lives of purity, productivity, and hope.

First of all, God invites us to live in a way that honors Him while we wait for His coming. Do you ever wonder why we're not just beamed to Heaven upon salvation? Why do we have to wait on Earth at all? God leaves us on this planet for many reasons, but an important one is to declare His glory through our righteous lives. This means that we do not conform to the temptations and patterns of the world around us, but we shine as lights in the darkness, modeling His holiness and purity.

Secondly, we're called to live productively. Our time on Earth isn't something to be taken for granted or carelessly thrown away or squandered for our own enjoyment. It's a precious resource from God to be wisely stewarded. This doesn't require us to race around frantically with groaning schedules and burgeoning to-do lists, but we are "making the best use of the time, because the days are evil" (Ephesians 5:16 ESV). When we live this way—from the perspective of Christ's soon return—we prioritize our service to Him, and we maximize each opportunity we have to share the news of His glory with those around us.

Finally, we live in hope! In a world that grows darker by the day, it's tempting to succumb to despair or surrender to defeat. The headlines in these times are particularly painful—sickness, economic crises, racial tensions, divisiveness and anger and grief. Yet against this dark backdrop, the hope of our calling shines like a beacon of joy. The enemy's apparent victories are not forever. We hold the peace in our hearts that comes from knowing this wonderful truth: Christ is returning to claim His church and set all to rights.

As I consider this, I'm reminded of a parable Jesus told about twelve bridesmaids at a wedding party. Some of the young women did not prepare for the coming of the groom, and as a result, they missed joining him at the feast. However, the wise bridesmaids were ready and waiting and accompanied the groom to a celebration. (You can read the entire parable in Matthew 25). That's the essence of our calling—to live in expectancy, waiting confidently for His return to unfold and His glory to be revealed.

The first days of September are here, and in this poignant season of changing times and blurring seasons, let's be aware of what the future will bring to our world. A shift is on the way. Others may scoff, but we know it to be true. And just like the martins, we can choose to prepare now for the season we don't see yet—living in purity, productivity, and peace. He is coming, and because we know that, we can rejoice!

In Love with LeConte

"I always…thank God for creating all this beauty for us humans to enjoy. 'Peace that passeth understanding' is possible for me when I sit there viewing the peak, which is sometimes wrapped in wisps of pink to violet mist."
– Gracie McNichol

It was downright chilly that day, especially as high in the mountains as I was. Yet as I clambered out of our two-door Jeep, not even the frosty air could dampen my spirits.

I was wearing a new pair of hiking boots—a charcoal black L.L. Bean model, with bright red laces—and a backpack with a patchwork design in pink and blue. Inside that backpack were all the supplies I would need for an overnight stay—toothbrush, comb, clothes to sleep in, and snacks to eat along the way. But I was hauling more than just necessities. I was also carrying the culmination of several years' worth of dreams…dreams that had once seemed futile and hopeless but that were now coming gloriously, unmistakably, true.

I can't remember when it was that I first heard about Mt. LeConte, only that it was a few years prior to that morning. Maybe a fellow hiker mentioned it in passing, or perhaps I saw photos in the

205

visitors' center or printed on postcards. Looking back now, it seems that LeConte has always been entwined around my heart, but somewhere, I must have learned that deep in the heart of the Great Smoky Mountains National Park was a wonderful place called LeConte Lodge. It was located at the summit of the Smokies' second-highest mountain, and the only way to access it was by any one of a series of hiking trails—the shortest of which was a steep and strenuous five-and-a-half-mile trek. "Lodge," I learned, referred not to the opulent accommodations of a flashy resort but to a much more spartan experience. Guests to this establishment were treated to an overnight stay in a rustic cabin, warmed only by a propane heater and lacking any electricity or running water.

Many people, I discovered, viewed LeConte only as a destination for thrill seekers and adventure addicts. After all, what would they do in a cabin with no electricity and, even more seriously, no Wi-Fi? However, I fell in love with the idea. An enormous fan of the Laura Ingalls books, I considered a trip to LeConte as my chance to relive Little House days, and I immediately added an overnight

 stay on the mountain to my (ever-expanding) bucket list. I couldn't be discouraged by any of the hurdles that stood in my way: the effort it would take to complete the hike, the discomfort of missing a shower, or even the seeming impossibility of an overnight stay away from my home. You see, I have a severe peanut allergy that has always prohibited me from eating in restaurants or staying in hotels. My allergy makes a simple birthday party or visit to a friend's house a daunting challenge…let alone a night on top of a mountain.

All practical considerations told me to abandon the idea, to relinquish the notion of climbing LeConte as something reserved for all the other people, the people who were braver and stronger than I. However, I've never been one for practicalities. So on October 19, 2009, when I stepped out of our Jeep in those scarlet-laced hiking boots, I was doing more than simply preparing for a unique wilderness experience. When I gripped the cables and trudged up the rocky slopes of the massive peak, I was realizing that faith and determination produced results. When I enjoyed my first meal away from home in the LeConte dining hall, I was proving to myself that the barriers that so often seemed to hold me back were nothing more than spiderwebs. (To this day, LeConte remains the only place where I have ever been able to "eat out" thanks to prior alerts from my family and me and careful planning on the part of the crew.) And most importantly, when I finally stood at 6,593 feet and watched the brilliant blaze of the fire-quenched sun, breathing the icy dusk of a snow-crusted mountain night, I was fulfilling a lifelong dream.

That day in 2009 was the culmination of my dream, but it was only the beginning of my love affair with LeConte. My parents and I stayed the night at the mountain many times, and the experience became an annual tradition. When I grew older and the burgeoning popularity of the lodge made it impossible for us to acquire overnight reservations, we transformed the overnight stay into a day hike, completing a round-trip distance of twelve or thirteen miles in a

single day. Since 2009, there have only been three years in which we haven't hiked LeConte due to circumstances beyond our control. In fact, in 2019, we celebrated my parents' fortieth wedding anniversary in our beloved Smoky Mountains, and our trip included (of course) the day-long excursion to LeConte. And when I entered the high alpine forest, when I caught the first glimpse of the weathered log cabins peeking through the trees, I felt no less excited than I did on that first trip a decade before. For me, LeConte never becomes mundane.

Others besides me have felt that same way. At the age of forty-five, a chronically ill woman named Margaret Stevenson decided to turn to the outdoors to find healing. She developed a habit of constant walking (in her lifetime, she is said to have hiked the equivalent of five and a half times around the globe) and discovered freedom from her nearly bedridden prior life. She first hiked LeConte in 1960 and went on to summit the mountain an amazing 718 times, the last one occurring when she was eighty-three years old. Margaret explored many other areas—becoming the first woman to hike all 900 miles of Smokies trails, forming several hiking groups, and helping initiate the Trails Forever program, which conducts restoration and maintenance work on Smokies trails—but LeConte was her first love and held a place in her heart to which nothing else could compare.[2] Today, her bronzed hiking boots adorn the Lodge's main office.

Like Margaret Stevenson, Gracie McNichol suffered from extremely debilitating health conditions. In fact, an accident in her thirties left her completely crippled until she taught herself how to walk again. She did not begin hiking until 1954, at the age of sixty-two, and made her first ascent of LeConte that same year. It was certainly not her last: she completed 244 summits of the mountain, 155 on foot and 89 on horseback, the last trip at the age of ninety-two. (These 244 ascents formed a record, shattered later by none other than Margaret Stevenson.) A woman of deep and abiding faith, Gracie used her hiking time on LeConte's slopes to pray and even presented the Lodge with an autographed Bible still on display today.[3] "Being out on Myrtle Point [on top of LeConte] was a spiritual experience for Gracie," recalls Lisa Line, a former LeConte Lodge manager.[4]

The obvious question arises: after hundreds of trips up LeConte, didn't the women become a bit bored with the well-known surroundings? Gracie herself addressed this in a discussion with her friend Emilie Powell, who later wrote a biography called *Gracie and the Mountain*: "People would say, 'Don't you get tired of going to the same place over and over and seeing the same things?' But I told them that it's different every trip."[5]

As the mountain was for those women, so it is for me—a joy-filled paradox. LeConte is at once completely familiar and completely new—both a warm homecoming and a delightful surprise bundled into every successful summit. And as I reflected on the never-ending source of wonder that LeConte has been for its admirers, it seemed in a small way to parallel our relationship with God.

You see, some people find the idea of an eternal God to be a bit dry, even boring. If God never changes, they reason, then how can He remain exciting to His followers? How can those who have served Him for a lifetime still maintain their passion?

There are two errors in this thinking. The first is that although God is eternal, and He is unchanging, He is never static. The One Who sang the stars into being, the Lord Who paints the autumn leaves, can never become uninteresting or drab. He is the energy behind every creative act, the music to which the universe dances. Yes, Jesus is the same "yesterday, today, and forever"

(Hebrews 13:8 NKJV)—His essential character and personality do not change. However, He is also the God of eternal joy Who triumphantly proclaims, "Behold, I make all things new" (Revelation 21:5 ESV) and "Behold, I am doing a new thing" (Isaiah 43:19 ESV).

I am reminded of a profound quotation by the great philosopher G. K. Chesterton: "Because children have abounding vitality, because they are in spirit fierce and free, therefore they want things repeated and unchanged. They always say, 'Do it again'; and the grown-up person does it again until he is nearly dead. For grown-up people are not strong enough to exult in monotony. But perhaps God is strong enough to exult in monotony. It is possible that God says every morning, 'Do it again' to the sun; and every evening, 'Do it again' to the moon. It may not be automatic necessity that makes all daisies alike; it may be that God makes every daisy separately, but has never got tired of making them. It may be that He has the eternal appetite of infancy; for we have sinned and grown old, and our Father is younger than we."[6]

Could it be our own sin-sick souls that grow weary, that demand continual stimulation in new and different forms? Perhaps eternal constancy is not a handicap, but a strength—a strength that our world, which jumps from fad to fad with every puff of the breeze, cannot comprehend.

But there is a second reason why God never becomes boring—one that escapes our culture, but one with which every follower of Christ can agree.

God never changes—but we do.

There is no process to choosing God's way; it begins as a simple, single decision. However, we don't stop there. As Christians, we constantly grow, continually striving to fashion our lives, our characters, and our futures into the image of Christ. And as we grow, as we learn, as we become stronger and braver and closer to His heart, we are able to discover more and more of Him that we never could have imagined.

This is illustrated by an exchange in one of C.S. Lewis's immortal books, *Prince Caspian*. In this book, the character Lucy reunites with the lion Aslan (a symbol of Christ) after an extended absence. The following dialogue ensues:

"Aslan, you're bigger."
"That is because you are older, little one."
"Not because you are?"

"I am not. But every year you grow, you will find me bigger."[7]

In reflecting on this passage, blogger Adam Winters remarks, "While God is unchangeable in His being, attributes, and power, our relationship to Him is mutable. As we grow and mature, our perception of God may change proportionally....Life experience exposes many of the heroes or ideals we admired as children as less impressive than we once thought. But thank God that our Savior continues to reveal himself as bigger than we could have ever imagined."[8]

This, then, is the secret, the reason why God will never be dull or boring. No traveler into the depths of God's love will tire of seeking Him, and no viewer of His glories will ever shrug and say, "Well, I've seen it all." Instead, those who love the Lord will forever be like Paul, who cried out, "The Lord will rescue me from every evil deed and bring me safely into his heavenly kingdom. To him be the glory forever and ever. Amen" (2 Timothy 4:18 ESV).

By the time he penned these words, part of the last biblical book he composed, Paul had been evangelizing for thirty years in a ministry that covered nearly every known region and even spanned continents. His singular message—"Jesus Christ and Him crucified" (1 Corinthians 2:2 ESV)—had been preached thousands, perhaps even millions of times. Yet the proclaiming of the gospel remained his consuming passion. And when he shared his story with Nero at the end of his life, days away from his execution, he was no less in love with Jesus than he had been when he'd first converted from Judaism years earlier.[9]

Yes, my first LeConte experience was amazing, but when I look back, I realize that I have grown much since then. Certainly, I've grown taller, and I've become stronger from increased hiking. But in addition to developing my physical capacity, I've also developed my capacity to cherish, respect, and appreciate the wilderness and discover the love of God as revealed in His world. For example, when I first visited the mountain, I would never have been capable of round-trip hiking it in one day. Now, however, that amazing experience is possible for me, and I know that my physical and spiritual stamina for the journey will only improve.

The same is true for all of us who have experienced the depths of God, who have sincerely prayed to know Him better and come ever closer to His heart. We cannot grow tired of Him, and we can never outgrow Him. He will remain the reassuringly familiar God we have always trusted for months or years or even decades. However, at the same time, He will continually surprise us with His boundless creativity, His amazing plans, and most of all, His infinite love.

"Breathe on me breath of God. Fill me with life anew that I may love with Thou dost love…and do what Thou wouldst do." – Gracie McNichol, 1967[10]

WELCOMING THE ELK

S eptember is a special month for me.

For one, it's the lazy-golden Indian summer month, when the sun is warm but the breeze is cool, and the birds are beginning to exchange their bright summer plumage for more drab winter hues. It's the month when summer surrenders to autumn, when the farmers near my home scrape bare their grassy fields, rolling all the wealth of the growing season into rotund bales of sun-dried hay. But more than that, more than the sweet-smelling breeze or playful white clouds, it's the month I return to Colorado.

Every year I look forward to this time with eager anticipation, counting the days and dreaming of this journey. As August slips into September, I can hardly contain the excitement, and when I'm finally headed west along the interstate, over the plains of Kansas, past the sign that proudly proclaims "WELCOME TO COLORFUL COLORADO," and up the long, winding road to Estes Park, it feels as if the whole long summer has been leading to this moment.

You see, September in Estes Park is a panorama of beauty, color, and action. In most locations across the country, tourism is winding down by this time of year; kids are back in school, and the lazy days of summer have given place to more mundane routines. However, for Estes Park, September is one of the busiest times of the year; during my stays there, I meet native Coloradans who have come for the weekend from Colorado Springs or Denver, right alongside visitors from Florida, Virginia, Oklahoma, Canada. One September, I even met a couple who had flown in from Switzerland! What draws all these people? They've come for the mountains' biggest celebration ever—the season when the elk come home.

I'll let you in on a secret—beyond the town council, the mayor, and other elected officials, it's actually the elk who own the city of Estes Park. I'm joking, but in many ways, it's true. Each spring, the town floods with elk who are giving birth to their young in the protection of this valley. However, during the summer months after the calves are born, the elk disappear. They return to the national park, leaving the town empty. They'll spend the summer in cool, secluded places on the High Peaks—wandering the windswept alpine tundra or enjoying the lush grass of a mountain pass. For three months or so, only an occasional elk will be spotted in Estes Park, and even tourists driving the roads of the national park will be unlikely to stumble upon a herd.

But that all changes in September.

September is the time when the elk return, when they come down from those remote mountain passes. When the aspens glow golden and the night air is frosty, the elk know it's time to move to lower ground ahead of the coming snows. So they stream back into the valleys—the glacial parks, or open meadows, as well as the town of Estes Park.

This return of the elk is a sight to behold. Unless you've witnessed it, it's difficult to describe just how grand and awe-inspiring it is. I can only tell you that it's amazing, that it's majestic beyond anything you can imagine. During my time in the Rockies, I spent many purple-dusk evenings seated on a glacial boulder, gazing out over a valley still strewn with granite fragments left behind when the last great sheet of ice melted. The harvest moon rose in golden perfection behind the rough-hewn outlines of the great peaks. And as twilight deepened the air, the elk filled the valley—dozens of them, neatly arranged in separate herds, each ruled by a massive bull elk. I watched the bulls—huge, shaggy fellows, with candelabra-like antlers weighing hundreds of pounds. And I watched the cows, quietly nestled in the brush, or delicately prancing across the valley, or (one night) cropping grass only a few yards from me.

The wind felt chilly, and the dusk approached, and the big bulls became even more exciting to watch as they jealously guarded their herds from interlopers. As one stretched out his neck and tipped back his head, I heard it—the eerie call, or "bugle," of a victorious bull elk. And then, as other males answered his challenge, the evening filled with the sound, ringing off the granite peaks and drifting with the nighttime breeze. Even later that night, in bed, I could still hear it, and I smiled in my sleep—because the elk had returned.

Of course, when the elk return to the valleys, they immediately begin infiltrating the town of Estes Park. I suppose the town is a relatively recent addition to a landscape they've ruled for centuries, and perhaps they still consider the city as a mere surface intrusion. At any rate, they demonstrate a complete and total lack of property rights. And as you can imagine, several dozen half-ton animals in a tiny mountain village can lead to some mayhem.

Elk are everywhere and anywhere, all at the same time. I've seen them jamming traffic on Main Street, forcing cars to wait patiently while they roamed the roads. They're also fond of nibbling homeowners' geraniums on Riverside Drive or meandering through Bond Park in the center of town. Indeed, bull elk will frequently usher their herds right through the downtown district or even spar with rival males on the carefully manicured turf of the local YMCA. One of their favorite activities is usurping the opulent nine-hole golf course on the outskirts of town, providing an interesting golf experience for patrons (to say the least). I've actually seen a photo of an adventurous elk who had managed to ascend the steep cliffs behind one house and then had made the next logical step—onto the roof!

You might think that the people of Estes Park would become annoyed with the elk. After all, the giant creatures can be inconvenient, bothersome, and even downright frightening. It would be easy for the town to view them as a nuisance to control or a pest to eliminate. However, the opposite is true.

The people of Estes Park don't shun the elk or dread their arrival. In fact, they welcome them! During "elk jams," drivers calmly wait, never honking or showing frustration. The residents who lose their flowering plants just laugh and remark how fortunate they are to live in a place where elk roam free. And during the last weekend in September, the town hosts the much-acclaimed Elk Festival, a staple on the calendar for over two decades—two days of singing, storytelling, traditional dancing, arts and crafts, food, games, and contests, all designed to celebrate the return of the elk.

For Estes Park, this arrival is not merely a seasonal phenomenon—it's a homecoming. That's because the elk are seen as a symbol of all the town has to offer—a flagship for Estes Park. If you visit the town's official website, you'll notice that the city emblem is a blue square with rounded corners—"ESTES PARK, COLORADO," it declares beneath a row of mountains. And standing on the mountains is none other than a massive bull elk with a tremendous rack of antlers.

It would be tragically ironic if the people of Estes Park proudly displayed an elk image as their logo, yet shunned the company of the real-life animals. How hypocritical it would be! Yet I worry that sometimes, we as Christians can fall victim to the same trap—professing our allegiance to Christ yet squirming from His ruling Presence in our lives.

We understand that we're people of God. We sing His songs, we quote His words, and we might even sport His cross around our neck or on our car bumper. And just as the town of Estes Park is owned by the elk, our lives belong to God. He can interrupt us in any way He desires, at any time He chooses.

All this is solid Christian doctrine, theology to which we can offer an "Amen!" But if we're being honest with ourselves, allowing God to work in our lives is a scary concept. That's because we instinctively know that most of the time, what God sees as progress resembles mayhem to us. When His Spirit moves, it is rarely a gentle breeze but more frequently a gale-force wind—a wind that blows our selfish desires out of sight and whips our human plans to shreds.

Consider the day of Pentecost (Acts 2). Oh, it began quietly enough. People from all over Israel were congregated in Jerusalem to observe a festival, and the disciples were tucked away in an upstairs room for a simple prayer meeting. But that was before God showed up. In a matter of moments, the rushing wind of the Spirit filled the room, complete with flickering tongues of holy fire. What a display of the Lord's power!

Can you imagine the chaos that must have surely erupted? Try to envision the scene. The disciples spilling frantically from their hideout, shouting the gospel in every known language and ecstatically praising God. Confused bystanders shoving their way through the crowd, seeking to catch a glimpse of these men gone mad. Mocking religious leaders hurling their judgments. Indeed, the scene was so disorderly that the disciples were accused of being drunk (Acts 2:13)!

Messy? Embarrassing? Unplanned? Yes. But Spirit-filled? Unquestionably! Seizing the moment, Peter began an impromptu gospel presentation that led to the salvation of three thousand people (Acts 2:41). What looked like sheer turmoil was actually the hand of God, igniting the flames of the Christian era.

And it didn't stop there. The history of the early church is full of such moments of divine chaos. Paul, surviving a shipwreck and a snakebite to the glory of God (Acts 27-28). Philip launching himself uninvited, with no regard for convention, into the chariot of an Ethiopian government official—and thus spreading the gospel to Africa (Acts 8). A formerly paralyzed man sprinting through the Temple whooping his praise (Acts 3). Exasperated government officials labeling the saints as "these that have turned the world upside down" (Acts 17:6 KJV)! (Would it not be wonderful if we Christians today could earn that title again?) Moments of chaos, but moments of God.

But it seems that somewhere along the way, the church ceased to be comfortable with chaos. Somehow, the Spirit's power—and what He might demand of us—became not exhilarating but terrifying. And slowly, we traded a life of miraculous messiness for the unspoken expectation that the Spirit would behave in a tame and orderly fashion, or at least respect our own plans.

And that's the root of our fear, isn't it? If we allow the Spirit free rein, He might turn our world upside down. But if we can check His work, our lives will be much neater and more orderly. Our routines won't be interrupted, and our plans won't be hijacked.

Consider the town of Estes Park again. Certainly, the elk could be removed. A squad of animal control officers, a few stout fences, and some strong deterrents, and the elk "problem" would be solved. And then wouldn't things be much nicer in the town? The golf course would be accessible. The geraniums would be undisturbed. Traffic would flow smoothly, the turf at the YMCA wouldn't suffer, and pedestrians wouldn't have to change their plans to avoid elk. But to me, to the people of Estes Park, and I suspect to you as well, that plan sounds inexpressibly sad. The town of Estes Park is all about the elk. In fact, you might say the elk are the whole point of the town. They distinguish Estes Park from any other small American town, provide common ground for the citizens, and bring visitors from all over the world. Without the elk, the town would be pristine...but it would also be dead.

And just as the townspeople of Estes Park hold the power to banish the elk, we can choose to shun God's work in our lives. For me, one of the most sobering statements in Scripture is found in Matthew 13:58: "And He did not do many mighty works there [in Nazareth], because of their unbelief" (ESV). Don't forget: this was Jesus' hometown! The people who scoffed at His message were His friends, His neighbors, His coworkers, maybe even His distant relatives. This town should have been for and about Jesus. He should have had free reign to do whatever He pleased. But notice the word *because*—He did not display His might *because* of the people's faithlessness. In fact, the Common English Bible (CEB) even translates "He did not" as "He was unable to do." Somehow, in ways we don't understand, our resistance to the Spirit hinders His work in our lives. Although it seems impossible that the omnipotent Son of God could have been prevented from performing His miracles just because of the skepticism of the people, that's exactly what this verse implies. I find that idea very scary, because it proves that in most cases, we are not waiting for God to move, as we often claim we are. Instead, He is waiting for us to allow Him to do so!

So which is more important—orderliness and predictability, or the wild abandon of grace? To return to my analogy, when I was in Estes Park, I had my share of elk run-ins. I was stuck in lines of traffic while the bull elk ushered their herds across the road. I was awakened at night by the bugles, right in the RV park where I was staying. I had to be watchful while I was running, and I had to pause on trails while elk crossed in front of me. But the elk didn't detract from my experience in Estes Park. Instead, they enhanced it beyond what it could have possibly been without their presence. So at the Elk Fest, I joined the community in celebrating the elk and everything they stand for. With them, the town can be chaotic, but it is also alive.

So today, take an honest moment to consider the ways in which you might have been limiting God's work in your life. Resolve once more to "quench not the Spirit" (1 Thessalonians 5:19 KJV). And then watch for the crazy miracles of God to begin unfolding around you. Instead of trying to control God, let's allow Him to control us. Because a life lived in harmony with the Lord may be chaotic at times—but it will never be boring, it will never be dry, and most importantly, it will never be dead.

FAITH AND THE FOOTHOLD

I t's basically the footprint of water.

Each time I return to my beloved mountains of Colorado, I visit the Rocky Mountain National Park Alluvial Fan. For the average tourist, it's not much to see. Compared with the windswept mountains and the majestic elk and the great arching higher-than-holy sky, it's only a collection of rocks.

There's a steep mountainside, over which the Roaring River tumbles, squirming through a crevice, then washing away across the flat expanse of meadow below—Horseshoe Park, it's called. And down the mountainside, on and in and around the river, are rocks, a great barrage of them, as if some giant hand had opened and poured marbles down the slope.

It's odd, this swath of stone, rocks marking their own trail down the hillside. They look like a mystery, or a failed building project, but they're actually a reminder of a great tragedy. On July 15, 1982, a sanitation truck driver was traveling through the National Park campground in Horseshoe Park when he heard a loud roaring noise that he couldn't pinpoint. Then, he saw an entire uprooted ponderosa pine crashing down the river. Frantic, he called park headquarters from an emergency phone, then used his truck to block unaware visitors from entering the area.

That roaring sound was the onslaught of water—the aftermath from the failed Lawn Lake Dam upstream. In one terrifying day, 30 million cubic feet of water submerged the landscape. Horseshoe Park was completely flooded, and three visitors to the park were killed. The flood wasn't done yet, though; it merged with Fall River, on the opposite side of Horseshoe Park, and left the town of Estes Park drowning in six feet of water. The damages cost $31 million, the devastation was complete, and the landscape struggled to recover. And as Roaring River, swollen with runoff, pounded down this mountainside, it carried the boulders with it, leaving them behind when the waters receded.[1]

Today, Horseshoe Park is mostly dry, except for a few marshy areas that provide the perfect habitat for moose. Trees have sprouted again, and the river obeys its banks. But the rocks remain. They're actually quite beautiful. Most are granite, fired by upheaval deep in the womb of the earth. Some are a sharp black-and-white, folds swirled in the stone. Some have light pink flakes, the confetti of rose quartz trapped inside. All are sharp to the touch, rough and bumpy, yet all sparkle in the sunlight like fairy stones. And the rocks are not only lovely; they also boast a high degree of traction. In dry weather and decent boots, walking or climbing on granite is relatively slip-proof.

And climbing is why most people, myself included, visit the Alluvial Fan. It's possible to struggle over, around, and through all those boulders, working one's way up the hillside. The process is known as rock scrambling, and despite its inglorious name, it's surprisingly challenging yet enjoyable at the same time, requiring not only strength and agility but also a great deal of strategy.
At the end of the Alluvial Fan scramble—the end of the designated route, but by no means the end of the boulder field—is the crowning challenge, a truly massive boulder—more like a rock cliff, at least thirty feet high. It sits next to the river like a king, its smaller subjects

of rocks paying homage all around. It too is granite—and it seems designed for climbing.

I've conquered its slopes many times by now, exulting in the challenge during my every visit to the Rockies. But I remember on my first visit that I was scared. I remember that I doubted my abilities. I remember that the rock face seemed very high and the risk of falling onto the rocks below very great. I also remember that if it hadn't been for the desire to conceal my fear and appear far braver than I truly was, I would never have agreed when my dad proposed we climb the rock together.

The first part was easy—well, not easy, but simple. A leap, a bracing of the hands, and then my feet found the ledge, a few horizontal inches creeping around the side of the rock. I shuffled along, working my way to the righthand side. Then another crevice appeared, just above that one. Pressing myself sideways into the rock, my outstretched arms clinging to its stone in the embrace of a climber, I moved up.

I remember a few other details. I remember that the granite was painfully sharp against my sweating hands, but it was also firm and stable. My boots had good traction on its uneven surface. I remember that it was very windy that day, which didn't help in the least. I also remember that, ironically, I was wearing a bracelet that read simply "Courage."

Which I was about to need.

I was feeling rather proud of myself as I inched my way along the narrow edges. And then I reached the top section of the rock—and it seemed that all options ended.

There I was, clinging to the side of this monolith, tiptoes squeezed onto a crevice, fingers tucked into cracks. The thin strip of rock I'd been trusting had died away into nothing. I craned my neck up—slowly and carefully, fighting vertigo—only to see that I was a paltry few yards from the top, and it seemed there was no way to get there.

I was ready to give up. My dad, however, insisted that there was a way—a very obvious one, according to him. He pointed out that I could move upwards on my hands and knees to a series of footholds—or what he called footholds—that would undoubtedly take me to the top. Easy, he assured me. Very easy.

Still trying to keep up the appearance of bravado, I stalled, pretending to examine the route. Actually, I thought he was crazy. Crawling across an exposed rock face on my hands and knees

220

sounded like a suicide wish. And the footholds he referred to were barely indentions in the rock. They looked unreliable. Precarious. Not at all what I wanted to trust.

So there I was. Trapped. Stuck. Unwilling to trade the illusion of safety—albeit immobility—for the danger of the proposed escape. I closed my eyes and pictured myself losing my grip, pictured my boot sliding even half an inch, and envisioned myself dropping through empty space toward the boulder field below.

No. I couldn't take the risk. So I was frozen—unable to go back, unwilling to go forward.

My dad assured me that the footholds would support me. He reminded me that even if I fell, he, being behind me, would catch me. (I remained skeptical that he would truly be able to do so while also hanging off a vertical rock face.) He promised me that I was quite capable of performing this feat.

And so, very carefully, heart pounding, "Courage" bracelet screaming at me, I crawled forward to the footholds. I pressed my palms into the granite, ignoring the sharp edges. I braced myself, I asked him one final time for reassurance, and I fought to keep the empty space out of my peripheral vision. And I moved my boot forward onto that foothold.

I truly didn't expect a miracle. I didn't expect to be able to summit the rock. I expected to go sliding right back down, hopefully into my dad's arms. But to my astonishment, the foothold was actually much deeper and firmer than it had appeared from below. Yes, the slope was steep, but I could manage it. One foot and then the other, I struggled upwards. And in less than fifteen minutes, I was standing with my dad on top of the rock, where we bragged about our accomplishment, enjoyed the amazing view, and took far too many selfies.

"Courage" bracelet aside, I don't see myself as a person of immeasurable faith. I've never been able to remain unflappable in the midst of pain, or discouragement, or seeming defeat. I don't take great risks and I don't gamble on the unknown and I rarely make any decision without the chattering of fear in my head. And that day on the Alluvial Fan, I didn't have any more faith than normal. I only had just enough faith to put my foot in a scratch on a rock because there was no other way. That's not sterling confidence. But that rock was strong. The little amount of faith I had in it didn't affect its power. And because I had just that tiny grain of faith, and because that rock was just that strong, I am here today.

Faith can be a scary word for Christians. After all, we never believe we have enough. *Faith* makes us think of trumpet tones, of bold believers ordering mountains to step aside, of Daniel in the lions' den and Gideon leading his tiny army and Peter casting out demons. It makes us think of the believers today who resolutely face illness, persecution, abandonment, and even martyrdom. We turn from these scenes to gaze at our daily struggles—complaining kids, irritable spouse, dead-end job, malfunctioning car, looming bills— and we shrink inside. Surely we lack faith—how could we survive the attacks of Hell or the persecution of the world if we cringe at the circumstances in our mundane days?

If that's you today, I have good news. Yes, we all lack faith at times, but the efficacy of God does not depend on our faith.

Did you catch that? Faith is for our benefit, not God's. Faith makes our spirit stronger, but it doesn't increase God's power. Faith makes us more willing to pray for impossible things, but it doesn't make it easier for God to answer our requests. Faith gives us assurance in God's will when we face disease, but it's not a prerequisite for God to heal us. The ups and downs of our faith do not correspond with fluctuations in the power of God. They only alter how we view Him.

Now, don't get me wrong: the Bible is clear that unbelief can hinder the work of the Lord. However, unbelief is far darker than the mere absence of faith; it's the stubborn, hardhearted insistence on disregarding God's leading or discarding His promises. It's the polar opposite of faith, and so yes, when faced with our unbelief, God may choose to remove His working from our life in whole or in part. However, faith—no matter how weak or small—invites God's Presence into our situation. And since God "does not give the Spirit by measure" (John 3:34b NKJV), the tiniest coal of faith is just as effective as a raging fire.

If you don't believe me, just consider the story related in Mark 9. A desperate father with a demon-possessed son begs Jesus' disciples for help. Despite their best efforts, however, the apostles can't cast out the demon. When Jesus approaches the group, the distraught father beseeches Him: "If you can do anything, have compassion on us and help us" (v. 22b).

"If you can do anything…" No faith there. That *if* is a closed door. Jesus gently reminds the man of his need for faith: "'If you can'! All things are possible for one who believes" (v. 23b). In response, the father cries out, "I believe; help my unbelief!" (v. 24b) Sometimes it takes faith to realize that we don't have enough faith.

This man wasn't a strong believer. He wasn't a mega-spiritualist or a super-saint. He had just enough faith to ask for Jesus' help—just enough faith, in fact, to realize he needed more. But that one tiny speck of faith was enough. And in front of a skeptical crowd, disillusioned disciples, and a man grasping at straws, Jesus casts out the demon.

Perhaps that is why Jesus promised His disciples that faith no bigger than a grain of mustard seed could move mountains (Matthew 17:20 KJV). Because you see, the amount of faith we have is irrelevant. What matters is the character of Whom we have placed our faith in. And because He is mighty, our faith is also mighty.

I had very little faith on the Alluvial Fan that day. I had just enough faith to put my foot on that rock and see what happened. But because that rock was firm and unwavering, that was all the faith I needed.

And throughout my life, that's often been the extent of my meager faith—close my eyes, hold my breath, and take that one step. And see what happens. And each time I have truly stepped out into the calling of God, I've never, not once, been disappointed. God has graciously overlooked my fears, my foibles, my insecurities. He hasn't demanded that I be a giant of belief or that I loudly proclaim my trust in Him. He has only asked for just enough faith to take that first step of obedience. And when I've taken that first step, I've never failed to feel Courage surging through my soul, and I've remembered what I always knew—the greatest blessings spring from the tiniest seed of faith.

WHERE THE WIND BLOWS

M y friends, welcome to autumn.

The vibrant riot of summer has quietly faded, the stirring symphony of the growing season dwindling to a slower cadence. At first the earth seemed to be undecided, balancing on the narrow knife-edge between summer and winter. But all through September, the days have dwindled. The evenings have come earlier, and the darkness has been thicker. The grass has withered into crispy stalks. The hay has been cut and the schools have resumed and the birds have flown south. And now, in these first days of October, the signs of autumn are all around us. This season is a breathtaking whirl of beautiful snapshots—painted leaves floating on quiet streams, the silvery arms of barren trees, the cries of the wild geese that wing southward in the crisp nights when the harvest moon scatters its magic over the earth.

Yet ironically, in this enchanted season of such beautiful pageantry, the truest harbinger of autumn's arrival is something you can't see—something that captures my heart each year—the autumn wind.

I'm not alone in my love for the autumn wind. Just listen to what has been written about it:

"Listen! The wind is rising, and the air is wild with leaves,/We have had our summer evenings, now for October eves!" – Humbert Wolfe[1]

"Wild is the music of autumnal winds/Among the faded woods." – William Wordsworth[2]

"The wind that makes music in November corn is in a hurry. The stalks hum, the loose husks whisk skyward in half-playing swirls, and the wind hurries on." – Aldo Leopold[3]

These quotations provide a glimpse of the spirit of the autumn. Yet what poet or playwright could truly capture the magic of the autumn wind?

I certainly can't. Any attempt to distill it into crude words is simply stripping the magic away—capturing a rainbow and attempting to dissect it. Even now, as I fumble for descriptions, only images come to mind. Roaming the October woods and hearing the wild whistle and roar of the wind, until the leaves scatter around me in a snow globe effect and the treetops roll and toss like a mighty ocean over my head. Running homeward over fields and pastures in the dusky twilight, racing the wild wind, laughing for the pure joy of the season. Lying in bed on chilly fall evenings, warm and secure, yet hearing the deliciously eerie sound of the wind creaking and muttering around the corners of my house. Common occurrences, everyday activities, but glorified by the touch of the autumn wind.

This wind is a mysterious thing. I've never glimpsed it. I've never touched it. I've never photographed it or captured it in a jar. I've never analyzed it or traced it back to the unknown lands from which it comes. But this I know—although I haven't seen the wind, I've watched its effects. I've been fortunate enough to stand in its path and encounter its mighty force. And I've witnessed it usher in a whole new season—completing the transition from summer to autumn.

I don't think it's happenstance that Jesus compared the wind to the Holy Spirit. "The wind blows where it wishes, and you hear its sound, but you do not know where it comes from or where it goes. So it is with everyone who is born of the Spirit" (John 3:8 ESV).

Like the autumn wind, the Holy Spirit is mysterious—we can only begin to scratch the surface of all He is and does. He is invisible—we cannot see Him go by or hear His footsteps or touch His form. As with the wind, we know He is nearby not because we see Him, but because we see His effects on everything else. In fact, the more we consider the aspects of the Spirit's work, the more parallels we find between the third Person of the Godhead and the mysterious autumn wind.

First of all, the Spirit breathes. Just think of the first time we're introduced to the Holy Spirit in Scripture, in Genesis 1:2. "The earth was without form and void, and darkness was over the face of the deep. And the Spirit of God was hovering over the face of the waters" (ESV). Did you know that the word translated "Spirit" here is actually *Ruach Elohim* in Hebrew?[4] This literally means "the breath of God." This verse is a perfect reminder of the first aspect of the Spirit's work—simply breathing over a person or situation, slowly beginning to bring God's purposes to bear on what is unfolding. Just as the Spirit hovered over the formless void at creation, He is also said to have hovered over Mary, or "overshadowed" her, when she conceived Jesus (Luke 1:35 ESV).

I read these verses, and I imagine the Spirit as the autumn wind. At the end of summer, before the season has fully begun to change, the wind rustles gently in the leaves. It doesn't at first manifest as a full-blown wind but simply a shift in the air, a faint stirring in the treetops. Just like the autumn wind, the Spirit begins to whisper across the landscapes of our lives in small ways. In fact, sometimes we aren't even aware of His Presence; we might look at our circumstances and see no reason to believe that God is working. But take heart! The same God Who breathed order over chaos at creation is breathing hope and resurrection over the confusing areas of your life.

Even better, we're promised that the Spirit doesn't just breathe; He also births. Imagine the autumn wind again. It doesn't rustle in the leaves and then vanish, allowing the world to return to summer. Instead, it remains and grows stronger and stronger until the season is brought to fullness. This is the beautiful reality of the Spirit's work in our lives: what He begins, He will see born. God leaves nothing unfinished (Philippians 1:6), so He doesn't blow across a person's life and then capriciously hop to the next project. If you have felt the stirring of the Spirit in your life—however small— be encouraged to know that He will not be derailed from His plans for you!

Lastly, the Spirit blesses. Now, by this, I'm certainly not implying that He loads us with material abundance or guarantees our comfort and security or gratifies our every whim. Instead, He blesses us by enabling us to do what we could not on our own. The blessing of the Spirit is revealed by the development of His plans in our lives.

Just think again about the autumn wind analogy. Did you know that the wind is responsible for many of the typical facets of autumn? For example, the wind brings in cooler temperatures that stimulate leaves to turn colors—and then helps the trees shed those very leaves.[5] The wind also contributes to the development of equinoctial storms that usher in the characteristic fall climate.[6] In fact, the changing wind patterns in the fall even help birds along the migratory pathways—enabling summer residents to escape to tropical locales and bringing our fall and winter visitors back to Arkansas.[7]

From our perspective, these changes "just happen," somehow unfolding all by themselves. Yet it's the wind, around and above and within it all, that is gently transforming the season into something magical.

My friends, that's how the Spirit works within our lives. He breathes—stirring our souls. He births—seeing His plans to completion. And He blesses—producing the transformation in us that would be impossible without His guidance. So, if the Spirit performs all of these roles, what is left for us to do? I believe our response to the Spirit can be summarized in a brief statement: stand in the wind.

What if I watched the trees blowing in the autumn wind while sitting inside on my couch? What if I read articles about the mechanics behind the wind flow but never felt its kiss on my cheeks? What if I loudly proclaimed my love for the wind, and wrote poems about it, and drew pictures of pretty leaves blowing to earth, but I never actually went outside and stood in the wind? Then my relationship with it would be shallow and meaningless, based not on experience but on hearsay, and my professions of love for it would be artificial.

You see, if we want the Spirit to operate in our lives, we have to stand in the wind. We can't be content with listening to sermons, or reading devotionals, or talking about the Spirit to others. To be sure, these are all excellent activities; however, they can't replace a personal encounter with the Spirit. The power and passion of the "breath of God" can't be replicated.

And the Spirit will not force Himself on us. He won't rush into our lives like an unstoppable gale, sweeping away all our resistance. Instead, He might begin as a quiet breeze, a gentle stirring in the corners of our hearts. The decision to allow Him to proceed further belongs solely to us. We, and we alone, can choose day by day to give Him free rein to work in our lives.

It's autumn—the season of transformation. The wind is blowing even now—chasing the scudding clouds, swirling the leaves like confetti, rising beneath the wings of the wild geese. And day by day, it's blowing in a new season. Do you feel it? Let's believe today that the season is changing. Let's believe that the Wind is truly stirring. And let's give Him full rein to transform us until His Presence is a "mighty rushing wind" (Acts 2:2 ESV) across our hearts and lives.

DARING TO DREAM

This is the season of acorns.

Every fall, I encounter them, a familiar note in the symphony of the autumn woods. I roam the arching corridors of the flaming forests, shuffling through the papery carpet of fallen leaves. And there, rolling about under my feet, are the acorns, like forgotten marbles from a game of the woodland angels.

They're plenteous now, but all summer they've been practically invisible. First they were nothing more than tiny buds on the fingers of the branches. Then the buds gave way to the atypical "flowers" of an oak tree, pollen-dusted catkins swinging in the spring breezes. And from this embryonic form, infant acorns stretched— tiny and timid and the velvety green of growing things. But autumn is their time to ripen, to perfect their polished brown shade, to be released from the trees like a gift. In fact, if I'm in just the right place on a windy day, I can watch them showering down, see them releasing their hold on their parent oaks and bouncing to the forest floor.

It's amazing to me that although these little items are commonplace, they are, in a quiet way, stunningly unique. What most people don't realize is that not all acorns are created equal; my home state of Arkansas features a staggering twenty-nine different species of oak trees, and each of them produces acorns in a signature style.[1] Some have tapered forms, elongated and elegant. Others are fat and round, cheery cheeks shining. Some are no bigger than my thumbnail, while others are giants the size of golf balls, with magnificent furry toppings. But despite their external variations, all acorns share the same basic design: a jaunty cap perched atop a sleek shell.

But acorns are more than just interesting objects to observe; in the ecology of the forest, they serve a variety of vital, if unsung, functions. For one thing, they're a primary food source for wildlife; over a hundred species of animals including deer, bears, ducks, and rabbits glean valuable calories from nutrient-rich acorns. Wildlife scientist Roger di Silvestro jokes that "the acorn is the cheeseburger of the forest ecosystem—fairly easy to find and nicely packaged."[2] And when animals consume acorns, they contribute to the nut's second function: fertilizer. Shell fragments and crushed acorns join the organic material on the forest floor, known as leaf litter or humus; the purposes of humus are varied but include enriching the soil, harboring beneficial invertebrates, and promoting the growth of new vegetation.[3]

Food and fertilizer are important functions, but the acorn's primary purpose is not only the most famous but also the most inspiring: to grow an oak tree.

The process by which an acorn grows into an oak is nothing short of miraculous. Inside that tough external capsule nestles the oak tree's most precious offering: its seed. If the acorn comes to rest in the right conditions—nutritious soil, adequate moisture, and ample sunlight—then the outer shell will crack. A tiny root will burrow its finger into the loam, and a miniature set of twin leaves will reach skyward. These humble beginnings are the first shoot and root of the oak. Over time, four or five years to be exact, the root system will develop, and branches will sprout farther. By the end of that period, a sapling oak will be standing over the heart of the former acorn.[4]

It's impossible to hear this information without gaining a whole new perspective on acorns. Instead of scuffing them underfoot, I sometimes pause and gently extract one from the forest floor. I brush it clean with my thumb and wrap my fingers around its lightweight design. And with awe, I realize that I'm cradling a hundred-foot oak in my hand.

It's amazing when you think about it: the life of an acorn doesn't come from itself. The stylish cap and slender body don't hold any power of their own. There's nothing about the acorn itself that gives it life. What keeps it alive is that it holds something bigger than itself.

Could the same be true for us?

You see, on our own, we are just as lifeless and lost as that tiny acorn. Our culture tries so hard to conjure life, but despite our best efforts, our frail humanity can't replicate vitality. Instead, our life comes from being filled with something bigger than ourselves.

"We, as humans, have an innate desire to be courageous. Woven into our hearts is the desire to live lives that matter, to live great stories, to be the courageous heroes that overcome our greatest fears just in time to save the day," writes author and blogger Stephanie May Wilson.[5] I love her words, because I believe it's true. We have to live filled with something far bigger than ourselves—or we won't live at all.

Just consider the acorn again. What makes it precious is that it is holding a miracle inside it. The future is wrapped in its shiny skin and capped by its jaunty hat. It is a time capsule protecting the embryo of an oak-to-be, a treasure chest hugging a rich gem of possibility. The purpose of an acorn is to harbor a dream—and to allow God, in His timing, to release it.

We have more in common with the acorn than we think. You see, we may not look like much on the outside. But our value comes from the fact that we are filled with something bigger than ourselves. By the power of the Holy Spirit, we've been seeded with infinite possibilities—dreams and visions of the great works we can do, the mighty oaks we can grow, for the Kingdom of God. Nestled within the capsules of our hearts are the seeds—the dreams, the hopes, the visions. As the acorn holds within itself a magnificent oak tree, so we carry dreams far bigger than ourselves.

And it is these dreams that are the secret to our existence. As Proverbs 29:18 states, "Where there is no vision, the people perish" (KJV). The blunt wording of this verse describes the state of soul of a person who lives without a sense of the future. Without God-given dreams and plans, we will quite literally perish—choked by convenience, stifled by silence, muffled by mundanity. Our life only flows when we are dancing in step with the Spirit, partnering with Him to bring His calling over our lives into vivid reality.

To many of us, this sounds wistfully wonderful—a charmed way to live, vastly different from anything we could accomplish. Sure, pursuing a passion and daring with boldness and dreaming oversized dreams sounds great...at least in theory. But then we look around—at our own insecurities, or our woeful lack of talent, or our embarrassing mistakes. And anyway, modern life is forever tugging on our sleeve and harping for our attention like a spoiled child. Really, if we're not even motivated to wash the breakfast dishes, what makes us think we can change the world?

If that's you, I understand. Discouragement has shrouded me in its fog many times. But in those moments of shadowing insecurity, this is the brilliant truth with which we illuminate our hearts: *God has a dream for all people.* Not just wealthy people. Not just talented people. Not just methodical people. Not even just people who have color-coded sock drawers! *All people.* Look no further than Ephesians 2:10: "For we are his workmanship, created in Christ Jesus for good works, *which God prepared beforehand, that we should walk in them*" (ESV; emphasis mine). Along the splendid trail of life, God has carefully laid out good works for us all through the years—a pathway of dreams and dares and decisions.

And if God has ordained all this, what is left for us to do? Simply to choose to walk the pathway He has prepared. And truly, it's no choice at all...the choice to exist or to live. And it's a choice we can make here, today, no matter how many years we've lived or how much time we've wasted or how many fears we combat or how many mistakes we've made.

But how do we start? In the dusty corners of our hearts, the seeds of our dreams often lie forgotten or unnoticed. How do we find those precious gems of our calling? Once again, the humble acorn has much to say.

The first step in finding your God dream is to check your DNA. You see, if you were to examine the genetic material of an acorn, you'd find that it was the DNA of an oak. Even in that stage, it bears the image of its true identity, and it's hardwired to become the future. So what passions are woven into your character? What excites you? What fills your soul with wonder? What would you love to wake up every morning and do?

Once you find that spark, evaluate your dream. God dreams, like acorns, come in all shapes and sizes, but they should share a few commonalities. First of all, they are bigger than ourselves. Just as the towering oak is immeasurably larger than the tiny acorn, so our

232

dreams should be wildly disproportional to our capabilities. Our culture is fond of miniaturized dreams, but only a God-sized dream is worth pursuing through a lifetime.

Secondly, God dreams outlive us. The acorn will be absorbed into the forest floor within a single brief season, but the oak it plants may live for many centuries.[6] In the same way, our visions should lead us to make contributions that extend beyond the scope of earthly time—touching hearts, creating a legacy, leaving a testament to the faithfulness of God in our lives.

Thirdly, and most importantly, God dreams should bring glory to their divine Author. I've never seen an oak that wasn't stretching its arms to Heaven in praise. And in the same way, our dreams should not leave people marveling at our ingenuity, or tenacity, or creativity. They should instead sing the praise of God Almighty in a way that even effaces our own contribution.

To see a God dream in action, look no further than the story of David—an overlooked and undergrown teenage boy to whom God promised the throne of Israel. If ever there was a God dream, this was it. It was outsized—definitely bigger than anything an impoverished teenager could have hoped to have achieved on his own. It was long-lasting—David's contributions are still felt today in his legacy, his political work, and of course, his psalms. It brought glory to God—although he stumbled at times, David remained a man after God's own heart, and his story is a testament to the power of the Almighty at work in his life.

Yet there's a part of David's story that we often overlook—one that tells us something important about God dreams. You see, David wasn't anointed king and installed on the throne the next day. He had to wait—not a week, not a month, not a year, but almost fifteen years (2 Samuel 5:4)!

This waiting is a commonality of God dreams, and it is the stage of the process where people are perhaps most likely to falter and flail. The spark of a God dream ignites within us, and we expect it to immediately billow into a roaring flame. But dreams aren't preformed commodities, and they don't spring into being overnight. They grow—steadily, and slowly, and often silently.

Again, there's a parallel with the acorn. For an acorn to become an oak, it has to follow the stages of growth: embedding itself into the soil and being nurtured with light, water, and essential nutrients. Then, it has to wait—patience is required as possibility incarnates into reality. But at no time do we see an acorn frantically trying to make itself grow or attempting to squeeze the oak into existence! Instead, we see it lying trustingly in the damp soil of the autumn ground—knowing that the God Who deposited the dream inside it will bring it forth in His time.

And it is in these same humble stages that we find our dreams growing. We must sow ourselves deeply into the firm foundation of God—burying ourselves in His Word, rooting ourselves in His grace (Ephesians 3:17). We must nurture our dream with His nutrients, like the fellowship of other believers, prayer, giving—as commonplace as sunlight and water, yet as essential. And finally, we must perform that hardest calling of humans—to bear the weight of the wait, to open ourselves to the Spirit and be still in Him as He works invisible realities in our hearts and souls. In such an atmosphere, with such a mindset, growth is not only probable—it's inevitable.

The acorn—such a humble object. Yet its value is derived from the treasure it holds within itself—a treasure far bigger than itself. Like the acorn, we're all carrying dreams. God has given each of us a vision and a future as unique as our fingerprint, and it's woven into our hearts, just waiting to be discovered. So begin today to search for your dream—your outsized, long-lasting, God-glorifying dream—and commit yourself to its growth. And just as the acorn transforms—small roots stretching forth under stars and sunlight—so too will your dream. My friends, allow yourself to feel the hope now, for God has spoken: "I am doing a work in your days that you would not believe even if told" (Habakkuk 1:5 ESV). Be encouraged: from the hearts of humble acorns, He's still bringing mighty oaks.

Watching in the Woods

D on't look now, but the woods are full of eyes.

When I roam the October forests, there's no escaping them. I climb the hills, and the eyes peer from behind bushes. I stroll along the rivers, and the eyes are glimmering through the trees. I plunge into the thickets, and the eyes are staring from the shadows.

This might sound alarming, but it doesn't cause me to fear—because I know the "eyes" aren't spies documenting my every move or wild animals with sinister intents. In fact, they're not truly eyes at all. They're a kind of seed called buckeyes—a hallmark of fall in Arkansas.

You may already be quite familiar with buckeyes if you live in the Midwest, especially in Ohio, where buckeyes inspired the state nickname, the state flag, and even the state sports mascot! But many people don't realize that Arkansas has plenty of buckeye trees as well. And this season is their time to shine.

The trees themselves are less than impressive—slender and short, with fragile-appearing limbs. However, they're still incredibly lovely. Their lush foliage is a particularly elegant shade of green, their spiky flowers are a stunning scarlet, and their namesake seeds are

235

amazingly unique. All during the growing season, each buckeye seed slowly developed within a protective husk. But now, those soft brown husks are withering, revealing the mature buckeye inside.

Each buckeye seed is actually a hard case containing anywhere from one to three embryonic trees. The buckeyes are slightly smaller than a golf ball and not quite as spherical, with a lovely brown, glossy sheen that gives them the appearance of polished wood, and a round white spot on one side. It's this spot that inspired their name—to Native Americans, they resembled the glistening eyes of deer peering from the undergrowth.

Every part of the buckeye tree—leaves, branches, and the seeds themselves—is highly toxic; in fact, it is said that the only animals that can safely consume raw buckeyes are squirrels.[1] (I have never seen any animal gnawing on a buckeye, so this may be a myth.) However, these trees still boast a variety of surprising uses. Roasting the buckeyes will negate their poisonous components and render them not only edible but highly nutritious; indigenous peoples used buckeyes extensively as a protein-rich food source known as hetuck and as a medicine for injuries and inflammation, digestive troubles, and even cerebrospinal and hormonal afflictions. The acid from the nuts was used in leatherworking, and the dried seeds were incorporated into jewelry. The wood itself is in high demand as well; in pioneer days, its light weight made it a good candidate for utensils, hats, and baskets; and today, that same property makes it the wood of choice for artificial limbs.[2]

But perhaps the greatest value of buckeyes isn't as food or pharmaceuticals but simply as objects of beauty. There are few other natural items that rival their aesthetic properties. In fact, at this time of year, my mother and I have a tradition of roaming the woods together, searching for these treasures. We scuff through the fallen leaves and laugh at the antics of the busy squirrels and maybe even see a deer flash away, slender legs twinkling, antlered head held proudly high. And when we find the slender limbs heavy with their shining seeds, we carefully peel back the leathery-soft husks and fill a basket with these glowing eyes of the autumn woods.

When we return to our house, in the crisp shadows of the autumn evening, it's time to decorate! Over the years, we've devised plenty of creative ways to use buckeyes in festive adornments, combining them with other natural fall finds such as pumpkins, acorns, pinecones, dried leaves, and even hickory nut shells. I smile when I see them festooning our home—the magic of the season, the shining seeds of fall.

Of course, despite their name, I know buckeyes aren't really watching me. The "eyes" that haunt the woods right now don't keep track of my every move. However, they do remind me of the One Who truly sees all—our omniscient God.

Just as buckeyes seem to be constantly "watching" the woods, God's gaze is never wavering. There is nothing hidden from His sight. His eyes discern the microscopic crustaceans on the depths of the ocean floor as easily as they identify the stars at the furthest edge of the expanding universe. He can watch a snowflake fall in the Himalayas, a palm tree sway in Hawaii, a meteor crash into an unknown planet, and a human heart break—*all at the same time.* I'm reminded of David's words in Psalm 139: "Even before a word is on my tongue, behold, O Lord, you know it altogether....My frame was not hidden from you, when I was being made in secret, intricately woven in the depths of the earth. Your eyes saw my unformed substance; in your book were written, every one of them, the days that were formed for me, when as yet there was none of them" (verses 4, 15-16 ESV). If God sees even unborn children in their embryonic states, we can be assured that He is watching every detail of our lives.

David's words are echoed by those of the prophet Hanani in 2 Chronicles 16:9: "For the eyes of the LORD run to and fro throughout the whole earth" (ESV). At first glance, we might wonder if this verse is meant as a threat or an unsettling "Big Brother is watching" scenario. But it's actually a reassurance! Just look at the second half of the verse: "to give strong support to those whose heart is blameless toward him." God isn't eyeing us with a scowl, waiting to crush us for our misbehavior. He's gazing on us with eyes of love—eyes that see our cries for Him and also see the future He has orchestrated for us.

One of the best illustrations of the watchful care of God is the account of Abram, Sarai, and Hagar in Genesis 16. As the wife of Abram (who would later be known as Abraham), Sarai had been promised a child by God. However, as time elapsed, she grew desperate and hatched her own scheme for fulfilling the promise: present her Egyptian slave Hagar to Abram as a surrogate so that an heir could be produced. (This was obviously not God's will, although it was a common cultural practice at the time.) Shockingly enough, Abram, the man known for his rock-solid faith, agreed. And the plan worked—sort of. Hagar did become pregnant, but there were unforeseen repercussions (as there usually are when we act out of our flesh). Evidently, Hagar began to scorn Sarai and act arrogantly toward her, and Sarai retaliated so abusively that Hagar ended up on the run.

As we read this passage, we can't help but wonder: if God sees everything, where is He now? Sarai's scheming and Abram's complicity seem to transpire unchecked. We might begin to think that God was asleep or distracted or simply overlooked this situation. But in verse 7, we realize that God knew what was going on all along. Always the God of the outcasts, He appears not to Abram or Sarai but to Hagar—frightened, rebellious, lonely, desperate Hagar. And His encounter with her demonstrates some encouraging truths about the loving watchfulness of God.

First of all, this account teaches us that God sees our hearts. He had a window to the motives of everyone involved in this situation. He knew not just the actions of these people but the forces leading them toward the actions: Abram's aversion to conflict, Sarai's restless desperation, Hagar's longing for escape. As humans, our view of others is dreadfully shortsighted. We don't have the ability to see into the minds and hearts of those around us; we can only judge based on externals, and as a result, we sometimes jump to terrible assumptions. But God's discernment penetrates to our deepest parts, the areas of our hearts and minds that are hidden even from us. He reminds us in Jeremiah 17:10, "I the LORD search the heart and test the mind" (ESV). And no matter what His probing reveals—He loves us anyway!

Secondly, God sees our distress. Just look at Genesis 16 again. Author and Bible teacher Denise Kohlmeyer has pointed out that God is the first one in this passage to refer to Hagar by name.[3] Abram and Sarai dismissively refer to her as the "slave"; but when God encounters Hagar, His very first word to her was her name. What comfort this must have been to a woman who probably felt perpetually overlooked—because if God knew her name, she could be confident that He knew her identity, her nature, and her story. When she was forced to cooperate with her owners' scheme, He saw. When her emotions, her rights, and even her personhood were invalidated, He saw. When she was pregnant and desperate, He saw. "Behold, you are pregnant and shall bear a son. You shall call his name Ishmael ['God listens'], *because the LORD has listened to your affliction*" (Genesis 16:11 ESV, emphasis mine). What a powerful statement! And just as God knew Hagar's distress, He is well-acquainted with ours as well. No headache or heartbreak escapes His eyes.

But what makes God's perspective truly unique is that His view is not limited to our present mindsets and current circumstances; He sees the outcome as well. What He is allowing now is leading to a carefully orchestrated future. Standing outside space and time, He views the events of our lives in a non-chronological way that we cannot even fathom. This was revealed in His words to Hagar; He encouraged her that her unborn son would be a mighty leader and the father of a great nation. (Many groups of Arabic people today are descendants of Ishmael.) And with this future-oriented vision, He was able to instruct her to return to Abram and Sarai, knowing this was for her ultimate good.

God sees the hearts, the tears, and the future—and He shared all of this with Hagar. And how did she respond? This had to be overwhelming. She was a female slave—the lowest of the low. She was an Egyptian—doubtless she had been involved in idolatry. It's possible she knew very little about God at all. But she responded to His words in a powerful way—by giving God a name. "So Hagar gave this name to the LORD who had spoken to her: 'You are the God who sees me,' for she said, "Here I have seen the One who sees me!" (Genesis 16:13 BSB).

The God who sees me. Hagar could have chosen any title for God. She could have called Him "The God Who reveals Himself," or "The God Who promises," or "The God Who intervenes." But instead, she named Him "The God Who sees." For this woman who had likely felt very unseen all her life, knowing that God saw her intimately was the most powerful truth. And that certainty gave her the courage to trust His vision and respond in obedience—returning to the house where she had been mistreated, continuing to be faithful to her duties, and, nearly two decades later, calling upon God's provision when she was once again in a desperate situation (Genesis 21).

My friends, if you go to the woods these days, you'll be surrounded by "eyes." The buckeyes will seem to stare at you from every nook and cranny. However, you don't need to go to any specific location to be seen by the Father. His loving eyes have been fastened on you since before you were even conceived, and His watchful gaze knows no interruption. He sees your motives, He sees your pain, and He sees the future He has designed for you. What amazing love! Let's respond in faith—rejoicing in His care for us and responding with the implicit trust of obedience. "Behold, the eye of the Lord is on those who fear him, on those who hope in his steadfast love" (Psalm 33:18 ESV).

LESSON FROM LEAVES

*"'A magic time of year,' Caddie called it to herself. She loved both spring and fall.
At the turning of the year things seemed to stir in her that were lost sight of in the
commonplace stretches of winter and summer."*
– Carol Ryrie Brink, Caddie Woodlawn[1]

L et me begin with this disclaimer: I love every season.
The still silver of winter's hush, the shy budding of
chartreuse spring, the riotous symphony of
abundantly golden summer—each touches me in a special way, unlike
any other. But if I had to choose a favorite, if I could select one
season to stretch its days and linger longer than all the others, I
would pick autumn.

When autumn arrives, some hidden part of me throbs to life.
This is the time when the fall flowers flaunt their flaming hues—
goldenrod and asters and balloon flowers. Wedges of wild geese slice
through the sky, their cries a harbinger of adventure and freedom.
Fields are bronzed with nodding heads of wheat and dotted with
rotund hay bales. In the ethereal mornings, a faint mist hovers over
the landscape like an angel, filtering the early light, and the breeze has
a sharpness to it, a tang that wakes up all that has become drowsy or
deadened during the heat of summer.

241

Autumn is a quieter time than summer, a time of reflection and gratitude. It's a milestone of fruition, of realizing that all the energy and adrenaline of the growing season has led to the moment of harvest. Soon the torpor of winter will seize the world, but for now, we rest in an interlude, a time of blessing and abundance and rich riots of beauty.

Some, however, don't share my love of autumn. They say autumn is a time of death, a season of decay and darkness and mourning for the bygone glories of summer. And certainly in autumn the night comes earlier, the earth is starker, and the many summertime birds have soared southward on fast-beating wings. I admit that when I gaze across the fields of serge stubble, when I hear the croak of a far-flying crow, then amongst all the beauty, loss hangs heavy in the October air.

Interestingly enough, some theologians have designated autumn as the month of mankind's original sin in the Garden of Eden, when the silk-speaking serpent whispered his nectar-laden lies and Eve plucked that fruit and her teeth crunched into its forbidden skin. It was autumn, they say, when she shared the fruit with Adam, when all creation shuddered to its core, when we received the tragic gift of the serpent—a moral compass without a moral backbone, a knowledge of evil and a lust for it. It was autumn, they say, when the earth was cursed, when the innocent leaves of the trees twisted into thorns and thistles, when friction clogged the gears of the universe, when the embryos of all that would come—disease, war, famine, tsunamis, hatred, child abuse, murder, misunderstanding, genocide—began to be conceived and grow slowly to their dreadful conclusion. And it was autumn, they say, when, millennia later, the heavens rained judgment and the waters of wrath swept away all mankind for their sickness of sin.[2]

As evidence for this theory, Christian anthropologists point to the prevalence of autumnal festivals celebrating the dead. This season seems to be designated by nearly every culture as a time of focusing on the afterlife and commemorating ancestors—sometimes even descending into necromancy and the occult. Consider, for example, the Samhain observance of Celtic peoples, the Día de los Muertos in Latin American culture, the Hungry Ghost Festival in China, and our own Halloween observance in the United States. Biblically-minded anthropologists presume that this autumnal obsession with death and dying stems has been a part of our shared story since Adam and Eve's first descendants commemorated the day of their parents' sin, or possibly since the survivors of the Great Flood mourned the world before the waters. Since then, the fragmentation and dispersal of people groups around the world has created a diversity of ways to mark the occasion. However, at the root of each festival, no matter how we attempt to "celebrate," we are all actually mourning millennia-old events—the first autumn day when we let the golden grain of paradise slip through our fingers, and the second when we saw for ourselves the price that sin demanded.[3]

So what, then, is autumn? Is it a glorious exhibition of beauty or a ghastly reminder of death? When we stroll through the autumn woods, are we touring an art gallery or a cemetery? And in this season of both Halloween and Thanksgiving, is it more appropriate to enumerate God's blessings or mourn our own inadequacy? In the tension between delight and death, to which side do we lean?

I've wrestled with this question a few times, and I've come to the conclusion that, as with so many things in this life, approaching this season properly doesn't mean resolving this tension but embracing it. Yes, autumn involves great loss—the greatest loss of all history. Yet, at the same time, the message this season offers is not one of bitter regret but of resounding hope. And this paradox is symbolized by one of the most universal and widely acclaimed hallmarks of this season—the beautiful leaves.

To understand this symbolism, it's necessary to first investigate the scientific process behind the annual loss of leaves. While some trees are "evergreen," retaining their foliage year-round, many others are "deciduous" trees that sprout leaves in spring and shed them in the fall. In the case of deciduous trees, leaf loss is necessary for a variety of reasons. First of all, although leaves are the tree's method of deriving food from sunlight, the weaker winter sun dramatically reduces the effectiveness of the process, making the retention of leaves inefficient. Also, in its dormant winter state, a tree simply doesn't require as much food.[4] Lastly, and perhaps most importantly, is the issue of added weight. Although a single leaf weighs only five grams, the combined weight of all those leaves can produce an extra 1,700 pounds on the tree![5] In addition, the broad, flat leaf surfaces are perfect for catching sunlight, but in the winter, they'll catch something far less helpful—snow. And if a tree's branches hold too much snow, the tree is at risk for losing large limbs or even toppling entirely. (You'll notice that the leaves of evergreen trees are mere scaly needles that won't collect snow as readily.)

Thus, as summer blurs into fall, the trees begin quietly preparing for the coming cold. A layer of cells forms across the stem of each leaf; these cells, known as the abscission layer, seal off the leaf from the rest of the tree and block the flow of nutrients. Ultimately, the abscission layer and the nutrient blockade it imposes will cause the leaf to die and fall from the tree. However, first the chlorophyll—the bright green pigment in leaves and grass—begins to disintegrate. And with the green coloring removed, the other pigments in the leaf are free to shine forth in a myriad of breathtaking hues.[6] The production of a special pigment called anthocyanin is triggered by autumnal weather and responsible for the vibrant scarlet hues. The trademark yellow of aspens and hickory trees is caused by carotenoid pigments that are always inherent in leaves but usually masked by the green color. Even the seemingly drab hue of brown leaves is caused not by an absence of color, but by an abundance of it; when all the pigments mix, brown is formed.[7]

This is the scientific process, but these sawdust-dry facts can't begin to capture the magic of the event. Autumn trees look as if they've been delicately hand-painted, every leaf unique in coloration and pattern from every other leaf on every other tree in the whole world. Almost overnight, dramatic waves of color race across the flanks of the summer's green hillsides. I've been on autumn walks in forests where the sunlight sifting through the vibrant leaves made the very air glow, as if I were surrounded by stained-glass windows. And every year, I look forward to the thrill of rushing headlong into an equinoctial wind, with handfuls of falling leaves pelting me like a dizzying whirlwind of God's confetti.

Yet in the sweetness of such moments, there's an odd flavor of regret. After all, despite their beauty, these leaves are dying. Their dramatic display of color is a signal of changes happening deep within the tree, changes that will ultimately lead to the stillness of winter and the barrenness of the forest. Yet even in their death—marking the end of a yearly epoch—there is great beauty that can be found nowhere else.

This dichotomy captured my attention so strongly years ago that I made it the subject of an original poem, "Lesson from Leaves."

Leaves are fluttering down to earth,
Scarlet and Tangerine.
Dancing down, skipping down,
All people here below have seen.

244

All people here below have seen,
But who has remembered what this means?
The leaves must drop their hold to soar,
Must let go, and hang no more.

Must let go, and hang no more;
Must cease to live, and die before
Turning hues of red and gold,
The colors so vivid and so bold.

O Leaf! how much we learn from thee;
In thee the Christian's life we see;
Like thee we must let go in trust
That God will use us as He must.

Like thee we must first die to self—
To self, to fame, to friends, to pelf—
Before we can at last shine forth
As beautiful, colorful things of worth.

When I wrote that poem in 2009, the truth I wove into its lines was firmly implanted in my mind. However, after more than a decade of living and learning and growing, it's now embedded in my heart. As believers, we are no strangers to death, but the thought holds no terror for us. In fact, we accept, even welcome, the death of our ungodly habits and behaviors as a necessary process. Consider the apostle Paul, who in recounting the ways he had practiced self-discipline and relinquished his own will for the sake of the gospel, boldly stated, "I die daily" (1 Corinthians 15:31 KJV).

To the world, this sounds off-putting. Who wants to follow a religion of dying? Even some Christians squirm at this concept. We'd rather showcase the more photogenic tenets of our faith, like the eternal home God has prepared for us, or the sweetness found in His love, or the triumph of Christ's Resurrection. But we must never forget that the keystone of Christianity is found in the day when God bowed His back to a cruel whip and staggered beneath the weight of a rough-sawn cross, when He stretched out His nail-torn arms and spilled His blood in an act of profound death. Our life began when our God died. And each day, He calls us to take our cross and follow Him (Matthew 16:24).

But in the same way as the leaves, the people of God need not fear death as an ugly process of defeat and weakness. Instead, it is an opportunity to shine forth the handiwork of our Lord to the world.

This, in fact, is one of God's signature habits—never, ever, allowing darkness to have the last word. Even on that dreadful autumn day, the day of the serpent and the deceit and the sin and the curse, God was already recycling the bitterness of mankind's rebellion into an epic display of His grace and might. Just look at Genesis 3:15; tucked into one of the darkest chapters of Scripture, it offers the guarantee of a coming Messiah.

And thus it is with us. In our daily death, in our daily struggle to relentlessly prune away the parts of ourselves that hinder our walk with God, in our constant reiteration of "Not my will, but Yours, be done" (Luke 22:42 ESV), we find a surprising fact. The death that the Bible speaks of is actually the path to life.

Unless we die to ourselves, we cannot live to God. And only in living to God can we find a joy and a purpose and a fruitfulness that surpasses our wildest dreams. Jesus spoke on this theme during His earthly ministry: "Truly, truly, I say to you, unless a grain of wheat falls into the earth and dies, it remains alone; but if it dies, it bears much fruit" (John 12:24 ESV). Our life is that grain of wheat. We can foolishly choose to harbor it for ourselves, stowing it away and refusing to allow it to die. But seeds are not meant to be hoarded. They're designed to be sown—because their temporary death produces a harvest of fruit beyond imagination.

This October, we're treated to the gift—and it is a gift—of another autumn. We'll see the bountiful rotundity of pumpkins, hear the rustle and whisper of the breeze in the shocks of corn, and taste the delicious desserts prepared from harvest bounty. And of course, we'll be surrounded by God's breathtaking palette of color, with every tree dipped in hues beyond compare. So when you see those brightly colored leaves fluttering and shining in the fading sunlight, smile. Because yes, autumn is a time of death. But it's also one of the most profound reminders that with God, death never has the final word, and from the ashes of our crucified selves are forged the lessons that will last an eternity.

PERSIMMON PROPHECY

L et me introduce you today to a very special tree. It's a massive one on the western border of our property, sprawled comfortably with dangling limbs and a broad trunk. It was there over thirty years ago when my parents first bought this land, and it's been unshaken by the intervening time. This tree is a persimmon tree.

You may not have ever seen a persimmon tree, but chances are good that you've seen, or at least heard of, the persimmons it produces. Perhaps you've even had a disagreeable run-in with one. Among my earliest wilderness lessons received from my parents, right there with "Don't go in the woods after dark," "Wolves are faster than you are," and "Wasps will hurt you," was "Don't eat a persimmon." My beloved dog Angel, however, didn't heed this warning. One bright autumn day, she and I were wandering along the property near this tree. Being a dog who routinely ingested everything from expensive dog beds to telephones to (plugged-in!) Christmas lights, she discovered a persimmon lying temptingly on the ground and promptly began chewing on it before I realized what was occurring. In a matter of a few seconds, she made a very odd noise— something between a cough, a sneeze, and a croak—and spit the persimmon as far as she could. Alerted by her odd noises, I turned around just in time to witness her nearly choking from the effects of the fruit. She recovered quickly but never touched a persimmon again.

That's not to say that the fruit of the persimmon is always worthless. Although it is bitter and highly astringent when unripe, after several weeks it turns a gorgeous crimson color and becomes soft and quite sweet. Most country dwellers attribute the transformation in taste to the effects of the first frost, but it's actually due mostly to the length of time needed for complete maturation (although freezing an unripe persimmon does give it a boost of sweetness).[1] The ripe fruit is said to be so palatable that an abundance of recipes exist for using persimmons in delicious dishes from breads to cookies to jams to cakes. I must admit these desserts sound appetizing, but knowing how terrible a "green" persimmon is, I've never been brave enough to sample a ripe one in any form. For me, the true value of this fruit lies not in its conduciveness to cooking but in something far less flashy—its seed.

Each autumn, when misty overtones begin to cloud the fruit's maroon skin, I collect a few persimmons. I bring them home and line them up on the ground outside my house. Then, with a sharp knife, I carefully slice through the pulpy fruit to the flat seed inside, which somewhat resembles a pumpkin seed. The next step is to cut the seed in half lengthwise (no easy task, since it is slender and slippery). But when the two halves of the seed are finally pried open, a wonderful surprise awaits.

The inside of the seed is pearlescent with a light green cast, and against this backdrop is a stark white outline—the embryo of the future persimmon tree. This outline can take three distinct forms—a spoon-shaped one, a slender one that resembles a knife, or one that looks amazingly like a three-tined fork. According to folklore, the shape of the embryo indicates the caliber of the coming winter. A fork predicts a mild winter, with little snow and less cold than normal. A knife signifies icy conditions, with wind that cuts like a knife. A spoon forecasts heavier than normal snowfall—according to tradition, the spoon is actually a snow shovel, which you will need if you find this shape in a persimmon seed.[2]

Yes, I know it sounds a bit odd (although, may I point out, no weirder than allowing the presence of a rodent's shadow to mark the official beginning of spring). And I have to admit, it's far from a foolproof method to make winter plans. I've seen well-defined spoons prior to a winter when I wore shorts at Christmastime, and I've spent a season shivering in heavy parkas after finding forks. My guess is that the embryo shape has more to do with the past—growing conditions, summer rainfall, and tree health—than the future. However, the hassle of cutting the seed, the inconclusive results I've received, and my own skepticism aren't enough to prevent me from slicing persimmons every fall. The fruits are beginning to blush even now, so some evening in the next few days, you might find me in the abbreviated autumn twilight, striding home across the serge-brown fields, breath dangling in the frosty air, with persimmons in my hands and my knife in my pocket.

Perhaps the persimmons were more truthful in the old days when the legend originated; or maybe the people of that time, farmers and ranchers who lived off the land in a precarious balance of hard work and capricious nature, were simply grappling for any indicator, no matter how ridiculous, of the characteristics of the winter and by extension of next year's crop. Today, in our computerized economy when hands don't touch dirt that often anymore and central heating is available at the flick of a finger, the persimmon's power is no longer needed. However, although living conditions may have changed, the lure of knowing the future has not. No matter where, when, or how they live, humans all share an insatiable desire to see into the future—not merely on a global or cosmic scale, but in their own private lives.

Who knows what drives this urge? Is it hope? Anticipation? Mere hubris? I've come to believe that although it may wear a veneer of idle curiosity, our desire to know the future is based more on fear than any other factor. Consider the fact that now, at this very moment, we are plunging forward into a future about which we know nothing, at a speed we cannot alter, toward a final destiny shrouded in mystery, and even the most courageous soul is bound to feel a quiver of anxiety. To know the future, then, is to control it, or at the very least to be equipped to handle its fallout. Just as the farmers applied the persimmon's "wisdom" to their preparations for the coming snows, bracing against nature's onslaught and storm-proofing barns and houses, people today seem to believe that if they are only warned, they can take precautions to shield themselves and their loved ones from coming mayhem. Thus, we are fascinated with the future—forever straining our eyes to see beyond the dim lantern of today into the black abyss that stretches before us.

When we think of looking to the future, we usually picture occult proceedings like tarot cards, horoscopes, and palm readers—demonically-inspired mediums leading gullible souls to disaster, or even corny newspaper astrologers issuing vague hints about our fate. We might envision Saul, who on the eve of a massive battle became so anxious over the outcome that he disobeyed the clear word of God (as well as his own decree) and visited a witch.[3] Too often, Christians assume that maintaining a healthy relationship with the future consists only of avoiding these practices. However, as long as he can shift our focus from God, the devil does not care how that is accomplished. And he has far more subtle traps for us that not only skew our perspective on the future but can also cause us to implicitly question the very nature of the God we serve.

One of these traps, which is becoming increasingly common in our world, is the mindset of ignoring the future. Yes, we know things are unpredictable, but we'd prefer not to remind ourselves of that. The reality of our own incapacity to direct our lives brings too much terror if we allow ourselves to think about it—so we banish it from our minds. In its place, we focus solely on the present, as though the details of daily life can freeze time. If we dare look ahead, we gaze complacently down a gently winding road of weeks and months and years; our own mortality, or even the certainty of painful seasons, is reduced to a vague blur that dangles forever in the distance. No wonder we are shocked when tragedy arrives!

This mindset is birthed in pride—the conviction that somehow, we alone are sufficient to chart our course. It's easy to believe that we have "conquered the future" through our intelligence, hard work, hefty savings account, college degree, or comfortable job. Jesus told a story about a man with this view: "The land of a rich man produced plentifully, and he thought to himself, 'What shall I do, for I have nowhere to store my crops?' And he said, 'I will do this: I will tear down my barns and build larger ones, and there I will store all my grain and my goods. And I will say to my soul, "Soul, you have ample goods laid up for many years; relax, eat, drink, be merry."' But God said to him, 'Fool! This night your soul is required of you, and the things you have prepared, whose will they be?' So is the one who lays up treasure for himself and is not rich toward God" (Luke 12:16b-21 ESV).

None of us ever want to be deemed a "fool" by God. Believing that we are sufficient unto ourselves, however, is truly the most foolish thing we could do. Our hopes for the future, no matter how stirring, must always be seasoned with a strong dose of humility and a recognition that "the mind of man plans his way, but the LORD directs his steps" (Proverbs 16:9 NASB).

250

It's very fitting that immediately after presenting this parable, Jesus begins His most famous teaching on the future: "Do not be anxious about your life, what you will eat, nor about your body, what you will put on" (Luke 12:22b ESV). The error warned about here is the opposite end of the spectrum from ignoring the future; this is obsessing over it. These people realize that they are completely unprepared for what might befall them, and they're right. Unfortunately, they allow this conviction not to drive them to God and His strength but to crush them beneath a load of anxiety they were never intended to bear. (I encourage you to read the rest of the chapter, although it is too long to completely include here.)

Like those who ignore the future, these people embrace an inflated understanding of their own power to control their fate. So they drown out the anxiety through planning, as though their feverish preparations can freeze time. They consider every contingency, envision every hypothetical scenario, and decide on their reactions to situations that are far from certain. How foolish it is to draw maps of terrain we've never seen!

And worry is not only foolish—it's also epically useless. Jesus continued His lesson on anxiety with a telling question: "And which of you by being anxious can add a single hour to his span of life? If then you are not able to do as small a thing as that, why are you anxious about the rest?" (Luke 12:25-26 ESV). When I feel the urge to fixate on a real or imagined future issue, drowning in the details, I often recall this sage quote by Corrie ten Boom. Imprisoned in the Nazi concentration camps, stripped of her most basic human rights, and bereaved of her family, Corrie certainly had more reason to worry than most of us today. However, she chose instead to trust God, soothing her soul with this truth: "Worrying is carrying tomorrow's load with today's strength—carrying two days at once. It is moving into tomorrow ahead of time. Worrying doesn't empty tomorrow of its sorrow, it empties today of its strength."[4]

In our culture, worry has been reincarnated as preparedness or even lauded as a symptom of being a meticulous person. However, we must not forget that according to Jesus, worry is not a mark of distinction but a trait of pagans—in other words, those who have no relationship with God. What a sad day when God's people begin to live like pagans, cowering from the future instead of embracing it as the story their Father is lovingly writing for them!

On the outside, these mindsets look very different. But inwardly, they are both rooted in a desperate bid for control and a distrust of God's character. One whispers that we are strong and God is unnecessary; the other hisses that we are weak and God is unreliable. Both result in a fixation on controlling the future through our own efforts.

Don't get me wrong—it's certainly not sinful to be prepared, and having Christ-centered goals is commendable. The problem arises not when we thoughtfully contemplate our stewardship over the time God has given us but when we begin to play God, as though by our efforts and strategizing we become the captain of our own destiny. James addressed this problem in his epistle: "You do not know what tomorrow will bring. What is your life? For you are a mist that appears for a little time and then vanishes. Instead you ought to say, 'If the Lord wills, we will live and do this or that'" (James 4:14-15 ESV). The solution, according to James, is not to waft aimlessly through life. Instead, we must relinquish both a white-knuckled need to plan and a staunch refusal to face our inadequacy, trading both for an intimate relationship with the God Who loves us.

Especially in the autumn, when dusk is stronger than daylight and the song of the year is dwindling to a much slower cadence, the ache to know the future deepens. Another year has slipped away and a new one is peeking over the horizon, and perhaps this is why the persimmons seem so alluring as they swing from the silver-barked branches. But persimmons are no wiser than people, and people are amazingly shortsighted when it comes to scanning the vistas of our lives. The only way to make peace with the finiteness of our knowledge is to fully accept that we don't know the future—neither the good or bad. Allow that understanding to sink into your soul. When he was tending his sheep and speaking God's Word, Abel had no idea he would be murdered by his own brother (Genesis 4). On the other hand, when he was forgotten in the fields, overlooked by his father and rejected by his brothers, David had no idea he would one day be the king of Israel (1 Samuel 16). God is constantly writing unpredictable plot twists in the stories of His children's lives. It is not up to us to anticipate His next move; instead, it is our privilege to rest in His promises and to trust that in the hands of our divine Author, our story will be written just as He desires.

Truth from the Trail Camera

Years ago, my parents came to a rural area of Arkansas and bought twenty-six acres of land in a small town where people are scarce and wilderness is abundant. When they decided to build our house on this land, my mother insisted it be positioned squarely in the middle of the acreage atop a rolling hill.

Unacquainted with the ideals of our family, the contractor tried to convince Mom that this was a foolish plan. He pointed out that if my parents would consent to build the house on one edge of the property, they could sell the other part of the acreage in the future. My mother lost no time in informing him that she had no plans to part with one square foot of her land, and the very reason she had moved to a remote country area was to avoid feeling cramped by close neighbors!

However, even though we are quite a distance from any human neighbors, we still have hundreds of "neighbors" of other kinds. The birdfeeders we provide year-round attract dozens of species of feathered friends—nuthatches, blue jays, cardinals, goldfinches, orioles, sparrows, and finches, just to name a few. On dewy spring evenings, we can usually see a rabbit or two cropping grass in our front yard. Chipmunks enjoy living in our landscaping, and it's not an infrequent event to hear the scurrying of feet overhead when hardworking squirrels scamper across our roof.

If you journey to the woods and mountains in the forested section of our property, farthest from our house, you'll find larger and more impressive "neighbors." Our property has long been a refuge for large herds of deer. They routinely come to our fruit trees, usually enjoying the harvest before we do, and it's quite common for me to find a whole family group bedded down near our creek in the early mornings.

Besides the deer, there are a few animals that are seen or heard only rarely but still make their presence unmistakable. The first time I heard the raspy bark of a red fox scrape across the dusk, I was terrified; it is a completely unnerving sound. Even more frightening than the fox's cry is the chorus of howling wolves to which I've been treated on many a night. They've been designed to scream in harmony with each other; this technique creates the impression of a larger pack than actually exists and strikes fear into the hearts of their prey. (I assure you that both of these objectives are met with admirable effectiveness.)

The rarest of all animals in our area are the big predators: the black bear and the mountain lion. It's been a few years since I've personally seen a bear in this region, but based on reports and photos from neighbors as well as the tracks and clawed trees I've come across, they're still active in my woods. I've seen mountain lions a few times, slouching through the trees or creeping across a lonely ridge—just like all cats, they seem to appear only when I'm not expecting them. I remember a few years ago when my father, noticing a large brown form near our creek, became convinced that my chocolate Lab, Angel, had gone wandering again. He began calling the supposed dog in an aggrieved tone, but when the form revealed itself as a large panther that made an eight-foot leap from the ground to a tree, he was highly thankful it hadn't responded to his calls!

With all these animals around me, perhaps it's not surprising that I grew up with a deep respect and a perpetual love for all the denizens of wild places. I've always been fascinated with watching for these creatures, especially the mountain lions. Together with Angel, and now my current dogs Mercy and Gailey, I've spent hours upon hours wandering the woods, teaching myself how to use the signs the animals left—a hollowed area where a deer had slept, a fresh wolf track in wet mud, a log that a bear had clawed to pieces—to gain a window into their very private lives.

Perhaps, then, you can imagine how excited I was when on my nineteenth birthday, my parents presented me with one of the best gifts I ever received. They had bought me something I'd long admired and craved from afar—a trail camera.

For those of you who are unfamiliar with this concept, a trail camera (also known as a game camera) is a motion-activated camera designed for outdoor use. Hunters, trackers, and outdoor enthusiasts place these camouflaged cameras in strategic outdoor locations, and when wildlife trigger the motion sensor, the camera discreetly snaps a photo and saves it to a preloaded memory card. A night vision component even allows for photos of nocturnal visitors.

I was absolutely thrilled to receive this device. In my mind's eye, I naïvely envisioned myself hanging it from the nearest tree and immediately capturing hundreds of pictures of the most elusive animals—even those seldom-seen bears and mountain lions. The day after my birthday, I headed to the woods and used the included bungee cords to secure it to a suitable tree. When I checked my camera a couple of days later and noticed that the memory card already held a promising number of photos, I lost no time in inserting it into my computer and preparing to admire the rare pictures I surely had acquired.

I was shocked, therefore, to realize that most of my photos were devoid of wildlife—just trees and branches and the landscape surrounding my camera. A few photos featured deer, but even those shots weren't impressive. My hopes dampened, but not destroyed, I repeated the process of setting the camera up and then checking the card in a couple of days. Again and again, I found the same results, until I began to become seriously discouraged. I knew there were abundant animals in the area. I'd heard their howls, seen their prints, even glimpsed them moving through the trees. So why wasn't my camera capturing them?

My passion for wildlife was still greater than my discouragement, so I didn't give up. Instead, I began researching. In online magazines, blogs, and even handouts at outdoors stores, I studied how successful trail camera users had conducted their setups, memorizing facts and poring over diagrams. At the same time, I also experimented with my camera, trying different angles, different locations, and different methods of securing it. The management and improvement of my trail camera became my favorite hobby.

It didn't take me long to learn the key facets of trail camera setup. And once I knew these essentials, it wasn't hard to figure out why my early attempts had been so unsuccessful. For starters, placing the camera in the woods wasn't enough; it also had to be near a stream, a deer trail, a gap in a fence, or some other location that naturally drew wildlife. Also, the dimensions had to be exact; it had to be at least two feet off the ground, facing north for the best lighting conditions. Furthermore, some sort of attractant was needed—I learned that deer preferred mineral licks, while bears found crushed acorns or (better yet) donuts irresistible. Lastly, and most importantly, the camera demanded patience—being left undisturbed for long periods of time. By checking it every couple of days, I was only leaving my scent more abundantly and making the whole area less inviting to wildlife.

These were just a few of the facts I had to learn, because although the trail camera was a gift, discovering how to use it was work—work I had to invest in order to enjoy the gift as it was intended.

Isn't this a lot like our relationship with God?

God "gives the Spirit without measure" (John 3:34 ESV). Each of us, upon adoption into God's family, receives the unconditional, unlimited gift of His Holy Spirit. There's nothing we can do to merit this blessing, and likewise, there's nothing we can do to disqualify ourselves from receiving it. It is God's promise that we truly have been saved and that we will live forever with Him. However, although we don't have to do anything to secure our salvation, we can't bypass the hard work of learning to use this gift properly.

To some, this sounds off-putting. Why would a free gift require work? If we are saved by grace, why do our actions matter?

To be clear, the works that we do don't in any way affect the gift of our salvation. Being adopted into God's family means that "by grace [we] have been saved through faith"; Paul even reminds us, "And this is not your own doing; it is the gift of God" (Ephesians 2:8 ESV). Our eternal salvation is assured. In theological terms, our justification—the act of being made right with God through Jesus' blood—is finished. However, our sanctification—the process of becoming more like Jesus, day by day—is ongoing.

Think again about my game camera. During the months it took to learn how to use my camera, my parents didn't retract their gift. My skill in using it didn't determine whether or not I was allowed to retain it. Even if I had never learned to use it, even if I had stuffed it into a cabinet and allowed it to sit there completely untouched, I would still have been able to claim ownership of it.

However, my parents would have been disappointed; they would probably have felt quite hurt that I valued their gift so lightly. In addition, I would never have received the full benefit of it. A trail camera is no good sitting in a cabinet. It is designed to be used, and to be hidden contradicts its very nature.

This, then, is how it is for us as Christians. We can know God and receive the promise of His eternal protection without ever utilizing the precious gift of the Holy Spirit. However, I can't help but believe that it saddens the heart of God when He sees His children indifferent to His wonderful gifts, like His Word, His Spirit, and the privilege of communicating with Him through prayer. Even more seriously, when we disregard the gifts of God, we stunt our own spiritual growth.

Some Christians assume, as I did with my camera, that being in the right environment is enough. I positioned my camera in an area where I knew there was abundant wildlife and hoped for the best. Regrettably, some people adopt this mindset when it comes to God. They feel that by immersing themselves in places full of God's Presence—a church, a Sunday school class, a godly family—they will somehow absorb spiritual growth automatically. Don't get me wrong; all of these places and activities are important. However, what's missing in the lives of these believers is intentionality.

The gift of walking with God each day takes practice. Just as I can't randomly abandon my camera in the woods and expect to find thousands of professional-quality photos on it in the morning, we can't leave our relationship with God to chance and still expect to cultivate strong character and abiding faith.

Consider this verse: "Do not lie to one another, seeing that you have put off the old self with its practices and have put on the new self....Put on then, as God's chosen ones, holy and beloved, compassionate hearts, kindness, humility, meekness, and patience" (Colossians 3:9-10a, 12 ESV). This passage shows the intentionality of our walk with God. We have to consciously choose to "put on" certain behaviors and mindsets, like empathy, gentleness, and a self-effacing disposition. Likewise, we have to "put off" or discard old habits and opinions.

This is the transformative work of living for God—learning to exchange the broken-down pieces of our lives for His firm foundation. And yes, this takes work. But here's the beautiful part: because we love God, the effort it takes to grow closer to Him is not drudgery but joy. Consider an artist practicing diligently to hone her craft by mixing colors, preparing canvases, and sketching subjects. Excellence in any of these areas takes a great deal of labor, but the artist does not mind. Why? Because she is focused on more than just producing a beautiful painting. She enjoys the process of painting itself.

And this is what I've discovered with my camera. When I first received it, I was completely focused on capturing those high-quality photos of the wildlife in my vicinity. I checked that memory card constantly and was perpetually frustrated with the lack of spectacular pictures.

But before I quite realized what had happened, I was no longer obsessed with the photos I was capturing. Instead, I became captivated by the experience.

Tinkering with my game camera setup is still one of my favorite hobbies. I still spend countless hours, especially in the fall and winter, tramping through the woods, scouting locations, selecting attractant, and even building bait stations. But now I'm motivated by a love of the process—a joy in sharpening my skills, in exploring the woods, in anticipating the moves of the animals around me.

And as we draw closer to God, as we seek to become better able to follow His voice, I'm convinced that we will have that same experience. We'll come to realize that the ultimate goal of this life isn't checking off all the spiritual boxes or receiving some divine stamp of approval. And God doesn't command us to become more like Him so that He can lay a crushing load of expectation on our shoulders or mercilessly flog us into rigorous obedience. As we know Him more, as we enter deeper into His embrace, we learn the lesson that has blossomed in the hearts of God's people for centuries—yes, living in His light requires diligent work, and the seeds of faith must be carefully tended. But the eternal "crown of righteousness" (2 Timothy 4:8 ESV) isn't our only compensation. Living day by day in the light of our Lord, leaning ever more fully into His loving arms, is a beautiful reward all its own.

TREASURES IN THE TREETOPS

M y yard is filled with treasure hunters.

Day after day, from the moment the sun first peeks over the hilltops until its last good-night as darkness settles, these treasure hunters are hard at work. They don't consult maps, and they don't utilize any equipment, but they still manage to locate an incredible amount of bounty—and they're committed to hoarding it in super-secret stashes. Who are these mysterious treasure hunters? They're none other than one of my favorite backyard animals—squirrels.

All my life, I've believed that God created squirrels just so He could laugh at their antics! Whether they're nibbling on nuts or basking on sun-warmed branches or impudently barking at strangers, these creatures are some of the most charming of backyard denizens. For one thing, they're quite attractive—both the sleek gray squirrels with their silver-tipped tails and the much larger red squirrels, their coats burnished as bronze as the autumn leaves. Secondly, as a single glance at their keen faces reveals, squirrels are highly intelligent. Scientists have discovered squirrels signaling to each other with their quirky tail positions, employing erratic maneuvering to avoid predators, and strategizing solutions to complex problems (like perfecting a method to outwit the supposedly "squirrel-proof" baffles on our birdfeeders).[1] But perhaps the most galvanizing characteristic of squirrels is their flair for the dramatic. These cheeky little acrobats of field and forest have no scruples about openly showing off. They delicately balance on the thinnest twigs and swing like trapeze artists from fragile vines and make themselves happily at home in the dizzying canopy of a hundred-foot patriarchal tree. I've even seen them perform death-defying leaps between trees, launching from the tips of the branches and soaring through the air in a reckless way that made me first catch my breath, then laughingly applaud their bravado.

Cute, clever, and courageous—squirrels are constantly active any time of the year. But right now, their usual playful antics have been replaced by "treasure hunting"—gathering and storing food for the long winter ahead.

For them, this is urgent business—a matter of life or death. Every week, an adult squirrel needs to eat its body weight—about 1.5 pounds—in nuts. During the winter, that food source won't be available, and squirrels feel the effects (they can lose 25% of their body weight in one season!). So it's imperative that squirrels collect every morsel they can find now to mitigate the hardships of the harsh weather to come. And these little creatures rise to the challenge in unbelievable ways. Working at a frantic rate of twenty-five nuts an hour, a squirrel will, in an entire fall season, stash away a whopping ten thousand nuts.[2]

At this time of year, our property is especially popular with the squirrels due to our abundance of black walnut trees. All summer long, the nuts have slowly ripened, snug within their bumpy green shells. And now they're hanging heavy on the branches, and the race is on for the squirrels to collect all they can. At any given time during the daylight hours, a glance outside our windows will reveal literally dozens of these little creatures scrambling frenetically around our land. Their speed and dexterity are mind-boggling—scrabbling up the tree trunks, claws scratching on the rough bark; bounding through the grass in arcing, oversized leaps; stretching their jaws around gigantic walnuts with self-satisfied airs. We even hear the staccato skittering as they dash across our roof! And as I watch them scurrying frantically about, I'm reminded that they aren't the only creatures who go treasure hunting. We humans do it too.

"Do not lay up for yourselves treasures on earth, where moth and rust destroy and where thieves break in and steal, but lay up for yourselves treasures in heaven, where neither moth nor rust destroys and where thieves do not break in and steal" (Matthew 6:19-20 ESV).

This command makes us pause, doesn't it? No, we don't jealously accrue black walnuts, but we certainly accumulate treasures for ourselves. Our "nuts" can take the form of new cars, sleek laptops, designer clothing, fat IRAs, coveted careers and dream vacations and a perfect appearance. But even though the treasures for which we hunt may be a bit different, the process of treasure hunting is much the same for both humans and squirrels.

First of all, it's fast-paced. The scurrying squirrels are working so hectically because they know they only have a short amount of time to collect all they can. In the same way, we humans can begin to treat our lives as one giant treasure hunt—the goal being to acquire as much as possible in this brief lifetime. Secondly, it's competitive. During the nut collection season, these usually amiable squirrels become quite territorial. They hide their acquisitions from other squirrels, they bark menacingly at those who threaten their personal space, and they rush to beat other squirrels to the supply of nuts. As humans, we're all out to compete as well—and we can be pretty ruthless in the process. Lastly, it's all-consuming. This time of year, gathering nuts is the sole pursuit of a squirrel, filling their waking hours. And the search for treasures can easily become just that obsessive to us, a whirling vortex that engulfs everything else.

But though our treasure hunting has much in common with that of the squirrels, there's one important difference: it's futile. Hoarding is a vital survival strategy for squirrels, ensuring their well-being during a cold, harsh winter. But for us, it's a distraction, a diversion, even a danger. And while the squirrels have a purpose for what they amass, we usually don't—our desires rapidly outpace our true needs. Even more sobering is the fact that our "treasures" are subject to decay, disappointment, and disaster. An elegant mansion can burn to ashes. A prized convertible can be involved in a crash. Money can be stolen, investments can plummet, and beauty can fade.

What's more, our frantic race for treasures only seems to create more emptiness. Have you ever noticed that one thrill is not enough? Over and over again, we learn that what we thought would satisfy doesn't deliver. As soon as one novelty fades, we're on to the next. The "treasure hunt" beguiles us down a path of craving more and more and more—stumbling after a mirage that never fulfills.

To see this in action, look no further than the story of Zacchaeus in Luke 19. This man's life revolved around literal "treasure": he was a tax collector. In Christ's day, tax collectors were some of the most despised members of Palestinian society. They were viewed as traitors by other Jews because they worked for the hated Roman government, and they were ostracized socially and culturally. Even worse, they also were known to be immoral and unethical, customarily inflating tax rates and padding their own pockets with the excess.

Yet for a man who had spent his whole life treasure-hunting, Zacchaeus must have come up empty-handed. What other reason would have driven him to join the crowds waiting to see Jesus walk by—even leading him to climb a sycamore tree for a better view? But the beauty of this story is that Zacchaeus didn't just *see* Jesus; He learned that he was *seen by* Jesus. Look what happened after his encounter with God: "And Zacchaeus stood and said to the Lord, 'Behold, Lord, the half of my goods I give to the poor. And if I have defrauded anyone of anything, I restore it fourfold'" (Luke 19:8 ESV).

In a strikingly redemptive response, Zacchaeus switched his script from getting to giving. But why? How could a man absorbed by material gains change his perspective so suddenly and completely? The reason is simple: after a lifetime of fruitless searching, Zacchaeus realized that he had finally found the true Treasure, compared to Whom all earthly trinkets paled. And now that he was no longer focused on money and possessions, he could share them with those in his path.

Zacchaeus's actions still provide the best antidote for those caught in the trap of treasure hunting today. This is the essence of becoming free from the never-ending search for more and more: not selfishly hoarding our treasures, but sharing them as the blessings they are.

Once again, watching the squirrels has illustrated this truth for me. (Who knew these little creatures could teach us so much?) You see, when squirrels are stashing nuts, they're doing more than greedily amassing resources. Instead, they're actually sowing seeds.

As you may already know, squirrels bury most of the nuts they find. During the bleak winter months, they're then able to locate them, using a memorized mental map and the identifying scent of their saliva. But squirrels don't reclaim all the nuts they bury; some are left underground to germinate. As a matter of fact, squirrels are instrumental agents of reforestation, credited with planting thousands of trees a year.[3]

Could it be that this example provides the antidote to frenzied treasure hunting in our own lives?

"[G]ive, and it will be given to you. Good measure, pressed down, shaken together, running over, will be put into your lap. For with the measure you use it will be measured back to you" (Luke 6:38 ESV). There's much that could be said about generosity and responsibility and good stewardship. There are many reasons to disentangle ourselves from the frenetic treasure hunt. But here's the decision in a nutshell (pun intended!): we can keep, or we can reap.

You see, if we keep to ourselves what God has given us—money, time, possessions—the blessings and benefits spread no further than ourselves. But if we turn the focus outward rather than inward—if we sow our blessings into the world around us—then we reap fruits that are multiplied beyond our wildest imagination. Think of the squirrels again. A nut that is eaten is just that...a single nut. It might provide a quick snack, but its impact is momentary and minimal. However, if that nut is planted, it becomes a tree—a tree that will in turn produce hundreds of thousands of nuts, year after year after year. I'm reminded of Jesus's words in John 12:24: "Truly, truly, I say to you, unless a grain of wheat falls into the earth and dies, it remains alone; but if it dies, it bears much fruit" (ESV).

This approach is far from easy. It's counterintuitive, to say the least, because we humans have a hard time loosening our grasp on our resources. Maybe it's pride—*I want more than he has!* Maybe it's fear—*I'm worried I won't have enough!* Maybe it's apathy—*I'm just not interested.* But regardless of our reasoning, learning to view our blessings biblically is a vital skill. It's the only mindset that will release us from the slavery of treasure hunting, and it's the only pathway to stop keeping and start reaping.

So this fall, when you see the "treasure hunt" of the energetic squirrels, take a moment to appreciate their antics. Laugh at their cockiness and admire their diligence and marvel at the ingenuity with which the Creator has blessed them. And remember something else...the very trees that now sustain these creatures are often products of the seeds sown by earlier generations of squirrels. Let's determine today to stop keeping and start reaping—to release the treasure God has given us and then watch it multiply beyond our wildest dreams. After all, our earthly resources can be a misery or a miracle...and the choice is ours.

Of Corn and Courage

L ike most good stories, this one begins in the woods.

It was many years ago, on a blustery fall day—the perfect kind of autumn afternoon when the last leaves rattle in the barren trees and the wind chases tattered clouds across the sky. My parents and I were enjoying a leisurely exploration of the forest behind our creek when the afternoon's tranquility was shattered by a shocking discovery: a patch of ground that had been completely destroyed. The grass was stomped into nothingness, and the earth was trampled into a putrid, muddy sinkhole. I was only nine years old at the time, but I knew what this meant: wild hogs had moved in.

Wild hogs were about the last creature we wanted to take refuge on our property. They are a non-native nuisance species in this country; initially introduced to America for sporting purposes by Spanish explorers in the 1500s, they quickly spread out of control thanks to their legendary reproduction rate (an old joke claims that "if a feral-hog sow produces a dozen piglets, thirteen survive"). Today, there are over five million wild hogs rampaging through the United States, two hundred thousand of which dwell right here in Arkansas.[1]

Not only are hogs invasive, they're destructive, a formidable threat to the natural ecosystems on which they intrude. Their incessant rooting habits pulverize the soil and vegetation; they've even been known to damage crop fields and roads. In addition, they "hog" (pun intended!) the resources of an area, forcing native species to compete. Furthermore, they carry an unnerving variety of parasites, diseases, and bacteria that are harmful not only to animals but also to humans. Perhaps most worrisome of all, they are quite savage. They can run at speeds of thirty miles an hour, weigh up to 220 pounds each, and leap six-foot-high fences. This athletic prowess combined with their surly temperaments renders them a hazard to other animals, livestock, and people.[2]

Considering all of these facts, you can imagine why we were far from thrilled to find evidence that the hogs had taken up residence in our woods. And as the weeks wore on, our not-so-welcome visitors showed no inclination to depart. They rooted along our creek, disturbing its banks and gouging the land. They harassed our wildlife and usurped meadows that had formerly been frequented by deer. They even curtailed our woodland walks, because we couldn't risk encountering the band of these belligerent animals.

We resolved to evict our unwelcome guests as soon as possible, but we were uncertain about how to do so. Searching for a plan, we learned that wildlife management officials have experimented with a variety of hog-busting tactics over the years, but the most successful one has been trapping the hogs and releasing them in controlled environments such as farms.[3] After some research, we were able to contact a local man who owned one of these hog farms, and he agreed to remove the hogs for us. However, he stipulated that we had to trap them ourselves, a feat which proved to be impossible simply because the hogs were so elusive. Days might pass with no sign of their presence, but just when we hoped they had possibly vanished, we would stumble upon those telltale stretches of decimated earth.

And then, one day, the story took a dramatic turn.

My mom and I were standing in our dining room on this particular afternoon when we were suddenly startled by a shadow of movement at the margin of our woods. To our astonishment, the "shadow" materialized into the entire tribe of wild hogs, casually trotting out of the forest—into our backyard! Eyes bright with curiosity, they wandered around our house, and after nosing through our landscaping and investigating our back patio, they discovered our birdfeeders and began happily gobbling the seeds on the ground underneath.

During this interval, my mother and I had been unable to do much more than simply stare out the windows in shock. But watching the hogs greedily feast on our birdseed, my mother abruptly declared that she was completely exasperated with this whole situation. It was bad enough that the hogs were cavorting through our woods. But she could not believe that they had now found the gall to brazenly maraud on our very doorstep and pillage our birdfeeders. She announced that something had to be done about the hogs once and for all, but in any case, they were not remaining in our backyard a moment longer.

With this proclamation, she was out the door, her parting words a caution to me to remain inside. I had no option but to watch helplessly from the window. In just a few seconds, I saw my mother sprinting across the backyard, straight toward the pack of hogs. She was whooping wildly and brandishing some long, threatening-looking object above her head. One glance from their beady eyes, and the entire band of hogs seemed to be convinced she meant business. The normally aggressive animals scurried down the hillside, stubby legs scrambling for refuge beyond the borders of our property. Exulting in her victory, my mother returned to the house and displayed her "weapon."

It was a bundle of three dried-out ears of Indian corn!

The corn had been displayed in our house as a fall decoration, but when it began to fade, it was relegated to the garage countertop, where it awaited disposal. My mother explained this unlikely weapon choice as mere impulse; she was passing through the garage on her way to confront the hogs and just snatched the first item she saw. Evidently the hogs found it impressive, and until my dying day, I will never forget the sight of my mother valiantly defending our home from wayward hogs—with three ears of Indian corn!

Within just a few days from this episode, we were able to trap the hogs in our barn (another exciting story for another day), and the farmer we had contacted earlier transported them to his property. The hog invasion was ended, and we've had no more porcine visitors since then.

But over the years, I've come to realize that while I might not have wild hogs roaming through my yard, I still face invaders in my life every single day. They don't mangle the ground, but they trample my hopes. They don't prevent me from hiking, but they can forbid me from dreaming. They're not a threat to my birdseed, but they're a threat to my soul. These invaders are the forces of darkness—Satan and his minions. As destructive and unwanted as wild hogs are, these enemies are far more deadly. And just as we could not hold open house for the hogs on our property, we can't allow these spiritual intruders to remain in our lives.

We shouldn't be surprised that we face invasions, because the Christian life is and always has been a call to warfare. Jesus Himself bluntly said, "Do not think that I have come to bring peace to the earth. I have not come to bring peace, but a sword" (Matthew 10:34 ESV). God doesn't summon us to a life of passivity. To be clear, salvation itself does not demand a struggle; Jesus has already conquered evil and won our eternal freedom once and for all! However, appropriating that salvation—walking in it day by day, refusing to settle for less than our divine birthright—does require us to put on our armor, because Satan and his legions are determined to resist our attempts to live for God. And in this battle with eternal consequences, our warfare must be carefully executed on heavenly principles.

First of all, we fight for what God has given us. When I think back to that day with the hogs, I remember that my mom wasn't about to let those invaders ruin our land or threaten our animals. She could have settled for the safest option, cowering in fear inside our house and letting the hogs roam unopposed. But instead, she went on the offensive against them. Why? Because she understood that our land and our family was something God had called her to protect.

I'm reminded of a Biblical hero named Shammah, a member of King David's renowned mighty men—an elite corps of soldiers with valiant hearts and incredible military ability. You'll find Shammah's brief but powerful story tucked away in 2 Samuel 23, the "hall of fame" of these fearless men. "And next…was Shammah, the son of Agee the Hararite. The Philistines gathered together at Lehi, where there was a plot of ground full of lentils, and the men fled from the Philistines. But he took his stand in the midst of the plot and defended it and struck down the Philistines, and the Lord worked a great victory" (v. 11-12 ESV). There's nothing in this verse that would lead us to believe that this particular patch of ground was anything remarkable; it sounds like nothing more than a common garden. So why did Shammah risk his life to defend this spot?

267

The answer lies in these words: "he took his stand." You see, we all have times in our lives when it's tempting to yield ground. Maybe your life seems too ordinary, or your marriage is too far gone, or your career can't be salvaged. In those moments, our human inclination is to count our losses and walk away. But imagine what would happen if we drew the line in the sand with Shammah's courage and said, "This doesn't seem like much, but it's what the Lord has asked me to defend. The enemy can come no further."

Once we've decided to defend the territory God has given us, what do we use for weapons? Too often, we lament that we can't repel the invaders because we don't have what we need to do so. We reason that if we had more money, better health, a more devoted spouse, or a different set of genes, then we could take our stand valiantly. But this is far from the truth—because your weapons are closer than you think. Just look at 2 Peter 1:3: "By his divine power, God has given us everything we need for living a godly life" (NLT). God has given us whatever we require for the battle. We just don't always recognize it!

Dried-up ears of Indian corn didn't seem like the best choice of weapon for my mom. But it was all she had on hand, so she decided to wield it fearlessly—and it worked! As it turns out, God loves to use humble means to accomplish amazing feats. Shamgar, a Hebrew judge, "saved Israel" by slaying six hundred Philistines with a simple ox goad (Judges 3:31 ESV). Facing defeat and arrest at the hands of God's enemies, Samson grabbed the abandoned jawbone of a donkey and with it killed a thousand soldiers (Judges 15)! Even Moses overcame the might of Egypt not with swords or spears but with a shepherd's staff through which God did wonders (Exodus 3). I'm reminded of the wise admonishment of Pastor Francis Anfuso: "What you need is often hidden in what you have."[4]

But God doesn't only delineate our territory and endow us with our weapons. He blesses us with something even more priceless: *Himself*. In this weary war, we aren't fighting alone. Because "we do not wrestle against flesh and blood" (Ephesians 3:10 ESV), the fight is in the spiritual realms, and it is God Who puts the strength in our souls to stand firm. Paul reminds us in 2 Corinthians 10:3-4 that "though we walk in the flesh, we are not waging war according to the flesh. For the weapons of our warfare are not of the flesh but have divine power to destroy strongholds" (ESV).

Divine power. You see, the fighting isn't up to us. We can be confused, outnumbered, or terrified—and that's ok. Nowhere are we commanded to fight in our own strength. We're instead assured that "the Lord your God is the one fighting for you" (Deuteronomy 3:22 NASB). And God does this in incredibly contradictory ways that fly in the face of all the world's standards:

When we are weak, we are strong in His strength. (2 Corinthians 12:10)

When we are outnumbered, there are still more on our side. (2 Kings 6:16)

When we seem to be defeated, we will rise again. (Micah 7:8)

When we are most afraid, we can find rest in His love. (1 John 4:18)

And that's the secret of the battle. You see, most of us can't claim to have pursued wild animals with Indian corn. In fact, my mom may be alone in the ability to reminisce about a memory like that! However, regardless of where we live, or what we do, or who we are, we can't escape invasions in our lives. And in our times of warfare, we face some crucial decisions. First, we determine not to relinquish what God has given us. Next, we fight with the weapons He has provided, even if they seem insufficient to us. And lastly, we yield to His authority over the battle. We need not fear the war— because when all is said and done, we watch Him provide the victory.

Soaring in Silence

T he winter is winning.

All around me, autumn is surrendering to the inevitability of winter. The dazzlingly decorated leaves are mostly fallen now, curled and crispy on the ground, leaving only a few faded ones clinging to the empty-handed trees. All crops of fruit and field are reaped; the pastures stretch in barren expanses of dry stubble. Even the air seems to have changed, transitioning from the blessing-bound expectancy of autumn to the hushed dormancy of winter. It's an odd time, a blurring line between seasons—a time of silence and stillness and perhaps, a bit of sadness too. Yet as the rich symphony of autumn dwindles to a decrescendo, the quiet of these days leaves the perfect backdrop for one of my favorite woodland creatures, one that seems to typify this silent time: the owl.

Four species of owls make their home in Arkansas year-round: the Eastern Screech-Owl, the Barn Owl, the Barred Owl, and the Great Horned Owl.[1] The first two are reclusive; in all my years of woodland wanderings, I've never seen or heard either. But the last two figure prominently in the natural world around me, welcomed denizens of the pastures and forests around my home.

270

Glimpsing an owl is rare; I can count on my hands the number of times I've had the privilege. Very occasionally, if I've looked up at just the right moment, I've caught sight of Barred Owls, brooding sentinels guarding the treetops. Once in Colorado, on an autumn afternoon slanted by silver sheets of misty rain, I unexpectedly came face-to-face with the secretive Great Horned Owl; for a few breathless moments we stared at each other, wrapped in the whirl of the foggy mist. But on the whole, owls are much more frequently heard than seen. And one of the best times to listen for their calls is now—during the enchanted evenings of late fall.

Step outside one of these nights, just at dusk, when the sky simmers in muted swaths of color and the trees are as starkly black as paper cutouts against the fading sunset. Wait in the crispy chill, in the layers of quiet, until the harvest moon floats above the horizon and spills light like golden streams across the landscape. And if you are patient, if you are silent, you will hear it—a haunting query echoing from the woods. Perhaps it will be the rhythmic inquiry of the Barred Owl, or the pensive baritone of the Great Horned, or even the strident neighing of the Screech-Owl. But all, in their different voices, will ask the age-old question of the owl: "Who? Whooo?"

There's a magic about these creatures—stealthy, silent, serene. For hundreds of years, they have remained steeped in a mysticism and mystery not shared by any other bird. Perhaps that's due in part to their elusiveness—as nocturnal creatures, they inhabit a different sphere from the prosaic daily world, hovering like ghosts around the edges of our awareness. Or perhaps it's their distinctive presence, their innate sense of dignity—anyone who's ever glimpsed an owl poised regally on a tree limb or floating gently across the sky has doubtless noticed their tranquil aplomb, their obvious confidence in their own supremacy. Then again, maybe it's their striking beauty—feathers streaked in a dozen shades of brown, elegant wings, piercing golden eyes.

All of this is impressive, but the characteristic of owls that is perhaps the most remarkable is often overlooked: silence. The color and pattern of their plumage forms the perfect disguise, allowing them to blend into the backdrop of the forest; the Barred Owl is the mottled brown of dry autumn leaves, while the Eastern Screech-Owl's silvery gray is uncannily identical to tree bark. Cloaked in their camouflage, they can perch unmoving on tree branches for long hours, as if suspended in time, completely unnoticed by the world. And amazingly, they're just as silent in motion as they are when at rest. Thanks to specially designed wingtip feathers that muffle noise by actually changing the airflow pattern, owls can fly soundlessly, giving no clue to their presence even when they are mere inches away.[2] And this silence is the key to their survival—enabling them to capture prey readily and avoid detection by other animals.

It's remarkable, really. Owls are creatures of immense strength—fearless hunters, dominant predators, speedy fliers with fierce talons and powerful wings. Yet the secret of their success is not found in their might or muscle but in a much humbler quality—their ability to be silent.

Might it be the same for us?

My friends, we live in a world that becomes louder by the day. Jumbo jets and freeways, rock concerts and subway trains, honking horns and squealing brakes and insistent doorbells rip the fabric of peace. But in this raucous world, we humans are still the loudest by far. We're told to "let our voice be heard," "speak up," "say something." We're bombarded by people confidently proclaiming their opinions. Especially in these tumultuous times, we're inundated with polarizing noise from government leaders, sports figures, celebrities, awareness groups, news anchors, and even our neighbors. Indeed, our culture seems obsessed with noise—and anyone with a social media account can choose to become a self-appointed steward of dissonance. But as the noise increases, our listening decreases. And now, it's out of control. What might have begun as a thoughtful discussion has long since disintegrated into a shouting match.

But as much as we might deplore the noise, we often feel unable to respond in any other way. Against the panoply of chaos, silence seems like a paradoxical choice. We view silence in contempt, as weakness ("I have to stand up for myself"), or vacuity ("I have to say something to prove my intelligence"), or defeat ("If I don't say anything, they'll think they're right"), or even irresponsibility ("I can't let THAT go unchallenged").

Changing minds begins to seem more important than changing hearts. Spreading truth takes a backseat to spreading our own opinions. Sympathizing is replaced by soapboxing. And so we jump into the fray, opinions blazing like firebrands—but instead of cutting through the noise, our words only augment it, and the ear-splitting cacophony of the culture continues. No helping, no healing, only a maelstrom of noise that whirls faster and faster. And frustration seethes in our souls—*what will it take to get these people to listen? I can't scream any louder!*

Could it be that the reason we're not celebrating results is that our approach is all wrong? What if quiet—so derided, so maligned—was not a weakness but a weapon? What if silence was for us what it is for the owl—our greatest strength?

There's a misconception that being silent equals being ignored, retreating to the shadows and skulking like wallflowers on the outskirts of important issues. But you see, practicing silence skillfully doesn't involve abandoning all words or muffling our opinions. What it does require is that we learn when well-chosen words are required, and when silence can speak more powerfully than any words we could say.

Scripture is replete with references to silence. "Be still, and know that I am God" (Psalm 46:10a ESV) is perhaps the best-known verse on this topic. Its message is echoed by Psalm 62:5: "My soul, wait in silence for God only, for my hope is from Him" (NASB). The prophet Jeremiah reminded his readers, "It is good that one should wait quietly for the salvation of the LORD" (Lamentations 3:26 ESV). And through Isaiah, God told the Hebrews, "In quietness and in trust shall be your strength" (Isaiah 30:15 ESV). Interestingly, all of these verses present silence not as apathetic passivity, but as a very dynamic state: a posture of trust before God and an essential precondition for spiritual victory.

But how could silence be effective? How could it be mightier than spoken words? For one powerful reason: silence enables us to listen.

Just think of the owl again. As impressive as its silence is, it's only a prerequisite for an even more vital talent: listening. The concave pattern of feathers on an owl's face, called the "facial disk," is carefully designed to collect a wide range of sounds, functioning somewhat similarly to a satellite dish. The sounds are then funneled directly to the owl's acutely sensitive ears, a miracle in their own right. In the marvelous wisdom of the Creator, an owl's ears are offset, with one just slightly higher than the other. This allows the owl to analyze sounds in a manner akin to modern triangulation, making complex depth calculations and pinpointing the exact location of prey. In fact, so keen is owls' sense of hearing that they can detect the scurrying movement of a single mouse under three feet of snow![3]

And so it is with us. When we have stripped away the noise and become "quick to listen" (James 1:19 ESV), on the bedrock of silence we can tune into what would have otherwise been ignored. We'll find that the things that lay beneath the surface of our lives, the things that were buried by layers of noise, become apparent.

So how can we practice such a controversial virtue in our very noisy lives? Like all things, silence must begin first with God. The prophet Habakkuk reminded his readers, "The LORD is in His holy temple; let all the earth keep silence before Him" (Habakkuk 2:20 ESV). This verse invites us to experience the Presence of God in extraordinary ways—basking in the wonder of His glory, soaking in His grace, calming our racing minds with His peace. But how rarely we obey this admonition! We fill the space between God and us not with reverent silence but with worship songs and church activities, Sunday school lessons and hurried prayers. We say so much *about* God, but we rarely leave room for Him to answer. That's why the practice of silence must begin with recognizing the sovereignty of our King. "Be not rash with your mouth, nor let your heart be hasty to utter a word before God, for God is in heaven and you are on earth. Therefore let your words be few" (Ecclesiastes 5:2 ESV). Renewal begins when we intentionally carve out time to be silent before the Lord—to suspend our human pompousness and hear His words of grace. As theologian and sage Henri Nouwen once commented, "Solitude is the furnace of transformation."[4]

Like a pebble tossed into a pond, silence before the Lord creates an epicenter of calm that spreads its ripples through our lives. The next step is to be silent with ourselves—and oh, how we seem to fear that. We cram our days full of activities—work, school, soccer practice, clubs, outings, appointments, vacations. And if we have a few scraps of time, a handful of moments when silence might begin to intrude, we reach for the anesthetic of our phones. Why are we so afraid of ourselves? Imagine if we disciplined our minds to think deeply, to ponder our strengths and weaknesses, our past and present, and how all of those fit into the story God is writing in our lives. We might find that the process involved was one of fine-tuning our spirits—and that when we listen to ourselves, we can course-correct before minor snags become major catastrophes.

When we're silent with God and silent with ourselves, we then have the freedom to be silent with others. Author and spiritual educator Tracy Balzer believes that "it is through solitude—through intentional times being alone with God only—that we are transformed into people who demonstrate compassion to others."[5]

What would that look like? Perhaps it would be the choice to practice silence when complaints and criticisms crowded our minds. Maybe, even better, it would resemble practicing silence when we ourselves are criticized—refusing to make a battleground out of small issues and thereby yield the peace in our spirits. And perhaps it would be choosing to listen, truly listen, to others—not just to what they say, but to how they say it. When we "let our words be few" and intentionally listen to someone else's heart instead of only their mouth, miracles of connection can take place.

But as amazing as silence and listening are, there's yet a third member of this sacred trinity of serenity—wisdom.

Did you know that in the mythology of nearly every western culture, owls represent wisdom?[6] They're presented as all-knowing guardians or helpful guides or enigmatic sages. Athena, the Greek goddess of wisdom, was portrayed as carrying an owl on her shoulder; owls were engraved on Greek coins. Native American tribes viewed owls as religious symbols or prophetic talismans. Owls even figure prominently in the iconography of academia today. Could it be that the owl's reputation for wisdom stems from its willingness to listen?

We think of wise people as those who disseminate their opinions with the world—professors, preachers, prophets. However, the main characteristic of wisdom is an eagerness not to speak but to listen. We live in an age with more access to knowledge and information than ever before—yet wisdom is on the decline for one simple reason: its parents, silence and listening, have been virtually exiled from our culture. Today, let's return to a different standard. Recognizing that there are more voices in the world than ours, gaining the empathy born of hearing others' viewpoints, striving to understand the motives of others instead of dismissing their perspectives—these are the ways we embrace wisdom.

"When words are many, transgression is not lacking, but whoever restrains his lips is prudent" (Proverbs 10:19 ESV). Our culture is living the first half of this verse—and the noise only grows louder each day. But as followers of Christ, we have the authority to change the trajectory. So the next time you hear an owl asking its haunting questions of the moon, or are fortunate enough to glimpse one roosting in the treetops, remember to make peace with silence and make room for listening. Then, and only then, will our hearts overflow with "the wisdom from above [that] is first pure, then peaceable, gentle, open to reason, full of mercy and good fruits, impartial and sincere" (James 3:17 ESV).

ADVENT AND ANIMALS

W inter is on its way.

Each year, the season sweeps down from the Far North, like an ancient king deigning to visit this land. The sky unrolls a carpet of silver clouds for his advance. The trees stretch their bare hands heavenward in welcome. The dry grass whispers the news to the last crispy leaves. And the winds rush ahead, blustering through the forest—eager heralds declaring the coming of the king.

And the event they predict is not far in the future. In a matter of weeks, we will experience the winter solstice—the year's shortest day and longest night and the official beginning of the coldest season.

As I brace for winter's coming, as I count down the days until the arrival, I'm reminded all over again that these are stern and surly days. The world wears an inhospitable face, and the myriad hues that grace all other seasons have dwindled to monochromatic tones. Indeed, the view from my window can be downright depressing some days: a shivering landscape cowering beneath a sullen sky.

But winter's negative effects on the landscape aren't nearly as serious as the threats it holds for wildlife. In a world of insulated buildings and warm cars and overflowing grocery stores, it's easy for us to forget that for the denizens of field and forest, winter can be an epically deadly time. Some creatures evade it altogether, like birds that soar southward or chipmunks that burrow underneath the ground or frogs that slumber in the mud. Many animals, however, choose to remain in place during the cold months—and in doing so, they face many challenges. For one thing, food supplies are scarce. The swarms of insects that thronged the golden meadows have disappeared, the grass that sustained the deer all summer is dead and dry, and the trees and shrubs no longer produce tender shoots or succulent fruit. Shelter, or lack thereof, is another problem. Leafless woods and withered underbrush are a far cry from the protective canopy of the growing season. And as if all this weren't bad enough, the temperatures are dangerously cold. Months of chilly days and freezing nights have to be survived before the creatures of the woodland can rejoice in the sun again.

Call it fancy, call it faith, but I like to think that in these gloomy months, the God Who watches the sparrows and tends the lilies sends woodland angels to watch over His creatures. Sometimes I imagine them, wings like wispy clouds against the sky, sheltering and defending and guiding the wildlife all winter long. Regardless of the exact nature of His provision, though, I do know that God doesn't forget His little animals. So in this time, the way I make ready for the coming of winter is by partnering with Him to prepare for the woodland residents.

This isn't as dramatic as it might sound. In fact, although there are plenty of ways we can help backyard wildlife, most of them involve surprisingly simple actions. For example, not raking the fallen leaves from garden plots until spring serves many vital functions, such as adding nutrients to the soil, providing habitat for animals like lizards and salamanders, and benefiting local insect populations. Also, while gardeners find it tempting to clip the withered heads of flowers that bloomed in the summer and fall, leaving those spent blooms alone allows birds to access the seeds hidden deep inside and use the fibers for nesting material. Building brush piles is another helpful action—small animals like mice and chipmunks prize them as essential shelter. Of course, birdfeeders are always an obvious choice. Just outside my kitchen window swing a half dozen feeders, each offering a particular kind of seed and catering to a certain group of birds. The feeders attract birds from cheeky chickadees and regal-crowned cardinals to inquisitive titmice, bossy blue jays, and streaky finches.[1]

These small acts for wildlife are the ways I prepare for the coming of winter—and I hope you might be inspired to join me in lending a hand for the animals as you also brace for this season. But my friends, as important as these preparations are, there's another kind of preparation in which we need to be engaged now—not for the coming of a season, but for the coming of a Savior. There is a King on His way—not my imaginative personification of winter, but the Ruler of all.

Christmas is coming, like a slowly rising star, and I feel the knowing all around me—as if even the creation pulses with joy to celebrate its Maker's birth. The sacredness of this time is as pure as the angels' song in Bethlehem, as ancient as the Jews' yearning anticipation of the Messiah. And each year, we relive the holy mystery through the tradition of Advent. Derived from the Latin word *adventus*, or "coming," this season of the church calendar is focused on the coming of Christ—on the Love that sent a Son to this rebel planet, the grace that descended into our darkness and shattered the shadows forever.[2]

The definitions and observances of Advent vary widely throughout different Christian traditions. But beyond any external variations, the primary feature of Advent remains the same—the focus on the imminent coming of Christ. No matter how it's celebrated, the liturgy of Advent invites us to prepare for a specific purpose: to receive Jesus' Presence.

If we're honest, though, sometimes this preparation can seem, well, unnecessary. After all, we've heard the story of the divine birth more times than we can count. We've memorized the lyrics to all the Christmas hymns. There's a well-loved crèche on our living room table. Yes, if we've spent any time at all in the church, we've probably heard about Advent year after year. And it can seem not only mundane but make-believe as well. Lingering in the back of our minds is the knowledge that Christ already came to this earth two thousand years ago. We engage in elaborate liturgy inviting His Presence, but do we really expect Him to descend among us again?

The secret is this: the preparation is not truly for Christ, or at least, not in the sense we're envisioning. We're not making it possible for Jesus to enjoy our company; we're making it possible for us to enjoy His. The preparation looks not out but in—making *ourselves* ready to receive the King.

The sad truth is that humans don't retain spiritual heat very well. Our hearts tend to grow as cold and barren as the winter days. And just as the chill of the season is inhospitable to life, the coldness in our hearts can bar the door against the work of the Spirit. The only way to combat this tendency is to thaw our souls again and again and again—to continually invite Christ to come. Are we asking repeatedly for salvation? No—that is a one-time decision. But must we ask Him daily, hourly, to make our hearts His home more and more fully—to expand the light of His grace in our lives? Absolutely.

Thus, Advent is not for Christ, but for us. If we want the King to come, we must prepare a place for His Presence within us. But with our hearts so apt to freeze, how can we make them ready for Jesus?

I'm reminded of a signature statement from the movie *Frozen*: "Only an act of true love can thaw a frozen heart."[3] When the sunshine of love hits our hearts, the ice of our self-sufficiency melts. However, the kind of love referred to is not romantic tingles or warm fuzzies or shallow affection. The only love powerful enough to be transformative is not the love we receive *from* others but instead the love we show *to* others.

At its core, love is simple. By this I don't mean that it's not sometimes messy, or uncomfortable, or inconvenient, or painful. It is often all of those things, but its underlying bedrock of selflessness is uncomplicated. And because of that, love delights in manifesting itself in the quietest and humblest of ways.

I'm reminded again of the acts I perform to prepare for the wildlife. I don't do anything extravagant. None of my actions require careful preparation, or exhaustive planning, or an enormous amount of time. In fact, none of them, with the exception of providing birdseed, cost anything monetarily. These are not ground-breaking, earth-shattering gestures of generosity. In fact, we might be inclined to dismiss these actions as insignificant—until we see what a profound impact these "unimportant" deeds have on the winter wildlife.

You see, this is how we thaw our hearts—not with one blazing bonfire, but with a hundred tiny candles. As Mother Teresa, herself an amazing example of devotion to Jesus, reminded us, "We can do no great things, only small things with great love."[4] In a culture so obsessed with grand gestures, this is the recipe for preparing for the King and thawing our hearts, little by little—small acts of service.

280

"Whoever receives you receives me, and whoever receives me receives him who sent me....and whoever gives one of these little ones even a cup of cold water because he is a disciple, truly, I say to you, he will by no means lose his reward" (Matthew 10:40, 42 ESV).

These words of Jesus remind us of the reason service is so powerful—because in every act of selflessness, we're serving Jesus Himself. He restated this point in Matthew 25 with a parable: Christ-followers are enthusiastically welcomed to Heaven by God the King, Who praises them for performing acts of love toward Him such as feeding and clothing Him, attending His medical needs, and visiting Him in prison. The followers respond in confusion, unable to recall ever rendering such mundane service to God Himself. Jesus concluded the illustration with this powerful statement: "And the King will answer them, 'Truly, I say to you, as you did it to one of the least of these my brothers, you did it to me'" (v. 40 ESV).

So in these drab days, I pull on my coat and lace up my work boots and head outside, into a chilly and churlish world. As the winter wind whistles from the north and the solstice draws irrevocably nearer, I prepare. I gather the stray branches that lurk under the trees and mound them into brush piles. I nod in approval at the dead flowers clinging to the dry branches. I fill my feeders and admire as the birds come, swooping toward the seed in a flurry of feathers. And I watch my breath swirl skyward and smile at the looming clouds and feel the crackling anticipation of Advent in the air. Because in these simple actions, I'm not just serving Jesus' little creatures. In some mysterious way that I will never fully understand until eternity, I'm serving Jesus Himself. And as seemingly insignificant as my deeds are, they aren't just preparation for winter. They're preparation for Christmas—for Jesus to come in my heart, all over again.

Small acts of kindness—how seemingly insignificant, yet how great. What are some you can do today? It might be finding a good cause for some extra cash. It might be phoning a friend who's going through a rough time. It might be writing a letter or lending an ear or sending a smile—or filling a birdfeeder. But whatever your act of love, remember this: it's for the King. He is coming—and we're priming our midwinter hearts to glow like summer in His love.

MIDWINTER MIRACLE

These are the darkest days of the year.

In many ways, winter is a time of mourning, a lonely dirge for the beauty that has been. Bitter winds mutter and growl through the spiderwebby branches of leafless trees. Ice glitters on every limb and crusts the ponds and lakes. The woods fade to muted tones—brown and silver and grey. The grass is dead and the ground is hard and the birds are mostly silent.

But perhaps the most disheartening feature of winter is the stinginess of the daylight. There's no warmth in the sunbeams at this time of year, and they frequently appear weak and watery, as if they barely have the energy to stretch through the frowning clouds. And what little daylight we do receive doesn't last long. Ever since Midsummer—the summer solstice, the longest day—the days have been shortening. And now, in Arkansas, we're experiencing well over fourteen hours of darkness each night.

And winter nights are black and long and empty enough to chill the nerves of even the bravest soul. When I step outside on a December night, the darkness seems to weigh on the world like a black shroud. I feel the air crackling with the bitter cold, and I watch my breath tumble away in floating puffs. Fingers of frost curl around every leaf and twig.

Yes, these days—and the accompanying bleak nights—are less than encouraging. But in the midst of this dreary season, when the days are growing shorter and the cold is becoming sharper and the dark seems to have the upper hand, something amazing happens—something that is borderline miraculous—the winter solstice.

The science behind it is fascinating. Technically speaking, this is the point in Earth's orbit when the tilt of the axis positions the Northern Hemisphere farthest from the sun. This is a gradual process, begun as early as the summer solstice in June, and the day of the solstice is the culmination of the journey before the North Pole will once more begin to swing sunward.[1] But the bare statistical facts can never begin to encapsulate the magic that is the winter solstice. It possesses an ethereal spiritual cadence that can't be dissected into dusty facts and figures. And it's that unknown magic—like a haunting tune whose lyrics I never quite remember—that keeps me waiting outside on the evening of the winter solstice. I pull on my warmest coat and stand atop our highest hill, waiting to welcome winter. The sunset smolders in the west, like blazing coals banked against the edge of the world. The silvery stalks of dry grass crunch under my feet, and the denuded trees stretch empty hands toward the heavens.

I stand there, the cold tingling inside my nose, and I see the darkness falling, the fine mist of shadow settling over all the world. And sometimes, if I'm very quiet, if I'm perfectly still, then there is a brief stirring in the air—more sensed than felt, more remnant than reality, just a quiet knowing that the season has changed. On the evening of the solstice, there are no outward fanfares, no extravagant displays. Indeed, it's difficult to tell anything has happened at all—the cold is still bitter, the dark is still insistent, the days are still bleak and the nights are still black.

In fact, the night of the solstice is the longest and darkest night of the entire year. But guess what? The night after that will be a smidgen shorter. There will be just a few more drops of daylight than there were the day before. And day by gentle day, the light will strengthen—a minute here, a moment there, until the world returns to the deliciously long days and brief nights of midsummer.

And that's the wonder—despite appearances, the dark is weakening. The light is winning. And it's nothing short of a miracle—that here, now, in the dead tomb of winter, a trajectory is launching that will carry us all the way to the glimmer of spring and the glamor of summer. And as I wait in the twilight on the darkest night of the year, I smile—because when I look beyond that blackness, I can almost, *almost*, smell summer in the wind.

Isn't it amazing? On the darkest night of the coldest season, when the year is at its bleakest, the winter solstice arrives with a very unexpected gift—hope.

My friends, we are shivering in some very dark nights right now. The state of our world has been like a leaden blanket draped over our dreams. We've endured terrible natural disasters—whipping wildfires, shuddering earthquakes, cataclysmic hurricanes. We've been divided as a nation—ripped apart by hatred and haughtiness, by broken promises and centuries of suspicion and political machinations. We've suffered a global pandemic—a virus that threatened our health, invaded our schools, blasted our economy, and left us lonely and desperate behind our masks. And through it all, we've watched the darkness appear to strengthen and its worshippers become more brazen in their idolatry. The world around us has seemed defiant in its attempts to squelch every trace of God. The darkness, always present, has become too blatant to ignore.

And having suffered all these things, here we are now—in the burnt-out end of the year, the coldest and darkest time. It's only natural to struggle with many emotions—from anger ("Why did this happen?"), to fear ("What will happen next?"), to grief ("I want everything to be ok again"), to finally, despair ("There's no way out").

These are the days when desperation squeezes our hearts in its iron fist—cold days, dark days, sad days, lonely days. But if you're looking upon a life that seems as desolate and barren as the December fields and woods, then I want you to remember something very important. In the same way as the winter solstice comes in the longest and blackest night, it is often just when things look bleakest—just when we cannot see the faintest glimmer of hope anywhere—that the Light of the World flings Himself into our darkness.

Don't believe me? Just consider the coming holiday—Christmas. What better example could there be? You see, we think of Christmas as presents and bells and carols and angel wings fluttering against the stars and a happy holy family snug in a stable. But we tend to forget how very dark the night was when Christ was born, how great the gulf of despair in which the Jews were drowning.

284

Despite what we see on Christmas cards or in nativity pageants, Palestine in the time of the birth of Christ was the epitome of hopelessness. For starters, God was silent. The prophecies that had studded the Old Testament like jewels suddenly ceased. With the promise of the coming Messiah at the end of the Book of Malachi,[2] God seemed to sign off. By the time of Christ's birth, the Jews had not received a word from God in four centuries! Imagine how abandoned they must have felt. In fact, Bible commentators refer to this period as "the four hundred silent years."[3]

And to make matters worse, those four hundred years were a time of turmoil and chaos. Israel was absorbed into the empire of Alexander the Great and later shuffled among many rulers in a time of political instability, religious oppression, and internal revolt. Then, the Roman Empire rose to world domination and began its systematic destruction of Israelite culture and independence. By this time, the Jews were crushed under foreign occupation, out of touch with their identity, threatened by persecution and political inveigling, and—seemingly—forgotten by God.[4]

If ever there was a dark night, this was it. Can't you imagine Bethlehem as it must have been on the night of Jesus' birth? Uneasy crowds grudgingly assembled for a foreign census. Harsh Roman authorities yelling insults in an unknown tongue. A culture disintegrating and a people divided and a nation carrying an ancient burden of weeping and woe. A Jew in Bethlehem at that time had every reason to believe he was living in the darkest night of Israel's history.

Yet on that dark night, in a lonely stable, God rewrote the story. Just as the solstice reverses the trajectory of the seasons in a single instant, God undid all the power of darkness with a single Baby's cry. The nights would still be dark in Bethlehem—but they would never again be as dark as they had been. The winter would still freeze the hearts of men for a time—but it would never again have the final say. And just as the winter solstice points a finger to summer, so the sleepy Baby in the manger on that dark night was the first step toward the bursting glory of the Resurrection.

My friends, Christmas was not an isolated event. God still specializes in stepping into dark nights. He enters our illness and injury, poverty and panic, depression and disaster, addiction and anxiety, strife and sin. No matter what starless night has engulfed us, He delights in abolishing the blackness and spotlighting us with His grace. And when He steps into our situation, it is dramatic. With the suddenness of the solstice, He defeats the relentless march of darkness and reverses the whole direction of our lives.

So in these bleak days and lengthy nights, invite God into your situation. I don't mean simply acknowledge His Presence as a hazy philosophical reality or mouth a trite prayer of surrender. It's time for us to see God not as a feeble candle-flicker Who can be easily snuffed out by long nights, but as the true Light of the World—the God with the power to shred every shadow.

And I'm convinced that when we do this, when we welcome God into our dark night, our perspective begins to change. First, we remember to walk by faith, not by sight. If we only stare at the soul-crushing blackness of our night, it will be easy to abandon hope and sink in despair. But if we expect God to blaze His glory into our circumstances—if we allow the future promise of summer to penetrate the present reality of our winter—then we will have hope. Secondly, if we are walking in faith, then we are also living in expectation of a miracle. Even as we wait for Him, we can begin to prepare our hearts for the work He will do, because we live in the confidence that He will fulfill His promises and hold true to His Word. Lastly, we rejoice! Certainly, when we are standing in the darkest and coldest night of our lives, then rejoicing can seem counterintuitive or counterproductive or even downright crazy. But when you are standing in the dark of December, dare to praise Him—knowing that the God of light will shatter the blackness. He is coming!

It's a beautiful paradox, isn't it—this mystical and magical time? The winter solstice is at once the darkest and bleakest night in all the year *and* the wellspring of hope for brighter days and greater light. And it's certainly fitting that the solstice coincides so closely with Christmas, because both hold the same golden promise of hope, and both remind us of one powerful truth—no matter how desolate the night can seem, the light always prevails. In fact, sometimes when we're standing in the dark, the transformation has already begun—even if we don't see it yet.

I don't know what dark night you're facing right now. I don't hear your desperate prayers or watch your hopeless tears or feel the particular pain that's slicing your soul. But I do know this: the solstice is coming. The nights will not be quite as dark as they once were. The days will begin to lengthen—slowly, yes, but steadily. To our human eyes, all may still appear unchanged, an unending empty night. But

286

there is a shift. The season is changing, and here, now, the light is breaking through.

My friends, dare to believe that no night, however dark, could ever quench the glory of the One Who is Hope Himself. Dare to believe that sometimes, the blackest nights can be transformed into the most glorious mornings. And most importantly, dare to believe in the miracle of Christmas—when all seems lost, when despair seems to reign, when the nights are darkest… Hope is born.

GOD'S CHRISTMAS TREE

T here's only one kind of Christmas tree for me.

These days, it seems that endless varieties of Christmas trees abound. Small firs perch unobtrusively on tabletops. Artificial trees offer a realistic look (without a realistic mess!). Flashier options include trees that light up in various hues, trees constructed entirely from sparkling tinsel, or even inflatable trees to be placed on a lawn.

But my family and I have always celebrated Christmas with one kind of tree—a real, living evergreen, one with soft branches and a sturdy trunk and the aroma of all the boreal woods. So every year, on Thanksgiving afternoon, we hop into the truck and head to a magical place—the Christmas tree farm.

This is a place like no other, a haven where these trees of winter have been quietly stretching taller all through the long summer months, like a living experiment in faith. Young Virginia pines march in orderly rows across the rolling hillsides; gaps in the rank and file indicate where a tree has already been claimed by a searching family. The trees range in size from stately giants over twelve feet tall to more slender specimens about my height. My favorite are the fluffy infants that don't even reach my knee. It's as if all the hope of Christmas resides in their tiny branches.

Every tree is distinctive and special, yet only one can come home with us. The selection process is taken seriously, and it's not uncommon for us to spend several hours at the farm, patiently wandering through the rows of trees and debating their finer points: is this one bare on the back? Does this one have limbs sturdy enough for ornaments? What about this one—does it seem too short? Does that one over there perhaps have greener needles?

At the end of the day, we will choose one of the trees to join us for our Christmas celebration, and we'll return to claim it once December begins. As the sun dips below the horizon and our breath clouds in the freezing air, we'll load our choice in the bed of the truck and drive slowly down the winding dirt road, and I'll look over my shoulder for one last glance of those stalwart evergreen trees, so straight and proud, with the evening stars beginning to tangle in their branches. And for all the days till Christmas, our chosen tree will sparkle in our living room, adorned with tiny lights and festive decorations—a little piece of the wilderness in our home.

Of course, evergreen trees aren't found only on tree farms. As I walk through the winter woods, I encounter them quite frequently. And they always appear remarkably striking. After all, by this point in the year, the trees around them are merely skeletal frameworks—silvery limbs bending barren, the remnants of their leafy crowns scattered across the forest floor. These are the deciduous trees, known for emblazoning the woods with vivid hues each autumn and afterwards relinquishing their leaves to conserve energy, hoard nutrients, and avoid damage from snow accumulation on full leafy branches.[1] Their show in autumn was spectacular, but now, they appear completely lifeless, as if all their energy fluttered away with their leaves.

Against this backdrop of seeming death, the evergreen glows with the polar opposite—abundant life. The miracle is in their name—they are "ever-green" and do not shed their leaves on a seasonal basis. Indeed, in some species, a needle might remain on an evergreen for fifty years![2] They're specially designed to weather the harshest conditions winter can fling at them. All of their characteristics, from a pyramidal architecture that discourages snow accumulation, to an energy-efficient leaf shape, to a waxy foliage coating that ensures optimal moisture retention, enable them to manufacture food for themselves even during the harshest times.[3] While other trees drowse in dormancy, struggling to survive inhospitable conditions, the evergreen not only survives—it thrives.

When I see an evergreen tree, I'm awed by its amazing design, and I'm grateful for its vivid green in the otherwise drab winter world. However, I'm also reminded of a startling and impactive truth—in the summer, both deciduous trees and evergreens look the same.

Imagine if visitors from an always-summer region near the equator explored a northern hardwood forest in near-July. Would they be able to distinguish which trees would soon turn bare and brown? In summer, all trees are leafy and fertile, flourishing in ideal conditions. Untrained observers can't possibly predict that in a few short months, some trees will become nothing more than barren sticks. The luxurious days of the growing season lack that one defining feature that would reveal the inner characteristics of the tree—adversity.

My friends, I notice the same phenomenon in our society as well. After all, during the "summers" of human lives, all people— godly or not—may react to their circumstances in quite similar ways. When the bank account is hefty, the marriage is happy, the promotion is granted, or the doctor's appointment is excellent, prosperity tends to mask the deeper distinctions. Indeed, in such times, the scales can seem a bit uneven: the most defiant atheist can appear to enjoy just as wonderful a life as the most devout of God's children.

But one day winter comes.

The bank account dwindles, the marriage sours, the career plummets, and the diagnosis is frightening. Conditions are not ideal. Summer is over. And suddenly, the divide between God's people and the world becomes as sharp and obvious as the disparity between the two types of trees. What makes the distinction so clear-cut? Simply this—when all the world fades away, God's people remain strong.

Consider the case of two completely different men—Judas and Peter. In the good times, both seemed much the same. Both were members of Jesus' elite following, both engaged in evangelistic work, and both ultimately betrayed their Master. However, in that dark abyss of guilt and fear, the difference between them was dramatically illustrated. When he was at his lowest point, Judas succumbed to grief and hanged himself in despair (Matthew 27). Peter, however, sought and received the forgiveness of Jesus and went on to become instrumental in the founding of the church (John 21). Both looked the same—until winter.

Or consider Psalm 37. Penned by David, this psalm is referred to by Charles Spurgeon as "the great riddle of the prosperity of the wicked and the affliction of the righteous."[4] In his lifetime, David had seen plenty of injustice; after being anointed king by Samuel, he spent at least fifteen years fleeing from a crazed tyrant who ruled his land and sought his life.[5] Even after he ascended the throne, he was constantly plagued by conspiracies and was forced to leave his capital after his own son Absalom staged a coup.[6] Yet this psalm opens with this gentle injunction: "Fret not yourself because of evildoers; be not envious of wrongdoers! For they will soon fade like the grass and wither like the green herb" (v. 1-2 ESV). Winter is coming, David assures us, and the prosperity of these people will be as transient as autumn leaves, while God's people will still stand strong.

This psalm touches on an evident truth: it's easy to derive strength and support from our circumstances. To be happy, says the world, all that is required is for our lives to go our way. However, the trademark of Christians is our ability to remain unmoved by our circumstances. Our hope is not found in our bank account, our marriage, our good health, or our career. Our hope is found in the promise of Jesus Christ, by Whom we inherit all the riches of God.

And that is the secret of the evergreen. When all other trees bow to the pressure of changing seasons, the evergreen stands tall and strong in the winter woods, drawing from a strength greater than itself. In the same manner, we as God's children remain "like a tree planted by streams of water that yields its fruit in its season...[whose] leaf does not wither" (Psalm 1:3 ESV), no matter what trials we may undergo.

And when eager tree-seekers converge on the Christmas tree farm, they are unwittingly paying homage to this truth. Whether in the form of branches over windows, wreaths upon doors, or trees within houses, the evergreen is considered the universal symbol of Christmas. Although the spiritual application behind these practices has long been ignored by the world, the evergreen's association with Christmas actually began as a reminder of the eternal life we possess.[7]

When the ultimate winter comes to this world and all that we cling to vanishes, when we depart this coordinate in time and space for the unknown realms of eternity—in this moment of seeming death, we will be revealed in our most brilliant life. Like the evergreen, we will be forever vibrant, unmoved by the greatest trial this fallen world can impose, rooted safely in the love of our God and warmed by the rays of His Son.

That's why I cherish the evergreen this time of year. I always enjoy wandering in the winter woods around Christmastime; in fact, my family has a very special tradition of hiking in the forests behind our property on the afternoon of Christmas Eve. We'll roam the leafless slopes and wander alongside the steel-gray streams. We'll glimpse the shy deer in their drab winter coats and head homeward just at dusk, when the air seems to crackle with excitement and the Christmas lights on our house are twinkling through the approaching darkness. And as we hike, we will see plenty of evergreens, as straight as the pillars of the heavens, cradling the stars close to their hearts— and we will smile. Because the evergreen reminds us that two thousand years ago, the deepest darkness man has ever known was shattered by the wail of a newborn baby and the soft crooning of a very young mother. The most bitter cold man has ever known was warmed by the adoration of angels and the worship of humble shepherds. And the greatest burden man has ever known was lifted by that same baby, now a man, who in spite of ourselves loved us to death—and back to life. And because of that baby, because of our Jesus, we are rooted in a wellspring of eternity that the world can only envy. We never need fear the "winter," because we are held safe through the storms of this life and loved fiercely in the joy of the next. Because He lives, we shall live also—ever-green in His love!

THANK YOU!

Friends, we've spent a whole year together exploring God's world with the lens of God's Word. I'm so thankful that you've taken this journey with me, and I pray that it has encouraged you and inspired you in your daily walk.

I want you to know that although the year may be over, the adventure is definitely not! Be sure to visit me on my blog at www.wordsfromthewilderness.com for new devotional writings, short stories, and more! Don't forget to stay up-to-date on all the latest content by following Wilderness Words on Facebook and @wildernessashlyn on Instagram. And if you want to reach out personally, feel free to email me at wildernessashlyn@gmail.com. Your presence alongside me is a blessing I don't take for granted, and I'm so grateful for you!

Truly, we live in a world of wonders. The oceans with their sunken secrets and moon-tugged tides…the mountains that wear sparkling snow like crowns…the scarlet surprise of the Northern Cardinals outside my window. Yet the greatest marvel is one that will never cease to stun my mind and capture my heart—the same God Who birthed all the beauty seeks to bring that same glory to our lives. My prayer is that the longer we linger in His Presence, the more our awe will overflow in praise. "Oh, the depth of the riches and wisdom and knowledge of God! How unsearchable are his judgments and how inscrutable his ways!....For from him and through him and to him are all things. To him be glory forever. Amen" (Romans 11:33, 36 ESV).

– Ashlyn McKayla Ohm

ABOUT THE AUTHOR

A passionate follower of Jesus Christ, Ashlyn McKayla Ohm finds her writing calling where her heart for God and her love for His creation intersect. Born and raised in rural Arkansas on the shoulders of the Ouachita Mountains, she's most at home where the streetlights die and the pavement ends—roaming the woods, counting the stars, watching for wolves, and breathing the mountain air. When she's not hiking, running, or writing about her adventures, you're likely to find her reading, playing the piano, birdwatching, or praise dancing. She has two wonderful dogs—Mercy, her loyal Labrador Retriever, and Gailey, her sassy Jack Russell Terrier—as well as a condescending cat, Noah Japheth, who graciously allows her the privilege of serving him.

After being homeschooled from kindergarten through twelfth grade, she earned a Bachelor of Arts degree in English from Central Baptist College. Today, she finds joy in weaving words into messages of hope and healing on a variety of platforms. She publishes monthly posts on her devotional nature blog, Words from the Wilderness, and she has also had the privilege of contributing devotionals to ministries such as Awake Our Hearts and Proverbs 31 Ministries. In addition, she is the author of the Climbing Higher series, a Christian fiction saga.

Ashlyn is forever grateful that God has given her the gift of not only exploring His beautiful world but also using her words to shout His praise and prayerfully draw others to Him. You can keep up with all her adventures at www.wordsfromthewilderness.com!

REFERENCES

"Acknowledgements/Dedication"
[1] Gene Stratton-Porter, *A Girl of the Limberlost* (Bedford, MA: Applewood Books, 1909), 219.

"Wild Goose Chase"
[1] Mark Batterson, *Wild Goose Chase* (Colorado Springs: Multnomah, 2008), 1.

"Forged in Fire"
[1] Ephesians 6:10-18.
[2] Don Enevoldsen, "Plerousthe," *counterthought.org*, April 28, 2012, https://counterthought.org/plerousthe/.

"Winter Woods"
[1] Amber C. Haines, "The Purpose of Loneliness," in *A Moment to Breathe*, ed. Denise J. Hughes (Nashville: DaySpring Cards, Inc., 2017), 366.
[2] You can read these accounts in the following passages: Exodus 14:21-31, Exodus 13:21-22, and Exodus 7:14-11:10.
[3] 1 Kings 18 contains the full account.

"Frozen Filigree"
[1] Kim Rutledge, et. al., "Frost," *National Geographic Encyclopedia*, September 6, 2011, https://www.nationalgeographic.org/encyclopedia/frost/.
[2] Ben Biddulph, Kelly Ryan, and Sarah Jackson, "The science of frost and frequently asked questions," *Government of Western Australia: Department of Primary Industries and Regional Development*, October 7, 2020, https://www.agric.wa.gov.au/frost/science-frost-and-frequently-asked-questions.
[3] Miriam Dixon, "Thriving in the Winter Season of the Soul," *Renovaré*, March 11, 2019, https://renovare.org/articles/thriving-in-the-winter-season-of-the-soul.
[4] Read Jonah 1-4 for this account.
[5] Job 1 provides the backdrop of these tragic events.

"True North"
[1] Proverbs 3:5 ESV.

[2] Proverbs 4:23a NIV.
[3] Micah 6:8 ESV.
[4] Romans 8:28.

"Sleeping Under Snow"
[1] "Snug in the Snow," *Environmental Education for Kids*, 2020, https://www.eekwi.org/explore/seasonal-observations/snug-snow.
[2] Ibid.
[3] Andy Andrews, *The Heart Mender: A Story of Second Chances* (Nashville: Thomas Nelson, Inc., 2011), 101.
[4] Jeremiah 32:21.
[5] John 11:43.
[6] 2 Corinthians 1:22.
[7] Galatians 2:20.
[8] Romans 6:3-4.
[9] 1 Corinthians 15:31; Luke 9:23.
[10] 2 Timothy 1:10.

"The Pinecone Parable"
[1] Dixie Sandborn, "Fun facts about pine cones," *Michigan State University Extension*, December 29, 2017, https://www.canr.msu.edu/news/fun_facts_about_pine_cones.
[2] Megan Arnett, "Unlocking the Secrets of the Pinecone," *Scientific American*, December 15, 2016, https://www.scientificamerican.com/article/unlocking-the-secrets-of-the-pinecone/.
[3] Katie Burns, "Q & A – Why do pine cones open and close?," *San Diego Union-Tribune*, February 11, 2001, https://www.sandiegouniontribune.com/sdut-q-a-why-do-pine-cones-open-and-close-2001feb11-story.html.
[4] Linda Dillow and Lorraine Pintus, *Gift-Wrapped by God: Secret Answers to the Question, "Why Wait?"* (Colorado Springs, CO: WaterBrook Press, 2002), 55-59, quoted in Max Lucado, *Cast of Characters: Encounters with the Living God* (Nashville, TN: Thomas Nelson, 2012), 163-164.

"Warmer Winter"
[1] "Climate in Little Rock, Arkansas," *Sperling's Best Places*, https://www.bestplaces.net/climate/city/arkansas/little_rock.
[2] "Climate in Estes Park, Colorado," *Sperling's Best Places*, https://www.bestplaces.net/climate/city/colorado/estes_park.
[3] Socrates, qtd. in *Essential Thinkers* (New York: Barnes and Noble

Collector's Library, 2004).

[4] Benjamin Franklin, *Wit and Wisdom from Poor Richard's Almanack* (North Chelmsford, MA: Courier Corporation, 2012), 4.

[5] See 1 Kings 3 for more about Solomon's extravagance.

[6] See Exodus 20 for this warning.

[7] C. S. Lewis, *Mere Christianity* (New York: HarperCollins, 1952), 227.

"Growing with Gailey"

[1] Mark 3:20.

[2] Luke 5:1-11.

"The Daffodil Dare"

[1] Suzanne Eller, "Do It Afraid," in *A Moment to Breathe*, ed. Denise J. Hughes (Nashville: DaySpring Cards, Inc., 2017), 43.

[2] Matthew 4:18-19.

"Growing Green"

[1] "Purple Martin," *All About Birds*, https://www.allaboutbirds.org/guide/Purple_Martin/maps-range.

[2] Joseph's full story is found in Genesis 37-50.

"Of Flowers and Faithfulness"

[1] Exodus 7:1.

[2] 2 Samuel 12.

[3] Matthew 1:24.

"Butterfly Blessing"

[1] "Butterfly Life Cycle," *The Academy of Natural Sciences of Drexel University*, 2018, https://ansp.org/exhibits/online-exhibits/butterflies/lifecycle/.

[2] Ferris Jabr, "How Does a Caterpillar Turn into a Butterfly?," *Scientific American*, August 10, 2012, https://www.scientificamerican.com/article/caterpillar-butterfly-metamorphosis-explainer/.

[3] Ibid.

"April Showers"

[1] John Cristiano Ramon, "Deserts of Israel," *USA Today*, March 21, 2018, https://traveltips.usatoday.com/deserts-israel-107879.html.

[2] Leviticus 26:3-4.

[3] Marvin H. Pope, "Baal Worship," *Jewish Virtual Library*, 2008, https://www.jewishvirtuallibrary.org/baal-worship-jewish-virtual-library.

"Under His Wings"
[1] "Eastern Phoebe," *All About Birds*, https://www.allaboutbirds.org/guide/Eastern_Phoebe/overview.

"Mini Miracles"
[1] "Spring Peeper," *National Wildlife Federation*, https://www.nwf.org/Educational-Resources/Wildlife-Guide/Amphibians/Spring-Peeper.
[2] Jonathan Lipnick, "On the Road to Emmaus," *Israel Institute of Biblical Studies*, May 8, 2016, https://blog.israelbiblicalstudies.com/holy-land-studies/on-the-road-to-emmaus.

"The Trail to Nowhere"
[1] Danny Bernstein, "Hiking All the Trails in the Great Smoky Mountains National Park," *National Parks Traveler*, March 3, 2011, https://www.nationalparkstraveler.org/2011/02/hiking-all-trails-great-smoky-mountains-national-park7651.
[2] Acts 7:30.
[3] See Genesis 37-50 for Joseph's full story.

"Hope from a Hummingbird"
[1] "Ruby-throated Hummingbird," *All About Birds*, https://www.allaboutbirds.org/guide/Ruby-throated_Hummingbird/id.
[2] Lanny Chambers, "Ecology," *Journey North*, https://journeynorth.org/tm/humm/facts_ecology.html.
[3] Margaret Feinberg, *Taste and See: Discovering God among Butchers, Bakers, and Fresh Food Makers* (Grand Rapids: Zondervan, 2019).

"Thin Places"
[1] Kenneth C. Stevens, *Iona: Poems* (Edinburgh: Saint Andrew Press, 2000), 18, qtd. in Tracy Balzer, *Thin Places: An Evangelical Journey into Celtic Christianity* (Abilene, TX: Leafwood, 2007), 31-32.
[2] Tracy Balzer, *Thin Places: An Evangelical Journey into Celtic Christianity* (Abilene, TX: Leafwood, 2007).

"12,000 Feet"

298

[1] Jadie Aranda, "High Altitude Cooking: What You Need to Know," *Denver Parent*, July 9, 2019, https://denverparent.net/2019/07/high-altitude-cooking-what-you-need-to-know/.

[2] Nate A. Miller, "Highest continuous paved road in U.S. opens for the season," *Greeley (CO) Tribune*, May 31, 2017, https://www.greeleytribune.com/2017/05/31/highest-continuous-paved-road-in-u-s-opens-for-the-season/.

[3] "Alpine Tundra Ecosystem," *National Park Service*, https://www.nps.gov/romo/learn/nature/alpine_tundra_ecosystem.htm.

[4] "Altitude Sickness," *Cleveland Clinic*, September 23, 2020, https://my.clevelandclinic.org/health/diseases/15111-altitude-sickness.

"Homesick"
[1] Jim Reeves, "This World Is Not My Home," track 2 on *We Thank Thee*, RCA Victor, 1962, vinyl record.

[2] C. S. Lewis, *The Screwtape Letters* (New York: HarperCollins, 1942), 155.

"Lost and Found"
[1] "1 in 60 Rule (Nano)," *SKYbrary*, September 10, 2012, https://www.skybrary.aero/index.php/1_in_60_Rule_(Nano).

[2] Stephanie May Wilson, "God Told Me Who I'm Going To Marry.," 2013, *Stephanie May Wilson*, https://stephaniemaywilson.com/2013/02/20/god-told-me-who-im-going-to-marry/.

"When the Trees Fall"
[1] Michael Dirr, *Manual of Woody Landscape Plants*, qtd. in "About Growth Rate," *Arbor Day Foundation*, 2015, https://www.arborday.org/trees/treeguide/growth.cfm.

"Midsummer Miracle"
[1] Stephen Schneider, "The science behind the summer solstice," *PBS*, June 20, 2018, https://www.pbs.org/newshour/science/the-science-behind-the-summer-solstice.

[2] Daisy Carrington, "Summer solstice: Traditions around the world," *CNN*, June 21, 2019, https://www.cnn.com/travel/article/summer-solstice-world-traditions/.

[3] Jaime McLeod, "Get Ready For The Arrival Of Midsummer!," *Farmers' Almanac*, December 5, 2020, https://www.farmersalmanac.com/midsummer-lore-12243.

[4] "Is An 'Equinox' The Same As A 'Solstice'?," *Dictionary.com*, https://www.dictionary.com/e/fall-equinox-solstice/.

"Lights in the Night"
[1] Marc Branham, "How and why do fireflies light up?," *Scientific American*, September 5, 2005, https://www.scientificamerican.com/article/how-and-why-do-fireflies/.
[2] Robert Gebelhoff, "Scientists are working with the light of fireflies to improve medical diagnoses," *Washington Post*, July 22, 2015, https://www.washingtonpost.com/news/to-your-health/wp/2015/07/22/scientists-are-working-with-the-light-of-fireflies-to-improve-medical-diagnoses/.
[3] "Facts about Fireflies," *Firefly.org*, https://www.firefly.org/facts-about-fireflies.html.
[4] Tye Morancy, "Re: How many fireflies does it take to produce enough light to read a book?," *MadSci Network*, April 12, 2006, http://www.madsci.org/posts/archives/2006-04/1144862955.Gb.r.html.
[5] "Synchronous Fireflies," *National Park Service*, https://www.nps.gov/grsm/learn/nature/fireflies.htm.
[6] Acts 2.

"Toads on the Roads"
[1] Robert L. Hill, "Cold-Blooded: What's It Mean?," *Zoo Atlanta*, May 30, 2019, https://zooatlanta.org/cold-blooded-whats-it-mean/.

"Flowers in the Ditch"
[1] Google Dictionary (search results for "ditch definition").
[2] Ann Voskamp, *One Thousand Gifts* (Grand Rapids: Zondervan, 2010), 54.
[3] Ibid., 55.
[4] Ibid., 31.

"Song of Summertime"
[1] Julie Kohl, "Arkansas Frogs," *Only in Arkansas*, March 17, 2020, https://onlyinark.com/homegrown/arkansas-frogs/.
[2] "Cicadas," *National Geographic*, https://www.nationalgeographic.com/animals/invertebrates/group/cicadas/.

"When the Creek Dries Up"

[1] Jentezen Franklin, "The Blessing of the Busted Nest," *Sermon.love*, 2021, https://sermons.love/jentezen-franklin/5822-jentezen-franklin-the-blessing-of-the-busted-nest.html.

"Lesson from a Lizard"
[1] "Reptiles," *Encyclopedia of Arkansas*, November 15, 2018, https://encyclopediaofarkansas.net/entries/reptiles-4509/.
[2] Jonathan Losos, "New Study on Color Change In Green Anoles," *Anole Annals*, February 24, 2012, https://www.anoleannals.org/2012/02/24/new-study-on-color-change-in-green-anoles/.
Linda Brown, "Beneficials in the Garden: Green Anole," *Texas A&M University*, 2004, https://aggie-horticulture.tamu.edu/galveston/beneficials/beneficial-19_lizard_green_anole.htm.
[3] Ben Team, "What Do The Colors Mean On Anole Lizards?," *Mom.com*, https://animals.mom.com/colors-mean-anole-lizards-8983.html.
[4] "Green Anole – *Anolis carolinensis*," *PBS*, https://nhpbs.org/natureworks/greenanole.htm.
[5] C. S. Lewis, *The Screwtape Letters* (New York: HarperCollins, 1942), 49-50.
[6] Daniel 1:7.
[7] "Introduction: Daniel," *Institute for Creation Research*, https://www.icr.org/books/defenders/4866.

"Itchy Issues"
[1] L. M. Montgomery, *Anne of Windy Poplars* (Canada: McClelland and Stewart, Ltd., 1936), 8.
[2] Melissa Conrad Stöppler, "Chiggers (Bites) Symptoms, Pictures, Home Remedies, Medicine, and Cures," *MedicineNet*, https://www.medicinenet.com/chiggers_bites/article.htm.
[3] *Life Application Study Bible* (Carol Stream, IL: Tyndale House Publishers, Inc., 1988), 979.
[4] Genesis 27, 33.
[5] 1 Samuel 18-20.

"The Miracle of the Moth"
[1] Gene Stratton-Porter, *A Girl of the Limberlost* (Bedford, MA: Applewood Books, 1909), 207-208.
[2] "Lives of moths," *Butterfly Conservation*, https://butterfly-conservation.org/sites/default/files/lives_of_moths-factsheet.pdf.

"The Beauty of Bats"
[1] "Myths and Facts," *Bat World Sanctuary*, https://batworld.org/myths_facts_page/.
[2] "Celebrate the Mom Bats!," *Bat Conservation International*, May 8, 2016, https://www.batcon.org/celebrate-the-mom-bats/.
[3] "Echolocation," *National Park Service*, https://www.nps.gov/subjects/bats/echolocation.htm
[4] "Myths and Facts."
[5] Acts 9:19-23.
[6] Acts 9:26-27.
[7] Acts 15:1-2.
[8] 2 Corinthians 10:1-11.
[9] Christina Patterson, "Knowing the Source of Your Calling," *First 5*, https://app.first5.org/book/Galatians/ff_galatians_1/.

"Dark Sky"
[1] Ralph Waldo Emerson, "Nature," in *Nature and Selected Essays* (England: Penguin Classics, 2003).
[2] "How Does Our Sun Compare With Other Stars?," *NASA Science*, https://spaceplace.nasa.gov/sun-compare/en/.
[3] Fraser Cain, "How Many Stars In The Universe?," *Universe Today*, June 3, 2013, https://www.universetoday.com/102630/how-many-stars-are-there-in-the-universe/.
[4] "How long does it take for the light from stars to be visible here on Earth?," *NASA's Imagine the Universe!*, July 10, 1997, http://teacherlink.ed.usu.edu/tlnasa/reference/imaginedvd/files/imagine/docs/ask_astro/answers/970710c.html.
[5] "Light Pollution Effects on Wildlife and Ecosystems," *International Dark-Sky Association*, https://www.darksky.org/light-pollution/wildlife/.

"The Missing Martins"
[1] "About Purple Martins," *Wisconsin Purple Martin Association*, http://www.wisconsinpurplemartins.org/purple-martins.html.
[2] Bridget J. M. Stutchbury, "Tracing Purple Martin Migration To Brazil, And Back!," *Purple Martin Conservation Association*, https://www.purplemartin.org/uploads/media/18-2-geolocators-345.pdf.

"In Love with LeConte"

[1] Gracie McNichol, qtd. in Courtney Lix, *No Place for the Weary Kind: Women of the Smokies* (Gatlinburg: Great Smoky Mountains Association, 2016), 250.

[2] Lix, 228-237.

[3] Ibid., 238-250.

[4] Ibid., 238.

[5] Ibid., 238.

[6] G. K. Chesterton, *Orthodoxy* (Salt Lake City, UT: Waking Lion Press, 2008).

[7] C. S. Lewis, *Prince Caspian* (England: C. S. Lewis Pte. Ltd., 1979), in C. S. Lewis, *The Chronicles of Narnia* (New York, NY: HarperCollins), 380.

[8] Adam Winters, "Christ, the Lion who Keeps Getting Bigger?," *Standing on Shoulders*, February 7, 2011, https://standingonshoulders. wordpress.com/2011/02/07/christ-the-lion-who-keeps-getting-bigger/.

[9] E. P. Sanders, "St. Paul the Apostle," *Britannica*, https://www.britannica.com/biography/Saint-Paul-the-Apostle.

[10] Gracie McNichol, qtd. in Lix, 246.

"Faith and the Foothold"

[1] "Flood!," *National Park Service*, https://www.nps.gov/romo/ planyourvisit/upload/flood_2009.pdf.
Associated Press, "Four campers feared dead in flooding," *St. Petersburg (FL) Evening Independent*, July 16, 1982, http:// www.gendisasters.com/colorado/19335/estes-park-co-dam-collapse-flood-july-1982.

"Where the Wind Blows"

[1] Humbert Wolfe, https://www.goodreads.com/quotes/107268-listen-the-wind-is-rising-and-the-air-is-wild.

[2] William Wordsworth, "Book VI: The Churchyard among the Mountains," in *The Excursion*, 1814.

[3] Aldo Leopold, https://www.azquotes.com/quote/549323.

[4] Elisha Ben Abuya, "Ruach Elohim," *Hebrew Meanings*, March 31, 2016, http://hebrewmeanings.blogspot.com/2016/03/ruach-elohim.html.

[5] Joe Martucci, "How does the Wind Impact Temperatures?," *WeatherWorks*, November 17, 2015, https://weatherworksinc.com/news/Wind-Temperature-Relationship.

[6] Brendan McWilliams, "High winds in September," *Dublin Irish Times*, September 16, 1998, https://www.irishtimes.com/news/high-winds-in-september-1.193645.

[7] "Weather and Fall Migration," *National Environmental Education Foundation*, https://www.neefusa.org/nature/plants-and-animals/weather-and-fall-migration.

"Daring to Dream"
[1] Kimberly Mitchell, "Arkansas Trees," *Only in Arkansas*, June 29, 2016, https://onlyinark.com/homegrown/arkansas-trees/.

[2] Roger Di Silvestro, "The Wildlife Benefits of Acorns and Oaks," *National Wildlife Federation*, October 16, 2013, https://blog.nwf.org/2013/10/the-wildlife-benefits-of-acorns-and-oaks/.

[3] "Humus," *National Geographic*, https://www.nationalgeographic.org/encyclopedia/humus/

[4] Adrian Grahams, "The Life Cycle of an Acorn Seedling Into a Tree," *Sciencing*, August 17, 2018, https://sciencing.com/the-life-cycle-of-an-acorn-seedling-into-a-tree-12486565.html.

[5] Stephanie May Wilson, "Don't Short Circuit Your Love Story," *Stephanie May Wilson*, August 2013, https://stephaniemaywilson.com/2013/08/13/dontshortcircuityourlovestory/.

[6] Ken Lloyd, "Q. What is the life span of an oak tree?," *New York Botanical Garden Plant Information Service*, January 25, 2021, https://libanswers.nybg.org/faq/270776.

"Watching in the Woods"
[1] Cindy Decker, "Cindy Decker commentary: Squirrels the only foe a buckeye can't defeat," *Columbus (OH) Dispatch*, September 25, 2015, https://www.dispatch.com/article/20150925/LIFESTYLE/309259671.

[2] Bethney Foster, "Uses for Buckeye Trees," *Sciencing*, November 22, 2019, https://sciencing.com/uses-buckeye-trees-5465217.html.

[3] Denise Kohlmeyer, "Hagar and El Roi, the God Who Sees," *Unlocking the Bible*, August 21, 2019, https://unlockingthebible.org/2019/08/hagar-el-roi-god-sees/.

"Lesson from Leaves"
[1] Carol Ryrie Brink, *Caddie Woodlawn* (New York: Macmillan Publishers, 1935), 204.
[2] Donald Simanek, "Bishop Ussher Dates the World: 4004 BC," https://www.lockhaven.edu/~dsimanek/ussher.htm.
[3] Bodie Hodge, "Halloween Origin: Halloween History and the Bible," *Answers in Genesis*, October 29, 2013, https://answersingenesis.org/holidays/halloween-history-and-the-bible/.
[4] Beth Daley, "Curious Kids: why do leaves fall off trees?," *The Conversation*, https://theconversation.com/curious-kids-why-do-leaves-fall-off-trees-111914.
[5] "How much more does a tree weigh when it is in leaf?," reply #3 by [dentstudent], *the nakedscientists.com*, September 6, 2007, https://www.thenakedscientists.com/forum/index.php?topic=8277.0.
[6] "Why Do Leaves Change Color?," *Environmental Education for Kids*, https://www.eekwi.org/plants/why-do-leaves-change-color. "The Process of Leaf Color Change," *Harvard Forest*, https://harvardforest.fas.harvard.edu/leaves/process.
[7] Daniel Engber, "FYI: Why Do Leaves Turn Different Colors?," *Popular Science*, October 28, 2013, https://www.popsci.com/article/science/fyi-why-do-leaves-turn-different-colors/.

"Persimmon Prophecy"
[1] Kelly Bostian, "The World Around You: Persimmons ripen without frost for the 2016-2017 winter forecast," *Tulsa (OK) World*, November 13, 2016, https://tulsaworld.com/sports/the-world-around-you-persimmons-ripen-without-frost-for-the-2016-17-winter-forecast/article_d2e6c732-3665-5822-bb87-c27811337f27.html.
[2] Catherine Boeckmann, "Predicting Weather Using a Persimmon Seed," *The Old Farmer's Almanac*, September 10, 2020, https://www.almanac.com/predicting-weather-using-persimmon-seed.
[3] See 1 Samuel 28 for the full story.
[4] Corrie ten Boom, https://www.goodreads.com/quotes/110765-worrying-is-carrying-tomorrow-s-load-with-today-s-strength--carrying-two.

"Treasures in the Treetops"
[1] "Squirrel," *One Kind Planet*, https://onekindplanet.org/animal/squirrel/.

[2] "Fun Facts About Squirrels," *Wild Birds Unlimited*, https://annarbor.wbu.com/squirrel-facts.

[3] "Role in the ecosystem," *Rosso Scoiattolo*, May 30, 2016, http://www.rossoscoiattolo.eu/en/role-ecosystem.

"Of Corn and Courage"

[1] Kimberly Mitchell, "The Story Behind the Real Razorbacks," *Only in Arkansas*, September 12, 2017, https://onlyinark.com/arkansas-women-bloggers/story-behind-real-razorbacks/.

[2] "Feral Hogs are Pests," *Arkansas Game and Fish Commission*, https://www.agfc.com/en/hunting/feral-hogs/.

[3] Mitchell, "Real Razorbacks."

[4] Francis Anfuso [@francisanfuso1], "Hidden Seeds," Facebook, November 4, 2020, https://www.facebook.com/permalink.php?id=720931754618722&story_fbid=3683273648384503.

"Soaring in Silence"

[1] Keith Sutton, "The whooo!, what, when, where and why of some of our most fascinating birds," *Arkansas Democrat-Gazette*, January 27, 2013, https://www.arkansasonline.com/news/2013/jan/27/whooo-what-when-where-and-why-some-our-most/.

[2] "Wing feathers enable near-silent flight," *Ask Nature*, September 20, 2019, https://asknature.org/strategy/wing-feathers-enable-near-silent-flight/.

[3] *I Saw A Bird*, episode 13, "I Saw A Bird with Audubon: Episode 13," produced by Elizabeth Sorrell, aired October 29, 2020, on YouTube, https://www.youtube.com/watch?v=TXAZMioi9A0&feature=emb_logo

[4] Henri Nouwen, *The Way of the Heart* (New York, NY: HarperCollins, Publishers, 1981), 25, qtd. in Tracy Balzer, *Thin Places: An Evangelical Journey into Celtic Christianity* (Abilene, TX: Leafwood, 2007), 127.

[5] Balzer, 126.

[6] Deane Lewis, "Owls in Mythology & Culture," *The Owl Pages*, March 23, 2006, https://www.owlpages.com/owls/articles.php?a=62.

"Advent and Animals"

[1] Jennifer Bové, "How You and your Kids Can Help Wildlife This Winter—In Your Own Backyard!," *National Wildlife Federation*, November 4, 2010, https://blog.nwf.org/2010/11/how-you-and-your-kids-can-help-wildlife-this-winter-in-your-own-backyard/.

[2] Justin Holcomb, "What is Advent?," *Christianity.com*, November 6, 2020, https://www.christianity.com/christian-life/christmas/what-is-advent.html.

[3] *Frozen*, directed by Jennifer Lee and Chris Buck (2013; Burbank, CA: Buena Vista Home Entertainment, Inc., 2014), DVD.

[4] Mother Teresa, in *The Words and Wisdom of Mother Teresa* (Boulder, CO: Blue Mountain Press, 2007), 72-73.

"Midwinter Miracle"

[1] "What Is the Winter Solstice?," *Smithsonian Science Education Center*, https://ssec.si.edu/stemvisions-blog/what-winter-solstice/.

[2] Malachi 3:1-5, 17.

[3] See, for example, the book of the same name by H. A. Ironside.

[4] "What were the 400 years of silence?," *Got Questions*, https://www.gotquestions.org/400-years-of-silence.html.

"God's Christmas Tree"

[1] Beth Daley, "Curious Kids: why do leaves fall off trees?," *The Conversation*, https://theconversation.com/curious-kids-why-do-leaves-fall-off-trees-111914.

[2] Barry Logan, "Why don't evergreen trees change color and drop their leaves?," *EarthSky*, November 1, 2019, https://earthsky.org/earth/why-dont-evergreen-trees-change-drop-leaves/.

[3] "Why do most evergreen trees have a pyramid shape?," *EarthSky*, December 19, 2014, https://earthsky.org/earth/evergreen-tree-shape/.

Juli Hennings and Harry Lynch, "Why Pines Are Evergreen," *EarthDate*, https://www.earthdate.org/node/139/.

[4] Charles H. Spurgeon, "Psalm 37," in *Treasury of David*, *The Spurgeon Archive*, https://archive.spurgeon.org/treasury/treasury.php.

[5] 2 Samuel 5:4.

[6] 2 Samuel 15-19.

[7] Dixie Sandborn, "How did evergreen trees become a symbol for Christmas?," *Michigan State University Extension*, December 6, 2016, https://www.canr.msu.edu/news/how_did_evergreen_trees_become_a_symbol_for_christmas/.

PHOTO CREDITS

I would like to express my heartfelt gratitude to Ralph Wood, who graciously allowed me to use his amazing photographs for "Wild Goose Chase" and "Soaring in Silence."

My sincere appreciation is also extended to Bettymaya Foott, Director of Engagement at the International Dark-Sky Association, for the beautiful photograph that adorns "Dark Sky." It was taken just outside Moab, Utah, in an area that is currently applying for acceptance to the Dark Sky community. For more information about the invaluable work of this organization, please visit darksky.org.

Some of the topics of these devotionals were not such for which I could acquire quality photographs; for these, I used common domain images downloaded from online sources. The devotionals for which these images were used are the following:

- "Lights in the Night" – downloaded image from Pixabay
- "Song of Summertime" – downloaded image by Laura Gilchrist on Unsplash
- "The Beauty of Bats" – downloaded image from Pixabay
- "Persimmon Prophecy" – downloaded image from Pixabay

Unless otherwise listed above, all photographs were taken by my family or me.

PRAYERS, PROMISES, PRAISES

The following pages are a quiet space for you to write or draw your personal words to and from the Lord. "My sheep hear my voice, and I know them, and they follow me" (John 10:27 ESV).

www.ingramcontent.com/pod-product-compliance
Lightning Source LLC
Chambersburg PA
CBHW071140130626
46553CB00004B/1450